A Nation Reformed?

A Nation Reformed?

American Education 20 Years after

A Nation at Risk

Edited by
DAVID T. GORDON

Foreword by
PATRICIA ALBJERG GRAHAM

HARVARD EDUCATION PRESS

Library of Congress Control Number   2002114347
ISBN 1-891792-09-1 (cloth)
ISBN 1-891792-08-3 (paper)

Published by the Harvard Education Press,
an imprint of the Harvard Education Publishing Group

Harvard Education Press
8 Story Street, 5th Floor
Cambridge, MA 02138

Cover Design: Alyssa Morris
Editorial Production: Dody Riggs
Typography: Sheila Walsh

The typefaces used in this book are Sabon for text and Gill Sans for display. Sabon is a descendant of the types of Claude Garamond. It was designed in 1964 by Jan Tschichold. Gill Sans was designed by Eric Gill around 1929. It is based on the typeface designed by Edward Johnston in 1916 for the signage of the London Underground.

Contents

Foreword

PATRICIA ALBJERG GRAHAM

Commemorating the publication of *A Nation at Risk*, which appeared twenty years ago, on April 26, 1983, challenges educators. Many winced at its critical tone, including the implied and sometimes explicit criticism of them and their efforts. Some rejected the arguments as overblown rhetoric. Some understood that the goal of the document was to stir up the citizenry in support of improved schooling for all children and that the rhetoric, while overblown, was perhaps necessary for Americans acculturated to fast-paced media. Indeed, the tone of the document illustrated the assumption of the authors that only such a piece could capture the attention of those who were receiving such superficial schooling. No extensive, analytical, philosophical, reflective prose for this commission and their staff, who rightly perceived that such reports were at best filed but neither read nor acted upon in late twentieth-century America. Presumably their goal was action based upon the principles enunciated in the document, which were essentially that the academic achievement of American schoolchildren was inadequate and needed to be improved.

The educators contributing essays to this volume two decades later write cogently and with fervor about the educational dilemmas Americans face. Their passion, while intense, is tempered for a more thoughtful audience. Three critical ideas emerge from their essays: 1) Americans have an incoherent sense of purpose for their schools; 2) changes in educational practice do not follow smoothly from changes in educational policy; and 3) formulating purpose, designing policy, or changing practice takes much longer than one expects or wants.

Jeff Howard reminds us that educators lack a clear consensus about the purpose of education, and that one is necessary. Two practitioners, Timothy Knowles and Kim Marshall, illustrate in their essays based on work with Boston schoolteachers and administrators just how these educators are experiencing the changing set of purposes for schooling that have evolved over the last two decades. In fact, publication of *A Nation at Risk* has been widely, if erroneously, accepted as the trigger for this changed external perception about what schooling is for: academic achievement as measured by improved test scores. What is apparent from these essays is the extent to which educators do not by themselves determine the purpose of schooling. Rather, they have traditionally participated in and been responsive to broader societal demands for what schooling should be doing to improve society, whether it is the assimilation of immigrant children in the first quarter of the century, or the psychological and social adjustment of youngsters in the middle years of the century, or facilitating access to public schools of those previously denied, either through desegregation by race or by inclusion of special needs students. In no instance has academic achievement for all been widely accepted as the primary purpose of schooling in America. That radical proposition lay at the base of *A Nation at Risk*.

Policymakers and researchers Susan Fuhrman, Richard Elmore, Pam Grossman, David Gordon, Maris Vinovskis, Robert Schwartz, and Nathan Glazer explain to us the discontinuity between what Americans want or expect from their schools and what they get. Each illustrates this disjuncture with pungent examples, whether from the business community (Schwartz), the teacher shortage (Grossman), or academic ideologies (Gordon). As Elmore notes, policy and practice in education are in "parallel play." Implementing "intensive instructional improvement interventions," Fuhrman observes, is not easy, swift, or effective. Yet Glazer raises a fundamental issue: that if the idea does not work as it is supposed to when it is implemented, perhaps the idea itself is not good. Vinovskis laments the lack of a research base for reform, although he does not emphasize that the staff of the commission for *A Nation at Risk* came largely from the old National Institute of Education, the federal government's educational research arm annihilated by the Reagan administration.

What properly troubles both the practitioners and the policy people is the sluggish response to changes that these authors and the constituencies they represent believe desirable. They are all eager for reform, concerned that children in America need better schooling, but youngsters are not receiving it because the adults responsible for providing it are not moving rapidly or efficiently enough to make the changes that would result in the improvement they seek. Some believe that accountability measures, particularly testing programs, are the best means to reach this outcome. Others disagree. Some recognize that outside forces are necessary to assist educators in moving their colleagues to a new sense of purpose and action. Everyone agrees, however, that this process of increasing academic achievement for American children through improved schooling takes longer and is more difficult to make happen than they would like.

Why should this be so? To understand this conundrum one needs to recognize the context in which this report was launched. First, it was one of many such efforts undertaken in the late 1970s and early 1980s attempting to bring a more academic or "traditional" focus to American schools, which for the past two decades had been predominantly wrestling with the perplexing issue of accommodating children of different races, different ethnicities, and various "handicaps" in classrooms from which they had previously been excluded. When such accommodations are the primary order of business, attention to academic learning is likely to decline. Thus, by the late 1970s the Twentieth Century Fund, the College Board, and the National Science Board, to name only three, had all commissioned reports on the state of the schools and the need for their improvement. Each was thoughtfully written, insightfully analytical, and each sank like a stone from public view. Together, though, they do indicate that many in the society recognized that the time was right for a change in the primary emphasis of American schooling.

Second, for teachers and administrators prepared in earlier generations and who were now senior figures in the schools, the emphasis in their training programs had been on helping children "adjust to life," as exemplified in the ideas of the 1944 Life Adjustment Commission, which did not stress academic learning for any but a few students. Thus, school people believed they had been doing their duty and following society's mandate to them in maintaining an emphasis on access and adjustment. As one New England superintendent explained to me at a conference of school administrators in fall 1981 when I inquired about the academic emphasis in his school, "You don't understand, we run social welfare institutions, not academic ones."

While I was appalled at the superintendent's inattention to academic priorities, he certainly reminded me of the many obligations that had been thrust upon schools in past decades and the degree to which academic matters had been deemphasized. Where, I wondered, in the world that children inhabited would they find an academic emphasis, if not in school? Many, of course, found it at home and in their communities, particularly if they lived in affluent settings in which getting into an elite college was part of their families' hopes and expectations for them. For some new immigrants, succeeding at school became their parents'—and sometimes their own—method of "Americanization." But for other immigrants, particularly those already settled in low-income jobs in this country, their form of Americanization meant acceding to the cultural expectations of their neighbors, who traditionally have not put a high premium on academic learning. The world of multimedia, of expensive items marketed to the young, of 20-hour-per-week jobs during the high school years all coalesce to minimize the attraction of the deferred gratification world of academic study. Many teenagers seek the more immediate gratifications of entertainment, fashion, and money.

Finally, in this environment of conflicting societal pressures on schools, what were the institutions doing that should be involved in shaping educational purpose, policy, and practice, university schools of education? Let us look simply at the one responsible for publishing this volume, the Harvard Graduate School of Education. Early in the 1970s it dropped its formerly highly regarded teacher education program (the Master of Arts in Education) and diminished significantly its principal and superintendent preparation effort (the Administrative Careers Program). In doing so it turned its attention to issues of research, social policy, planning, and learning environments (often those not connected with schools or colleges). Most other schools of education in leading research universities did the same thing, either eliminating their schools of education entirely (Duke, Yale, Johns Hopkins) or shifting their focus from schooling (Chicago, Stanford, Teachers College). Some came within a whisker of closing (University of California, Berkeley), some eventually did close (Chicago), and both Harvard and Stanford had discussions on their campuses about either closing or eliminating their status as schools and making them departments (as happened at Chicago before the department was eliminated).

By 1979, however, the then dean of the Harvard Graduate School of Education (HGSE), Paul Ylvisaker, appointed a faculty committee to address the school's appropriate role regarding public schools. Unlike many faculty committees, this one had a significant effect, and by February 1983 I, as the recently appointed (December 1981) new dean, reported to Derek Bok, then president of Harvard, that "within the last year the national mood toward school improvement has begun to change, with governmental and industrial leaders speaking out about the importance of investing in schools. With these changes, the time seems ripe—and the School well poised—for Harvard to take the lead in the improvement of educational practice and in the strengthening of schooling." The report highlighted the activities of the Committee on Schooling under the leadership of Harold Howe II, a former schoolteacher and administrator and Commissioner of the U.S. Office of Education in the 1960s. The Committee had spearheaded a new program in Interactive Technology in Education, the resumption of teacher education with an initial focus on mid-career math and science specialists, the growth of the new Principals' Center, and the planning, with the Harvard University Press, of the forthcoming *Harvard Education Letter* to bring the significant findings of educational research to practitioners in an accessible format. (In a later development, the *Harvard Education Letter* moved from the university press to the Harvard Education Publishing Group at HGSE.) The report concluded with the discussion of planning for the forthcoming summer meeting of presidents and deans of schools of education of Harvard, Stanford, Chicago, Columbia, Berkeley, Wisconsin, and Michigan to discuss how universities could be more effective in school reform.

In short, even before *A Nation at Risk* appeared, the country was shifting its attention to the need for school reform with a greater academic emphasis, and some schools of education and their university leaders were reallocating priorities to address these issues. No wonder, then, that the little blue report from the Excellence Commission fell on such fertile and well-watered soil. Growing a healthy plant, though, does not happen overnight, and the result sought in the report and in the many efforts of educational reformers to have all American children attain higher levels of academic achievement turns out to be a plant that grows slowly. It is alive, and it is sturdy, but it fruits slowly and sporadically.

Introduction

DAVID T. GORDON

T
he year 1983 saw the publication of several reports and studies diagnosing the illnesses of public education and prescribing treatments to restore schools to health. *A Nation at Risk*, issued by the National Commission on Excellence in Education, was just one of them. Yet with its dramatic title and incendiary language, the report soon became a touchstone in the history of American education. Its opening lines are now legendary, a permanent part of the school reform lexicon. We were warned of a "rising tide of mediocrity" that threatened to swamp our schools and imperil the future not only of today's young people but tomorrow's, too. We were told that "[i]f an unfriendly foreign power had attempted to impose on America the mediocre educational performance that exists today, we might well have viewed it as an act of war."

That same year, Joe Clark roamed the halls of Eastside High in Paterson, New Jersey, with a bullhorn and a baseball bat, shouting words of admonition and encouragement in a voice cultivated as an Army drill instructor. Clark vowed to clean up a school that was a social and academic disaster zone, plagued by vandalism, violence, and underachievement. Just a few years later, the governor of New Jersey would point to Eastside High as a model school, one where kids could study safely and with esteem-building encouragement. Clark landed on *60 Minutes* and on the cover of *Time*. President Ronald Reagan offered him a post as an education policy advisor, which he refused. Oscar-winner Morgan Free-man played him in the Warner Bros. movie, *Lean on Me.* Joe Clark's "tough love" manner turned him into a folk hero, a symbol of the kind of drastic measures many Americans thought were necessary to save their education system. Schools, it was thought, needed a good kick in the pants.

The authors of *A Nation at Risk* wielded the rhetorical equivalent of Joe Clark's bullhorn and baseball bat. They admonished and encour-aged. They expressed many of the common frustrations and hopes of ed-ucators, parents, and policymakers. Over-the-top in places and dead-on in others, they cemented a growing national consensus that school im-provement by any means necessary must be a priority. *A Nation at Risk* got our attention and inspired action. Of course, the report was more than just a broadside. As Al Shanker, late president of the American Fed-eration of Teachers, noted at the tenth anniversary of its publication, *A Nation at Risk* was "an exposition of what we would now call 'systemic reform': figuring out what we want students to know and be able to do and making sure that all parts of the education system—standards, cur-riculum, textbooks, assessments, teacher training—move simulta-neously toward the achievement of agreed-upon goals."[1]

In this book, which includes the report itself, we get to step out from beneath the trees to see the forest of two decades of reforms. School leaders, teachers, policymakers, researchers, parents, and students have all played a role in the widespread efforts to make our schools better. The twentieth anniversary of the report's publication is an ideal moment to take stock. What have we accomplished? Was the nation really ever "at risk" and, if so, is it now? Has all the time, effort, and money been well spent? Which reforms have made a difference and which haven't? And where do we go from here?

To set the stage for exploring such questions, Susan H. Fuhrman guides us through the various stages of reform, from the *excellence* movement of the mid 1980s—with its top-down reforms focused on raising course requirements and rules for teacher licensure and certifica-tion—to the bottom-up *restructuring* movement that offered schools more local control in return for accountability, to the *standards* move-ment, the "third wave" we've been riding for more than a decade. The standards movement has drawn support from federal, state, and local governments with unprecedented scope and coordination. Innovations such as charter schools, voucher programs, and private management of public schools have increased the stakes for schools and districts by introducing some competition into the allocation of public resources. So has the more drastic measure of mayoral or state takeovers of schools. The growth in the volume, cost, and diversity of education initiatives was probably unimaginable two decades ago, Fuhrman writes, and there are hopeful signs that this work will pay off. Yet significant challenges remain, particularly in terms of equity, coherence, and scale.

Of course, these reforms have taught us emphatically that change is not the same as improvement, as Richard F. Elmore reminds us. Elmore addresses the disconnection between policy and practice. For all the time, money, and talk invested in reforms, the fundamental work of schools—classroom instruction—has not changed very much in many schools, he writes. Educators have been treated as part of the problem, not part of the solution, and so there has been little or no focus on helping teachers and administrators improve their understanding of and ability to perform the complex work that takes place in schools. If performance-based accountability is going to have any meaning, policymakers will have to invest in the kind of high-quality professional development that fundamentally improves the work that takes place in schools.

What administrators have learned, they've largely learned on the job. "The new K–12 landscape has redefined what good school leadership is, what it requires, how it is measured, and how it is developed," writes Timothy Knowles. "Not only must school leaders learn to reinvent their schools, many of them must also learn to reinvent themselves." The principal's job used to be one of making sure kids were safe, buses ran on time, budgets looked good, and parents and policymakers were satisfied. But in the past twenty years, school leaders have had to become much more savvy about and engaged in instruction. In schools that succeed, teaching and learning at the classroom level is the primary concern. What does it mean to be a good instructional leader? What special knowledge do principals need to address the "academic imperative" put forth in A Nation at Risk? And how can districts find the best leaders for their schools? Knowles addresses these questions by mapping out specific, school-based strategies for improvement.

After fifteen years as principal of the nation's oldest public school, Kim Marshall assesses "the false starts, detours, and regressions" at the Mather School as it rose from rock bottom to the top third in Boston's citywide standings. Among the treacherous shoals of leadership: teacher isolation, chronic negativism, mysterious grading criteria, and a lack of curricular coherence. In the end, the rigorous statewide standards and high-stakes tests gave both teachers and administrators a fresh focus and intensity in their efforts to improve.

The authors of *A Nation at Risk* suggested improving teacher salaries, professional opportunities, and prestige in order to attract and keep excellent candidates in the profession, which at the time was facing record shortages. Yet two decades later the profession of teaching itself is at risk, writes Pam Grossman. States have tried to draw teachers not by improving the conditions teachers work in and increasing opportunities for professional development, but by relaxing the requirements for entry into the profession. The result is that while groups such as the National Board for Professional Teaching Standards have had some success in promoting improved teacher knowledge and skill, policymakers continue to undermine efforts to professionalize teaching by creating conditions that lead to high turnover, burnout, and shoddy teacher standards.

When it comes to educating poor and minority students, a deeply rooted cultural prejudice undermines efforts to set high standards and hold both children and adults accountable for meeting them, writes Jeff Howard, founder of the Efficacy Institute. The idea that intelligence is fixed at birth and unequally distributed disables the very notion of equal-opportunity education by creating "relative standards and a sliding scale of expectations." Doing so has led to a two-tier system of education, in which some kids are pressed to develop the skills they need to function in our world while others, on the basis of thinly veiled prejudice, are excused from achieving at high levels.

Just as prejudice impedes effective classroom practices, so too does rigid adherence to ideological orthodoxy, as my own chapter contends. That lesson was made clear in the post–*Nation at Risk* period when policymakers and parents fought over how to teach reading and math. The partisanship of these curriculum wars interfered with efforts to implement evidence-based strategies to improve teaching and learning. Phonics and arithmetic became "conservative" while whole language and reform math became "liberal." Meanwhile, research continued to demonstrate the need for balanced instruction in math and reading that would build basic skills while finding ways of making those skills relevant to the real world.

One of the fundamental weaknesses of *A Nation at Risk* was the assumption that we already knew how to improve our public schools—that only the will to improve them was lacking, writes Maris A. Vinovskis. Thus, the report did not call for additional education research or development, and the White House and Congress even slashed the already small amount of funds allocated for these activities. That, it turns out, was a missed opportunity to build on public support for educational improvements by sponsoring large-scale projects that would identify promising strategies for academic improvement and rigorously test their validity. Instead Washington focused diagnostic services, improving education statistics and analysis—information that can help us tell what's wrong but not how to fix it. The 2001 No Child Left Behind Act called for more attention to "scientifically based" strategies. Vinovskis asks, How much farther along might we have been if the federal government had supported the same twenty years ago?

One reason Washington may have been reluctant to initiate and support reform efforts is that states were already leading the way. For an inside look at the emerging role states played in education reform, there is no better guide than Robert B. Schwartz. As a policy advisor, education program director at the Pew Charitable Trusts, and founding president of Achieve, Inc., the nonprofit created by governors and business leaders to expedite school improvement and accountability, Schwartz has seen firsthand the way state leaders have stepped forward to take charge in education reform and how their emphasis shifted over two decades to building a stronger teacher corps and to supporting bottom-up innovation rather than top-down mandates. From Aspen to Charlottesville to IBM's Palisades conference center, Schwartz provides a fascinating account of the steps and missteps states have taken in paving and improving the road to standards-based reforms.

Washington's reluctance—at least until No Child Left Behind—to insert itself prominently into reform efforts has another explanation: the great diversity of school systems, the dependence of schools on their communities for resources, and the traditional commitment of Americans to local control of educational institutions. These, writes Nathan Glazer, help define the "American way of school reform," one in which efforts to create large-scale, comprehensive reforms run headlong into bedrock skepticism of centralization. Glazer draws on his own experiences as a close observer of the development of the ATLAS whole-school reform model, showing how from state to state, district to district, and school to school, reform efforts will likely differ in methods, means, and sometimes motives. "We can celebrate this diversity, or mourn it, but it is not likely to change," notes Glazer.

A theme that emerges time and again in these chapters is the central role of teachers and administrators in school improvement. Too often reforms have focused on big-picture issues—school governance, organization, curriculum, accountability, and so forth—without taking into account how decisions affect what happens on the front lines, where improvement is most needed. Because education is an enterprise focused on people, not products, the greatest challenge is to bring out the best in those who spend their days in schools themselves, one teacher and one student at a time.

CHAPTER ONE

Riding Waves, Trading Horses: The Twenty-Year Effort to Reform Education

SUSAN H. FUHRMAN

When the National Commission on Excellence in Education issued *A Nation at Risk* in 1983, who could have predicted that education reform would top the domestic policy agenda for the next twenty years? Prior to that time, education had cycled in and out of policymakers' agendas, rising to the top when there were particular concerns about poor or handicapped children, for example, and then falling back into relative neglect. In the early 1980s, a serious recession, terrible state budget deficits, and the Reagan administration's efforts to cut domestic programs put education policy on the bottom rung. Its recovery in 1983 and its persistence as a central issue is nothing less than startling.

This chapter is an effort to review the past twenty years of education reform. I begin with an overview of the various "movements" that have captured policymaker and public attention. Then I examine a few themes that have characterized the period and marked a change from prior years. Finally, I conclude with some challenges that remain with us despite, and sometimes because of, this era of unprecedented attention to education.

WAVES OF REFORM

So many seemingly different approaches to reform have been with us since 1983 that commentators have, for some time now, been comparing them to "waves." They come steadily and rapidly, wash over us, and sometimes leave only traces over the long run. As we'll see later, they are united by a number of themes, but typically they have had different primary champions, taken different points of departure, and been addressed at different targets.

Immediately after *A Nation at Risk*, policymakers took up the document's challenge to reverse the "rising tide of mediocrity" that had overtaken American education. In a set of policy efforts called the *excellence* movement, they focused on raising standards for students and teachers by, among other things, increasing course requirements for graduation, instituting more student assessment, specifying particular courses deemed important, lengthening the school day or year, and stiffening requirements for teacher certification and relicensure. Most of these efforts occurred at the state level, where large, comprehensive packages or omnibus bills combined several excellence policies with additional funding. The emergence from the recession made more funding possible; the reforms, which made the demands on schools tougher, made funding increases politically palatable.

Some states had already begun to put together reform packages prior to *A Nation at Risk*, particularly some in the South that had been working with the Southern Regional Education Board to identify many of the same problems and remedies. However, many more were spurred on by the report's stirring rhetoric and the unparalleled press attention it received. Business elites in particular were taken by its arguments about the importance of education's role in the national economy and by the specter of lost competitiveness due to educational weaknesses. They became important allies for political leaders, while education groups, puzzled by what was then a new level of state activism, largely sat on the sidelines. These reforms truly marked a change in state policy in education, which had in the past been preoccupied with finance formulas. Now states were getting into what was taught and by whom, issues they had previously left to local governments.[1]

Because the excellence reforms were so state directed, they were quickly characterized by many in the field as "top down." Within three to four years, a backlash emerged in the shape of another reform wave focused on more "bottom-up" approaches to educational improvement. Known as the *restructuring* movement, the new efforts, which sometimes found their way into state policy and frequently shaped district reform programs, were championed primarily by educators and their associations. Arguing that reform cannot be mandated from the center, restructuring advocates proposed in-school reforms, like more time for teachers to plan together and longer classes for particular subjects, and governance changes, particularly school-site management.

Although policymakers were not the leaders of the restructuring movement, they bought into the idea of giving schools more autonomy, as long as it was in return for greater accountability for results. Such reforms paralleled what was happening in business, where companies focused on flattening management structures and providing flexibility for teams of workers. The latter would be expected to improve production and efficiency in exchange for control over their own procedures. Policymakers applied these ideas in popular currency to education, as evidenced by Lamar Alexander's offer of a "horse trade" to educators when he was chair of the National Governors' Association. In return for accountability for performance, schools would be free to design their own processes, implying that states would back off the kind of micromanagement critics saw in the excellence reforms.[2]

Neither the excellence nor the restructuring movement produced the results their proponents desired. Student performance remained relatively flat. Researchers found that excellence reforms frequently led to superficial change; for example, more math and science courses were offered in the wake of higher graduation requirements, but the courses were often remedial.[3] With respect to restructuring reforms, these did not necessarily lead to changes in instruction. While involving teachers in decisionmaking, for instance, might give them opportunities to work collegially on hard issues of curriculum and instruction, they did not necessarily do so. Many used new arenas to work on tangential issues— for example, focusing on how the new governance structures would operate rather than on the substance of teaching and learning.[4]

A major characteristic of reforms in this period was their fragmentation. The excellence and restructuring movements sometimes resulted in contradictory policies—for example, state curricular mandates at the same time as efforts to enhance teacher roles in curriculum decisionmaking. Even within the same policies, there were conflicting specifications. Bills mandating higher standards for teacher preparation and licensure included loopholes permitting noncredentialed individuals to teach. Laws that promoted local autonomy through local school councils also mandated the exact composition of those councils.

Researchers and commentators began to notice this fragmentation and contrasted it to the way most of the rest of the world (which, by the way, was outscoring U.S. students on international assessments) operated, with central curricular direction and coordinated assessment and teacher development policies. In the late 1980s, a few pioneering states, like California, began to create more coherent policies, using substantive expectations for what students should know and be able to do in different subjects—content and performance standards—as anchors to which policies on textbook adoption, student assessment, and teacher certification could be tied.

So began the *standards* reform movement, which in many ways was able to bring the excellence and restructuring movements together and was sometimes called a "third wave" of reform. While "top-down" actors—state policymakers—would explicate standards or expectations for student learning and hold schools accountable for achieving them, "bottom-up" actors—teachers and local educators—would have great authority to restructure their own processes. Further, teachers, particularly in their disciplinary associations, were actively involved in standards development and so played a role in state-level activity as well. The National Council of Teachers of Mathematics showed that it was possible to reach consensus on sophisticated standards and provided a model for states and other subject-area associations.[5] Standards reforms were also seen as important remedies to prime failures of the earlier reform waves. The new approaches did not rely on empty mandates like course requirements, which had resulted in many low-level courses, but specified instead the challenging content students were expected to know. The new reforms did not rely on individual schools or districts to decide to restructure themselves one by one, an approach that would make improving education at scale impossible, but provided a supportive environment and incentives for all schools to reform.[6]

The standards movement has lasted for over twelve years, an extraordinary time, with support from virtually every constituency and level of government. By now, forty-nine states have content standards, which draw on models developed by disciplinary associations in every subject, and assessments said to be aligned to them; most have performance standards; most have made some effort to tie teacher certification to standards. The federal government supported and gave impetus to standards reforms with the 1994 and 2001 reauthorizations of the Elementary and Secondary Education Acts (ESEA). Now Title I students must be included in standards-based accountability systems.

There is some evidence that the standards movement is having desired effects. Performance on the National Assessment of Educational Progress (NAEP) and other national exams such as the SAT and ACT has risen, particularly in math, which was a big focus of the standards movement, given the leadership of the National Council of Teachers of Mathematics (NCTM) and the investment of hundreds of millions of dollars by the National Science Foundation in systemic reform initiatives. Some researchers have found that states with strong accountability have stronger student performance gains.[7] However, not all aspects of the standards reforms have been fully realized. Curricular improvement was never as widespread as hoped; policymakers left developing curriculum tied to standards up to schools rather than investing deliberately in it. Moreover, the standards often were vague, too vague to guide decisions about specific curricula, and many schools took the traditional route of equating curriculum decisionmaking with choosing a textbook series. Although new standards called for more challenging instructional approaches, teachers frequently lacked the requisite knowledge and skills in specific content areas or the belief that habitually low-performing students could really achieve the standards. Investments in capacity, such as improving teacher development, lagged relative to the need.

Another concern is that the standards reforms have been dominated by what was originally only one theme: test-driven accountability. The assessment policies that came to characterize the standards movement developed in ways very different from the visions of early standards reformers. Instead of sophisticated performance assessments with open-ended formats that could cover many domains of the standards and mirror good instruction with their challenging tasks, commercial tests with multiple-choice formats dominate. The latter are cheaper, take up less classroom time, and are better able to produce scores for individual students, something parents value. But they are also more amenable to test preparation and encourage teachers to focus narrowly on specific knowledge and skills. Instead of accountability systems that featured strategic technical assistance and support for failing schools, accountability remedies and sanctions are frequently meaningless, like permitting students to choose other public schools when options are really not available because of overcrowding or distance, and are aimed at only a small proportion of low-performing schools. Districts and states simply lack the capacity to provide intensive instructional improvement interventions.

At about the same time the standards movement was developing, some "bottom-up" advocates argued that, despite lip service to the "horse trade" of accountability for autonomy, the restructuring movement failed to go far enough in granting schools autonomy—especially in the key areas of budget, personnel, and curriculum—because these schools were still part of the existing district bureaucracies. It was argued that if schools were truly freed from regulations, except perhaps those pertaining to health and safety and civil rights, they could better design programs to meet the needs of their students, innovate, and develop creative solutions to meeting accountability expectations. A new contract with schools was envisioned: produce results, and all the rest is up to you. Thus was born the *charter school* movement, characterized by legislation in many states to encourage groups of teachers, parents, and other citizens to start new, innovative schools or to convert existing schools to freer status. In theory, the charter school movement was very compatible with standards reforms. Charters would be held accountable for meeting standards just like other schools, except that they would be exempt from any policies about how they should go about meeting them.

Minnesota passed the first charter school law in 1992. By 2001, there were more than 2,300 charter schools in thirty-four states and the District of Columbia. There's little evidence that as a class of reform they lead to improved student achievement or greater instructional innovation. This is not surprising; the charter approach is a structural reform that can, but doesn't necessarily, lead to improvements in instruction. Like restructuring more generally, how the governance changes are linked to instruction can vary from site to site. Further, the government side of accountability—the "horse trade" idea—does not seem to be working as intended. Few charters have been closed for poor performance. Those that have been closed have had managerial or financial problems. However, charters rank high in parental satisfaction and involvement. That students and parents choose to go to charter schools provides an important accountability mechanism that seems to be working as intended. Popular schools have waiting lists, while others close.[8]

Taking market accountability to an even greater level, there are a few examples of publicly funded *voucher* programs whereby students can choose to use public funding to attend private as well as public schools. Florida permits students in failing schools to attend private schools with public funding. In Milwaukee and Cleveland, public programs limited to low-income students permit students to use the voucher as a partial or full scholarship for both religious and secular private schools. A number of other cities, including New York and Washington, DC, have privately funded voucher schemes. The U.S. Supreme Court's 2002 decision in *Zelman v. Simmons-Harris*, which held that Cleveland's program does not abridge the First Amendment's prohibition against aiding religion, could encourage the development of more voucher programs, although state-specific prohibitions against sectarian aid could pose obstacles.

Voucher programs have had proponents over many years and exist in several other countries, like Colombia, Sweden, and Chile, but the examples in the previous paragraph all developed in the 1990s, stimulated by goals similar to those that animated the restructuring and charter movements. With vouchers, governments get out of the business of regulating schools, turning choices and authority over to the parent and student voucher holders. Accountability through the market theoretically holds schools responsible for results; the community of choice formed at the school is free to shape the operations and processes. In addition, vouchers may have been given a political push by new standards-based accountability systems that make school performance very public. Understandably, parents whose children attend schools labeled as failing want options. Inner-city parents who see private schools as the only viable alternative for their children have been among the most ardent voucher supporters. The right of students in a failing school to choose another (public) school is a specific provision in the accountability systems of many states and is now, through the No Child Left Behind Act (NCLB), the 2001 reauthorization of ESEA, required for Title I schools that still need improvement after a certain time period. As we've seen, Florida's accountability system permits choice of private schools; other states may follow in the wake of the *Zelman* decision.

As in the case of charters, the evidence on the effects of choice programs is mixed. Some students in some grades gain relative to public schools students; other students in the same schools of choice do not.[9] This finding reflects in part the lack of programs to study and the absence of rigorous research designs. But there is no question that, as more programs come on line, and on a larger scale than existing programs, interest in their effects will be intense. Adding to the interest is the fact that an increasing number of schools of choice, both private and public, regular and charter, are being managed by for-profit companies, or Education Management Organizations (EMOs).

Privatization became another important reform theme in the 1990s. Private firms originally interested in instruction—as opposed to transportation or food services, where they had long been involved—stuck to niche markets. Sylvan Learning, for example, offered instructional services for low-performing students, often in before- or afterschool settings. Eventually private firms began to take on whole schools and districts. Although two prominent cases of district management by private companies, in Baltimore and Hartford, ended in abrupt cessation of contracts and much controversy, the role of EMOs in school management has continued to grow. One recent estimate has these companies managing 15-20 percent of charter schools.[10] Edison Schools, Inc., the best known of the EMOs, is now managing 150 regular and charter schools throughout the nation, including twenty in Philadelphia as part of a state-directed remedy for school failure.

Evidence on the effects of EMOs, as in the case of charters and choice, is scarce. While Edison cites data about steady achievement gains, other studies question whether their schools are gaining any more than other schools in the same district. A recent study of charter schools in Michigan found that schools sponsored by Central Michigan University, many of which are managed by EMOs, generally had lower state test scores than other public schools. They also, however, enrolled higher percentages of disadvantaged children.[11]

We should not be surprised if there are no clear instructional or achievement effects of for-profit management. Like many of the reforms that devolved from the early restructuring movement, privatization is a structural change. Changing the provider of educational services doesn't necessarily change those services or their quality. We need to get under the banner of privatization to study specific instructional approaches and their effects and to determine the role that privatization per se plays in making those changes possible. It will be challenging to conduct such research in the case of private firms that may have different approaches to data sharing than public schools.

A final structurally focused reform coming to prominence in the last few years is the takeover of schools or districts by general government—states or cities. State takeover originated decades ago as a remedy for districts in financial trouble. By the late 1980s, states were beginning to include takeover for poor academic performance as the ultimate sanction in accountability plans. However, many states were reluctant to take that final step, knowing the limits of their own capacity to effect improvement in troubled districts and schools. In the cases we have of state takeover—in New Jersey and Pennsylvania, for example—new leadership has found it easier to clean up management and improve facilities than to improve instruction.[12] Most recently, a number of mayors in large cities have asserted control over school governance, arguing that accountability is best served when elected leaders, answerable to the public, have authority over the schools. They have taken a range of actions, from trying to influence board elections to seeking legislation permitting them to appoint school boards and chief executive officers. Michael Kirst sums up the impact of mayoral control: "Mayors are able to help balance the budget, improve buildings, and increase school supplies, but intervention in the classroom is more difficult."[13] Again, structural reforms do not necessarily lead to instructional improvement.

The last several reforms described—charters, choice, privatization, and state/mayoral takeover—are all theoretically compatible with standards reforms and have developed at the same time as the standards movement has taken a firmer hold. All place value on accountability for results, and the standards-based accountability approaches provide useful mechanisms. As we've seen, standards reforms can give impetus to some of these newer approaches by including choice or privatization or takeover as remedies for low-performance. However, taking a longer view, charters, choice, and privatization are exit options from the regular public school establishment on which standards reforms focus. They also move money from "regular" schools. If the standards movement fails to bring about substantial and sustained performance gains, despair over the possibility of improving public schools may lead to more support for these other options and a concomitant decline in support for public education.

REFORM THEMES

Despite the varied nature of the reform movements of the 1980s and 1990s—their "top-down" vs. "bottom-up" point of departure, for example—they share certain characteristics that define the last two decades. They have focused on educational quality as opposed to access to educational services; they have all used the rhetoric of accountability, which has become the strongest leitmotif over the last twenty years; and they have vastly increased the volume of reform activity and the number and diversity of players.

Emphasis on Quality

The reforms since *A Nation at Risk* have highlighted educational quality, not access to educational services, which had been the emphasis at both the state and federal levels in the past. Historically, with curriculum and teacher quality largely left up to local districts, states concentrated mostly on finance equity and minimum regulations about access to educational services. In the pre–World War II years, states began to try to compensate for differences in local ability to fund education with grants to school districts, generally flat per pupil amounts. In the 1970s, evidence was mounting that the flat amounts did not adjust for the growing gaps in the tax base among districts and that, in fact, because the flat grants were given to both wealthy and poor districts, they exacerbated the problem. Lawsuits challenging the constitutionality of inequitable court decisions multiplied, and most states reformed their finance systems to guarantee either a certain level of funding or the equivalent of a certain tax base to all districts.

Because they were responsible for providing the money, states also sought to assure that the services funded as a consequence met certain minimal requirements. To guarantee that students in all districts had access to certain basic services in order to meet state constitutional requirements for educational provision, states mandated minimal levels of courses to be provided, minimum numbers of days of the school year, minimum hours of instruction, and the like. They periodically checked to make sure that districts had curriculum policies in place and monitored district reports of teacher assignments to guarantee that teachers had valid state certificates.

It was only in the period surrounding *A Nation at Risk* that states turned to more substantive education policy issues like whether graduation requirements or teacher certification provisions were leading to an education system of sufficient quality, as opposed to a system that relied on minimal standards. Certainly the report's publication was not the only force at work. The growing amount of money that states were spending to reform their school finance systems and the consequent large increases in the state share of educational spending led policymakers to seek more control over how the money was spent. Also, state governments had modernized in the postwar period; with reapportioned and more professionalized legislatures, more executive branch capacity, and diversified tax systems, they were more capable of making substantive policy decisions and more aggressive about doing so.

As we've seen, the excellence movement was an early manifestation of the new emphasis on quality at the state level, and that emphasis has persisted throughout the other reform waves. Restructuring was about enhancing school-level ability to improve education, as was the charter movement. The standards movement ratcheted up the quality focus by relying on explicit statements of the knowledge and skills expected of students and by emphasizing challenging content. The choice and privatization movements are about letting other providers compete with public school districts on quality grounds.

As remarkable as the shift to a focus on quality was at the state level, the federal government's growing interest in educational quality is even more interesting. Historically, the federal government's role has focused on assuring that all citizens have equal protection under the law and providing additional resources for children with special needs. Sometimes, in the wake of what was deemed a national crisis, the federal government strayed beyond these limits to engage more substantively in educational matters. Such was the case in the post-Sputnik years when the National Defense Education Act of 1958 was seen as a way of making American students competitive with the best scientific minds elsewhere in the world. *A Nation at Risk* had somewhat of the same effect; it spelled out a crisis to which the government needed to react. Because it was issued during the Reagan administration, whose initial goal was to dismantle the U.S. Department of Education, much of what the federal government did in the 1980s was to cheer on the states in their excellence-related policymaking. But by the end of the decade, the president had joined the nation's governors in promulgating the National Education Goals, the National Science Foundation had begun a program to support standards-based systemic reform in the states, and the administration was supporting disciplinary associations to write standards in a number of subject areas.

In the early 1990s, a panel formed by the first President Bush to deliberate the implications of the education goals recommended the development of voluntary national education standards and a voluntary national assessment system. Presidents Bush and Clinton both acted on the recommendations and proposed legislation to support state standards reform and the development of the voluntary national standards and assessment system. Eventually, Goals 2000, which included grants to states and federal support for the development of voluntary standards, became law, in March 1994.

Political shifts in the mid-1990s and opposition to a Goals 2000 provision for a national council to approve standards meant that the voluntary national standards and assessment systems were never formally developed. Instead, the federal government focused on laws that encouraged the states to pursue standards reforms. The 1994 reauthorization of the Elementary and Secondary Education Act, the Improving America's Schools Act (IASA), tied aid for Title I, bilingual education, and a number of other federal programs to state standards developed under Goals 2000. Children in Title I schools were expected to make progress with challenging content and the performance standards expected of all children. The 2001 reauthorization, NCLB, continues the standards-based reform approach of IASA, but is less open to a variety of approaches to standards, assessment, and accountability policies, and more constraining about the policies states must have in place to receive Title I funding. Title I, which has been mostly a funding stream to direct money to districts and schools serving low-income students, is now bound up in a number of quality-related provisions.

The federal government has also supported charter and choice reforms. As this is written, Congress is likely to debate whether or not to maintain a provision in the 2002 tax package giving tax relief to parents sending children to private schools.

Accountability

It should already be clear that much of the policymaking following *A Nation at Risk* had to do with increased accountability for the resources that governments were investing in education. Accountability was not a new concept, but in the past districts were held accountable by the federal government and the states mostly for assuring that money flowed correctly and/or for compliance with regulations about minimal services. In the 1980s and 1990s, new approaches to accountability were developed.

The new systems are centered around student performance on statewide assessments, not on inputs like appropriate student/teacher ratios. Schools are held accountable for achieving either a certain level of performance (e.g., a percentage of students achieving at a "proficient" level) and/or for increasing performance from assessment period to assessment period. The new systems are focused on schools and students, not on districts. Test scores and other measures incorporated into indices are collected at the school level. In addition, by 2008, twenty-eight states will require that students pass a state-administered test for high school graduation.[14] Finally, the new systems include consequences for poor performance. A majority of the states require school improvement planning for low-performing schools. Beyond that, remedies range from technical assistance to intervention, including state takeover. Nineteen states have policies enabling them to reconstitute schools by changing the staff and/or student body.[15]

As we've seen, the new accountability's focus on results gained impetus from the influence of business leaders and ideas in education policy after *A Nation at Risk*. Since policymakers depended on business support for the large, costly, comprehensive reform packages they promoted in the excellence movement, it's not surprising that business ideas about accountability were influential.

The other reforms we have discussed have also all been tied to the emerging notion of accountability for performance. Restructuring, charter schools, choice, and contracting for provision of services with private firms are predicated on the notion that autonomy would come only in return for enhanced accountability for results. The standards movement gave added impetus. If standards were to be the primary focus, then achievement of the standards should be what schools were held accountable for, not compliance to regulations that might or might not contribute to greater achievement of the standards.

Most recently, the NCLB act heightened the emphasis on accountability even further. The law specifies the nature of state accountability systems, putting states at risk of losing their share of Title I funds if they do not base accountability on annual performance in math and reading and measure progress in a way spelled out by the federal government.

It is important to note that while accountability policies seem to be developing in a way that centralizes power—for example, the federal government holding states accountable, states taking over failing schools, etc.—the U.S. education system is still relatively decentralized and very complicated, especially when compared to the rest of the world. The federal government has not had significant success in enforcing its policies; one of the reasons for NCLB's strict provisions is Congress' dissatisfaction with state compliance with the 1994 ESEA reauthorization. States may find ways, such as lowering the definition of "proficiency" that schools must meet, to evade the spirit of the law. Further, some of the reforms that encompass notions of accountability move authority to new providers, like private firms or nongovernmental charter school authorizers, dispersing rather than concentrating power.

Growth of the Education Sector

Whatever the various reforms purport for educational improvement, they certainly have meant significant growth in the volume of educational policy, the size of the education sector of our economy, and the number and variety of players on the education scene. With each new cycle of school reform, governments at all levels began to develop more and more policy.[16] Some states that had confined themselves mainly to finance formula adjustments every few legislative sessions now had hundreds of education provisions come through the legislature. According to one estimate, there were one thousand bills on teacher quality alone between 1983 and 1986.[17]

Spending has grown accordingly. In constant 2000–2001 dollars, total elementary and secondary spending in the United States rose from about $200 billion in 1980 to about $350 billion today; per pupil spending rose from close to $5,000 to about $7,500 over the same period.[18] If one adds the private money invested in and spent on elementary and secondary education, expenditures come up to over $400 billion.

All this money both reflects and attracts new players to the education scene. Not only are there private firms operating schools and directly providing educational services, but there are also associations offering curricular materials, foundations supporting specific reform initiatives, organizations providing professional development, textbook and test publishers.[19] As education policy has grown in volume and cost, so too have the number and diversity of providers.

CHALLENGES

Despite twenty years of reforms, major challenges remain with us. First, the reforms have left us with significant *inequities* in our educational system. Poorer schools still generally spend less than wealthier counterparts; lower-performing students typically have less prepared and less qualified teachers than higher-achieving students; achievement gaps between minorities and whites and more and less advantaged students remain large. Equity has not been a focus of the last twenty years. This is not to say it was entirely neglected in favor of the emphasis on quality; spending continued to increase in part to continue to compensate for differences in wealth, standards policies were meant to bring all students to high levels of achievement, and accountability systems included technical assistance and support for low-performing schools. However, as we've seen, states and districts have lacked the capacity to mount serious interventions to improve instruction, to turn around low-performing schools, and to close achievement gaps significantly. Very recently, there's some indication that at least some aspects of inequality are beginning to get greater attention. The Maryland legislature passed a bill aimed at providing an "adequate" education for all students; court cases aimed at that goal have also been mounted. New evidence on the high percentage of unqualified teachers in high-poverty and high-minority schools is generating significant comment.[20]

A second challenge concerns the difficulty of improving the system at *scale*. While each reform has had some successes, none has brought improvement in every school it touched or helped large numbers of schools significantly. The successes of the standards movement seem to be limited to elementary schools, and all the other reforms have had mixed results and have been limited to relatively small numbers of schools. One problem is that many of the reforms were not aimed at instructional improvement but were largely structural fixes; but even the more instructionally oriented reforms, such as standards policies, have fallen short. As we've seen, reforms have stumbled on a lack of capacity—among the teaching force, for example, and in states and districts that must offer technical assistance. Investing in capacity is a long-term and expensive proposition, but it seems clear that without greater investment and more strategic thinking around teacher quality and curriculum, instructionally focused policies are not likely to encounter greater success.

The waves of education reform exacerbate a third major challenge that has remained with us throughout the last twenty years. Our system is very confusing; the more policy and players, the more conflicting messages we produce. When new reforms are enacted, the old policies remain on the books. A major challenge is to provide more *coherence* to the educational system, to permit greater focus, and to clarify the messages given to teachers. All the waves of reform failed to create a coherent instructional guidance system. Instead, they typified the American approach of turning to new solutions before the ink is even dry on existing policies.

A Nation at Risk sparked far-reaching changes in American education. Ever since, we have lived in an era of reform. It may be that the emphasis on "reform" itself is part of the problem. Every time we see a new problem, or an old problem in a new way, we craft a new policy solution. Since it's easier to fix the structure of schooling than to address deep issues of teaching and learning, we frequently turn to structural solutions. We assume the new approach will be "the" answer that has eluded us in the past. We never tire of "magic bullets." We also never ask how compatible the new approaches are with existing policies or anticipate the challenges of translating new policies into practice, given the residue of old policies and traditions that shape school and classroom activities. If we want improvement for all students, at scale, we'd better think less about new, different reform approaches and more about investing in the necessary capacity to bring about coherent, sustained, instructionally focused strategies.

CHAPTER TWO

Change and Improvement in Educational Reform

RICHARD F. ELMORE

E ducation policy in the U.S. has arguably not been much about education, at least the sort of education that occurs among teachers and students in classrooms. It has, however, been a great deal about policy, the kind of high-level political discourse that generates controversy and electoral credit for public officials. The great political and social struggles around education in the twentieth century have been about issues like the expansion of access to schooling (e.g., mandatory attendance), the institutional forms of schooling (the comprehensive high school, vocational education, what to do about the middle grades), and inequalities of opportunity among different types of children (financing inequities, compensatory education, desegregation, special education). While these struggles have been significant in their own right and have changed much about the institutional structure, rules of access, and social conditions of schooling in the United States, they have done little directly or intentionally about what teachers and students experience on a daily basis in classrooms. Indeed, the major theme of education policy seems, until recently, to have been the disconnect between policy and practice.[1]

Throughout the twentieth century, a rich and powerful series of debates about educational practice ran in parallel with policymaking—the struggle for the soul of progressive education, the emergence of child development theory and practice, the emergence of cognitive and behavioral approaches to instruction in reading and writing, and the like. But the two discourses of policy and practice have rarely intersected, and when they have, they have done little to inspire confidence in either policy or practice, as in the longstanding debate over evolution and creationism, or the more recent struggle between phonics and whole language instruction in reading.[2]

To say that policy and practice have been engaged in parallel play is not to say that the two discourses have not influenced each other, usually in unintentional and perverse ways. The emergence of the American comprehensive high school is a case in point. The comprehensive high school was a largely structural reform designed to accommodate huge increases in enrollment in the first half of the twentieth century, with only the thinnest of pedagogical theories behind it. This structure has been enduring and persistent, and has profoundly influenced access to learning for generations of high school students and the conditions of teaching for generations of teachers, often in manifestly destructive ways. But the reform itself was never much about how teachers taught and students learned. In fact, that may have been its major advantage as a policy idea. It was a largely empty structural vessel into which educators and communities could pour whatever content and pedagogy they wished. Those reformers who focused on issues of teaching and learning have typically moved outside the existing structure of the comprehensive high school to demonstrate that alternative conceptions of learning could coexist in other settings. And still, the comprehensive high school survives. Still, the parallel discourse about what good teaching and learning looks like for adolescents survives. The two have had not much to do with each other.[3]

Now, two decades after *A Nation at Risk*, this parallel relationship between policy and practice seems to be changing in ways that are unprecedented in American educational policy. The course of educational reform has led, probably inadvertently, over the past twenty years toward the classroom—toward a more explicit connection between what policy says and what teachers and students are expected to do. The question now is whether this connection will occur and, if it does, what influence it will have.

A Nation at Risk has relatively little to say about this issue. In fact, the report itself is a good example of old-style policy-as-usual—broad language carrying no specific proposals, designed to mobilize *others* to act, locating responsibility for its proposals in a broad array of actors distant from its point of origin in Washington, DC. It could hardly have done otherwise, originating in a presidential administration that had three years earlier run on a promise to dismantle the U.S. Department of Education and dramatically reduce the federal presence in education, declaring education to be wholly a state and local responsibility. Politically, the report was masterfully engineered by then-Secretary of Education Ted Bell as a way of positioning himself and an initially reluctant administration in a proactive role in education, and salvaging the Department, without committing the administration or the federal government to actually doing anything.[4]

Not surprisingly, then, the report is clearer on diagnosis than on prescription. It defines the central problem as low expectations for academic work in schools, weak preparation for teachers in academic content, and insufficient time on academic work in schools. It suggests that the remedies to these problems are the joint responsibility of teachers, local school administrators, school boards, and states—with a modest and vaguely defined role for the federal government in supporting others' work. More importantly, while the report is quite critical of the performance of schools in general, it is quite vague in its diagnosis of what has produced this problem. Presumably, the same institutional structure that produced the problem is the one that the report calls upon to exercise responsibility in solving it. It is as though the problems described in the report were a sort of unintentional side effect of teaching, administration, and governance of schools. Bringing these problems to the attention of teachers, school administrators, school board members, state legislators, and governors was sufficient to engage their full energy—suddenly—in a new, more powerful way. Not surprisingly, many educational practitioners saw in the report another example of policy-as-usual: a broad critique with vague prescriptions, ungrounded in anything that looked or smelled like a real school.

But *A Nation at Risk* did legitimize an already growing political movement that had begun in southern and border states, like Florida, South Carolina, and Kentucky, and, in time, gradually spread to virtually every other state. The so-called "reform movement" in the early 1980s was protean and incoherent, covering everything from increases in teachers' salaries to school finance reform to merit pay for teachers to school-site management and internal restructuring. It was a political cause in search of a theme, fueled largely by self-defined progressive southern politicians, like Richard Riley of South Carolina, Bob Graham of Florida, and Bill Clinton of Arkansas, looking for ways to bring their states into the mainstream economic and political life of the country.

It wasn't until the Education Summit of 1989 in Charlottesville, Virginia, between then-President George Bush and the governors, chaired by Bill Clinton, that what we currently regard as education reform began to emerge. The significance of this meeting was unprecedented in the history of U.S. educational policy: the chief elected executives from the states, sitting with the President of the United States to discuss a common strategy for educational reform. The vision of reform that emerged from this meeting probably would have surprised the authors of *A Nation at Risk* in its specificity and strategic focus. The deal—or the "horse trade" as then-Secretary of Education Lamar Alexander called it—was increased discretion for results. The federal government and states would focus their policy on results, defined as student learning, and schools and localities were expected to exercise their judgment and expertise to achieve those results. Only in cases of outright failure would the federal government or the states intervene in the affairs of local schools—and then only to remedy immediate causes and leave. This idea was the kernel of what we now call education reform: that the government's job is to regulate and reward *results*, and it is the job of school people to produce them. This idea began to work its way through state reforms and through successive reauthorizations of the federal Elementary and Secondary Education Act (ESEA) over the next decade-plus.

At the heart of this theory is the belief—shared by New Democrats and Republicans—that bureaucracy, government regulation, and institutional complexity sap human creativity and energy. Removing the dead hand of bureaucracy and overregulation by focusing government on results frees people to do what they know is right and effective. Education reform henceforth would come to mean accountability for results. And it is this theory that has been developed and modified in the laboratory of federalism for the last decade or so.

While accountability for results has proven to be a powerful and durable political idea, it has had no more basis in the reality of practice for most educators than previous policy ideas. Throughout the entire post–*Nation at Risk* period, education reform was largely *done to,* rather than *done with,* educational professionals. To a large degree, the dominant interests in state reform were general government officials and business interests. Educational interest groups—including the nominally powerful teachers unions—have been put in the role of responding to proposals initiated elsewhere, usually influencing policy only on the margins. Educators were largely considered to be part of the problem rather than part of the solution. The irony, of course, is that these same professionals were those who were charged with implementing performance-based accountability. The same people whose judgment and initiative is required to make accountability for results work are the people who produced the failures that created the occasion for reform. State reformers, obviously, do not have much sense of irony.[5]

Another deep irony of this reform period is that it is premised on the belief that focusing government regulation on performance frees people in schools to do what they know is right and effective, but, of course, most of what people in schools know how to do they have learned by working in the same schools that policymakers think are failing. What educators knew how to do was what they were already doing, not what policymakers were asking them to do.[6]

Fast-forward to the present: forty-eight or so of the fifty states now have some version of performance-based accountability systems, broadly defined as standards for content and student performance, assessments of student learning, public release of data on student and school performance, and some degree of consequences or "stakes" for poor performance. These systems vary widely in the specifics of their architecture—whether they involve specific stakes or consequences for schools and students, how frequently they test, how explicit the content and performance standards are, how difficult the tests are, etc.—but performance-based accountability has become the main theme of state education policy.[7] With the adoption of the No Child Left Behind Act in 2002—the centerpiece of federal education policy—the federal government is now in the position of being the chief enforcer of performance-based accountability at the state and local level. The new law is unprecedented in the specificity of its requirements on state and local agencies: annual testing in grades three through eight, specific targets for annual yearly progress in student performance, mandates for quality control in hiring of teachers, state and local remedial measures for failing schools, and exit options for parents of children in failing schools. No Child Left Behind goes far beyond any federal role envisioned by the 1989 educational summit, much less the calculatedly vague *A Nation at Risk*, and far beyond any previous definition of the federal role in education. Performance-based accountability is now federal *and* state policy.

The reform movement is far enough along at the state and local level to have revealed that the central idea behind the "horse trade" of performance for discretion and control is highly suspect. The premise that educators know what to do and all they need are the correct incentives to do it is essentially wrong. *Some* educators know what to do; *most* don't. *Some* are able to learn what to do on their own; *most* are not. About the same proportion of educators are capable of responding successfully to performance-based accountability as were successful under the previous regime. Educators, like most practitioners, learn most of what they know from what they do. It should not surprise us that the best predictor of what they will do at Time 2, other things being equal, is what they were doing at Time 1. The main lesson of the reform movement thus far is that increasing performance in schools is complex and difficult work —much more difficult than simply changing policy.

A large part of this difficulty has to do with the fact that performance-based accountability challenges the chronic and powerful disconnect historically between policy and practice in education. This disconnect is deeply rooted in the institutional structure of education in the United States. It is the consequence of a governance structure that promotes superficiality and instability in local leadership, that chronically under-invests in the knowledge and skills of teachers and school-level administrators, and that sends conflicting and multiple messages to people in schools about the nature and purpose of their work.[8] There is simply no way to solve the problem of large-scale improvement in educational performance without connecting policy and practice more directly and powerfully. It is this connection that we have been avoiding in variety of ways, through a variety of pretexts, throughout the twentieth century, but especially since *A Nation at Risk*. Schools simply cannot do what they are being asked to do without more explicit and powerful guidance and support for instructional practice and without major changes in investments in knowledge and skill for educational practitioners.

Put simply, educational reformers are gradually, unavoidably, and reluctantly approaching the inevitable conclusion that schools cannot simultaneously be the cause of failure and the source of success. Asking teachers and administrators to increase academic performance for students without fundamentally altering the conditions under which they failed to produce student learning in the first place is a dead end. Teachers and administrators generally do what they know how to do— they do not deliberately engage in actions they know will produce substandard performance, nor do they intentionally withhold knowledge that they know might be useful to student learning. If schools are not meeting expectations for student learning, it is largely because *they do not know what to do*. And, given the longstanding disconnect between policy and practice, neither do policymakers. In its least desirable face, educational reform can become a kind of conspiracy of ignorance: policymakers mandating results they do not themselves know how to achieve, and educators pretending they do know what to do but revealing through their actions that they don't.

Under these conditions, "change" can become an attractive nuisance. Policymakers "change" policy in order to keep faith with their constituents—raising standards, increasing the difficulty and frequency of testing, raising the stakes for students, threatening failing schools with adverse consequences. Practitioners reciprocate by engaging in their own brand of "change": teaching test items; expanding the amount of instructional time but not the actual content or quality of instruction for students who fail to meet standards; holding students out of testing grades who are at risk of failure; providing public recognition for students and teachers who meet performance expectations but not explaining how they did; and so forth. What's interesting about these conditions of "change" is that they are almost perfectly symbiotic—both sides are benefiting from the "changes" each is undertaking—and also almost perfectly pointless in educational terms. Both sides are operating in a mutually and tacitly acknowledged zone of ignorance.

This view of policymaking as "change making" also dovetails nicely with the pathologies of the governance structure for education in the United States. Administrators are selected and promoted largely on the basis of their ability to inspire confidence in communities and locally elected school boards, not usually on the basis of their knowledge of instructional practice. They seek approval and recognition by proposing agendas of "change" that maximize public visibility but minimize actual impact on instructional practice. Local board members collude in the dance of change by identifying themselves with the agenda of leaders. Since the effects of changes proposed by leaders are ephemeral, leaders often survive by moving on to other communities with other boards looking for "change." This phenomenon—called *policy churn*—is a powerful pattern in American education policy.[9]

And it runs exactly counter to the requirements of performance-based accountability. Over the long term, it is impossible to improve student performance without eventually improving the quality of teaching and learning that occurs in classrooms and schools. This work is hard, precisely because it is countercultural in virtually every respect: it requires the mobilization and use of knowledge that is not presently in schools and classrooms, it requires the active engagement of people whose knowledge is primarily about teaching and learning rather than about the tailoring of ideas to an unstable political environment, and it requires the design and operation of institutional structures that alter the way people learn to do their work.

In the default mode, the governance and organizational structure of American education is all about change and not much about improvement. Performance-based accountability forces the issue of whether schools and school systems can be about the improvement of learning for adults and children. There are two possible scenarios from here forward. The first is that the parallel play of policy and practice will continue, driven by deeply institutionalized forms and incentives, and, ultimately, it will become clear that performance-based accountability has failed to materially improve conditions of teaching and learning in schools, except for those schools that manage to succeed under any set of external conditions. The second scenario is that performance-based accountability will force the forms and incentives of American education into a new relationship to learning, which will actually improve conditions for learning in schools.

As should be clear, part of the problem here is semantic, and in this instance semantics matter a great deal. The term *change* has become so corrupted in its application to education, at least in the U.S., that it is practically useless as descriptor of anything related to the core functions of schooling. The problem of American education is not, as many proponents of change argue, that schools and the people in them "resist change." Quite the contrary, school boards, superintendents, and principals are all rewarded and reinforced for "changing" routinely and promiscuously. The problem is that schools are poorly equipped to *improve* the conditions of teaching and learning for teachers and students. To be sure, improvement requires change, in some sense. But the key semantic distinction is between *change* that has little or no measurable, cumulative effect on learning and that is driven by forces disconnected from teaching and learning, and *improvements* that are designed to direct attention and resources toward deliberate enhancements in the knowledge and skill of teachers and students designed to improve their performance. Another way of saying this is that change has a clear meaning only in an instrumental sense—change that *leads to* improvements in human capacity.

Thoughtful students of educational change acknowledge that few reforms ever reach teaching and learning, much less alter it in any fundamental way, and they agree in principle that useful change is, in some sense, about making the conditions of teaching and learning better.[10] But research on educational change, and its consulting spinoffs, are fundamentally concerned with advising people how to "manage change," rather than with questioning the value and role of change. The literature and practice of educational change is deeply concerned with how to convince people that they should change, how to make the need for change more compelling and palatable to a range of actors, how to hone and develop the skills of leaders to lead change, how to design organizations to be more or less perpetual change machines (because, after all, the world is constantly changing), and so forth. "Change in the service of what?" is a less compelling question in this literature. Even less compelling is the question of whether successful schools don't actually engage in less change of a visible sort, less fancy change-mastering and -leading, and more concentrated work on fewer big ideas directly connected to their core processes of teaching and learning than less successful schools. Even the most confirmed students of educational change would agree that the level of visible change activity in schools, or school systems, is no predictor of how successful they are likely to be.

The semantics of educational reform have traditionally been quite slippery around this issue, and the period since *A Nation at Risk* is no exception. The political rhetoric of reform, as we have seen, has been rather carefully designed (a) to mobilize commitment to change, but (b) to diffuse responsibility for the actions and consequences that follow from change, and (c) to avoid acknowledging that the problems that require change are produced by the very people and institutions that are being asked to engage in the changes required to fix these problems. The circularity here is obvious, and it can only be broken by teleology—that is, by assigning a purpose and direction to change and by assessing the value of change by the degree to which it makes progress toward that purpose.

Another semantic problem of educational reform is its tendency to substitute rhetoric for might be called a "theory of action." The "horse trade" underlying performance-based accountability is a classic example of this. "Discretion for results" sounds attractive as an organizing idea for a policy, but, in fact, there is no well-worked-out theory of how you get from performance-based accountability to improvements in teaching and learning. Performance-based accountability may have a powerful political logic behind it, but it has no causal theory that would explain how applying increased scrutiny to performance will in fact lead people in schools to do their work more effectively. Worse, as we begin to sketch out the details of what such a theory might look like, it is apparent that it doesn't much look like "discretion for results." In fact, it begins to look like *less* discretion of a particular kind for *greater consistency* and *higher levels* of results.[11]

With this congenital slipperiness of policy rhetoric in mind, let me stipulate a simple, some would say simplistic, definition of improvement: *Improvement equals increased quality and performance over time.* Put quality and performance on the vertical axis and time on the horizontal; improvement consists of moving in a roughly northeasterly direction. It is important to talk about both quality and performance as objectives of improvement for two reasons. First, agreement on what constitutes quality practice precedes and informs improvement in performance in education. In order to know what kind of performance we are trying to produce, we must first know what we are trying to do to produce that performance. Second, it is impossible to say whether performance has value unless one is prepared to defend the quality of the performance expected and the quality of the measures that act as proxies for that performance. So, for example, it makes no sense to talk about "improving reading performance" unless one has in mind some set of high-quality practices that would lead to increased proficiency in reading among students. Nor does it make sense to define reading performance in a way that is easily achievable but trivial in its value to students. Time, in the definition, speaks for itself. It takes time to improve, and we expect more or less steady progress in quality and performance over time.

Underneath this model of improvement lie two key ideas. The first is that there is such a thing as an *instructional core* that can be improved. In the United States, this is a controversial idea, since the culture of teaching has grown up around the idea that teaching practice is somehow irreducibly idiosyncratic and that "good" teaching is more an individual trait than a function of knowledge and skill. These beliefs about teaching are, of course, a dead end, because if there is no objective way to discriminate among more and less effective teaching practices and all practices are matters of personal taste and determined by individual traits, then there is no way to engage in any kind of discourse about teaching, much less improve it. In fact, all professional practices involve a core of knowledge that is relatively specifiable and teachable, surrounded by a zone of discretion in which practitioners are expected to use their judgment in adapting practice to specific circumstances. Trait theories of teaching are more a symptom of the intellectual underdevelopment of teaching practice than a valid characterization of the nature of the work.

The instructional core is defined by the relationship of the student and the teacher in the presence of content. In this model, it is possible to talk about the knowledge and skill of the teacher in relation to the content, the knowledge and skill of the teacher in relation to the student's mastery of the content, the knowledge and skill of the student in relation to the content and the students' knowledge of the teacher's expectations around the content, and the ways in which the content is refracted through the understanding of the teacher and student. There are, of course, many more things that education is about than instructional practice, and these things have value, but if education is not, in some fundamental sense, about the interaction of the teacher and student in the presence of the content, then it is, more likely than not, not about much.

The second key idea underneath the improvement model is that of *capacity* or *capability*, defined as the resources, knowledge, and skill that the teacher and student bring to the instructional core and the ability of the organizational surround—the school and the larger institutional environment—to enhance and support the resources, knowledge, and skill of the teacher and student. Capacity both *inheres in* teachers and students and it *comes to* them from external sources.

Improvement occurs, then, by raising the capacity of key relationships in the instructional core: by increasing teachers' knowledge of content and their knowledge of how to connect the content to specific students, by increasing the prerequisite knowledge that students bring to their interactions with teachers and by deepening their own knowledge of themselves as learners, by increasing the complexity and demand of content, etc.[12]

There is no other way to enhance capacity, as it is defined above, than by deliberately investing in the knowledge and skill of teachers and students to do the work of learning. This means literally using the school and the institutional structure that surrounds it as a mechanism to deliver resources and supports to teachers and students to enhance their learning. A controversial idea: that schools should become places dedicated to adult and student learning.

It is difficult to imagine schools succeeding on a large scale in responding to performance-based accountability without some deliberate theory of improvement. Some schools—those least in need of improvement—will no doubt manage their relationship to performance-based accountability systems by making more intensive use of the social capital that surrounds them in their affluent communities without actually doing much about teaching and learning. Some schools—those in need of improvement but out of range of the resources and opportunities necessary to improve the instructional core—will try to respond to performance-based accountability by doing what they have done in the past with greater focus and intensity. And many schools will try, at least initially, to meet the demands of performance-based accountability by gaming the system—teaching test items, moving content around in the calendar, holding students out of the testing stream, etc.—until they run out of such options. Sooner or later, if performance-based accountability is going to work as a policy, it will need a theory of improvement that is actually on the ground, in action, instantiated in an institutional structure, affecting the work of people in schools.

Notice I said "if performance-based accountability is going to work as a policy." In the world of policymaking, one always has to entertain the possibility that policies are more or less purely symbolic acts, and that the major point of policymaking may not be to influence the world but to display concern, generate short-term electoral credit, and move on to the next issue. It is quite possible that governors, state legislators, business interest groups, and now, after No Child Left Behind, bipartisan national political leaders, including the president and congressional leaders, are not primarily interested in the stated purposes of performance-based accountability but are using the issue of accountability to frame the issue of education for their electoral constituencies.

If performance-based accountability is a largely symbolic policy, then it is a peculiarly ill-suited one. The key distinction between performance-based accountability and earlier reforms, dating back to the beginning of the twentieth century, is that it actually carries the evidence of its own success. We will know whether the policy is working or not by the evidence that the policy itself produces. Symbolic policymaking requires a certain discrete distance between the rhetoric of policymaking and data on its effects, so that policymakers can always assert that they did not intend what the data show. In essence, policymakers are playing with fire by requiring the measurement of school performance: They are betting on a policy that essentially has no theory of action behind it, and they have bet the credibility of policymaking institutions (if not their own credibility) since elected.

What is at stake then in this experiment with performance-based accountability is the logic of confidence around public education. As long as the relationship between policy and practice was characterized as parallel play, everyone could be a winner. Policymakers and school leaders could engage in policy churn, reaping the benefits of new initiatives without ever having to deal with their consequences. Schools could manifest their commitment to "change" by engaging in activities that had little effect on their core functions, and by marginalizing those examples that did. The public could orient itself toward whichever aspects of schools they chose, since policymakers sent a welter of messages to multiple constituencies about how their interests were served by specific changes. Parallel play served everyone's interests well, except possibly the interest of students in learning. But then, students have never been a well-represented constituency in education.

The problem with performance-based accountability is that it stipulates the measures by which schools will be determined to be successful or not, those measures are in turn verdicts on the success of the policies themselves, and the policy disrupts the traditional logic of confidence around schools by asserting that schools are primarily responsible for student learning. As if this weren't enough, it is probably impossible to succeed at performance-based accountability without violating the principle of parallel play between policy and practice.

If the path to performance is primarily through deliberate practices of improvement, designed to enhance the resources, knowledge, and skill in the instructional core, then policy must necessarily be *about* practice, not about symbolic change and policy churn. This possibility is all the more problematical because the U.S. has little experience with policies that are designed to connect policy and practice in useful ways. A few examples will suffice.

It seems clear from both research and practice that professional development—highly focused on specific content and the pedagogy that goes with it and delivered as close as possible to the classrooms and schools in which it will be used—is a promising way to improve instructional practice. In most states and school districts and schools no infrastructure exists for delivering professional development in this way. The obvious remedy for this would be for policymakers at the state and local level to invest in building up an infrastructure of intermediary institutions that would work with schools and districts on the delivery of heavily content-focused professional development. The political incentives to support this kind of investment are extremely weak and the level of sophistication required to do it well is way beyond that of most political leaders.

It is dawning on a number of actors involved in serious work on instructional improvement that the "discretion for performance" model of accountability in the horse trade is deeply flawed. Teachers and their organizations are, in fact, asking for more explicit curriculum guidance in order to meet performance standards. And their analysis is compelling. Under the system of parallel play, the curriculum grew in response to essentially political imperatives—subjects were added to the curriculum in response to constituency pressures, textbooks ballooned in size and topic coverage in response to politically driven state adoption processes, activities in classrooms multiplied in response to teacher initiatives, and special programs constructed their own version of the curriculum for "their" students. Teachers who are actually trying to figure out how to respond to pressure for student performance very quickly understand that improvement of performance requires focus, and focus requires discipline, both in practice and in the external demands that administrators put on teachers. Under these circumstances, having a simpler, more explicit, more focused curriculum begins to seem to teachers to be more advantageous. And, of course, the policy structure around schools is designed to produce complexity, controversy, and flux, rather than stability, simplicity, and focus. Where are the political incentives that will draw policymakers and educational leaders into a different view of curriculum guidance?

One of the first things that dawns on schools and districts when they begin to receive performance data is the *range* of variability in student performance at any given grade level. This is certainly true in urban schools, but it is also true in nominally "high-performing" schools in more privileged communities. The trend in performance-based accountability systems, exemplified in No Child Left Behind, is toward *more* disaggregation of results by level of performance and type of student, directing attention away from average school performance levels and toward the way schools serve specific populations of students. As a matter of practice, we know very little about how to accelerate learning in specific domains from students whose performance is well below those of their peers. Most so-called remediation consists of putting students in the same kind of instructional settings in which they failed in the first place for longer periods of time, on the theory that it was the students who failed rather than the teachers who taught them. As the variability in student performance becomes clearer, the paucity of effective remediation and acceleration practices will become clearer, as will the relative lack of a knowledge base in this area and an institutional infrastructure to bring it into schools and classrooms. Who will own this problem politically, and who will generate the kind of sustained focus of resources and knowledge to address it?

These are a few examples of what happens when policy and practice move from parallel play to a necessary connection. The problems are daunting and the signs that policymakers are prepared for them are weak and erratic. It is unclear at the moment whether policymakers have any idea what they have done by unleashing performance-based accountability.

* * *

A Nation at Risk was a largely symbolic event in the early history of the current generation of education reform. It represented policy-as-usual in many respects, not the least of which was its tendency to define problems and push the responsibility for solving them onto other players in other settings, and to reinforce the idea of parallel play between policy and practice. It added legitimacy to a growing reform movement that did not begin to take on its present focus until 1989. And as the idea of performance-based accountability has developed, it has become progressively clearer that it is both highly subversive and vastly underspecified. If performance-based accountability is about anything other than symbolic action, then we are facing some major challenges in the way we think about schools and their improvement. The work of improvement is very different from the work of change as it has been traditionally defined in education. It requires more focus, more sustained effort, greater attention to the core processes of instruction, and more discipline in holding the policy agenda steady while providing the resources and support for teachers and students to respond. It is unclear whether either the policy system or the administrative structure of education are built for this work.

CHAPTER THREE

The Academic Imperative: New Challenges and Expectations Facing School Leaders

TIMOTHY KNOWLES

In the last two decades, public schools have faced a remarkable challenge: to ensure that all students are able to meet high academic standards. While one might assume that academic achievement has always been the primary purpose of American public schools, it has not. For the last century schools have attended to social goals that have had little to do with ensuring that students achieve at high levels, goals such as the assimilation of immigrants and extending the opportunities of education to those who had historically been excluded. Throughout most of the last century academic achievement was expected of few.[1]

In the early 1980s expectations for public schools began to shift. Business and political leaders sounded alarms about America's dwindling competitiveness, no more forcefully than in *A Nation at Risk*. The disparities in achievement among different racial, ethnic, and immigrant groups and classes became cause for public concern. At the same time, a growing chorus of questions was being raised about the capacity of teachers to prepare students for the new economy.[2]

The new "academic imperative" facing public schools has prompted change on almost every educational front. It has created armies of academics, entrepreneurs, and policymakers fortified with new ideas, technologies, and policies designed to get schools to address the new challenge. It has opened new frontiers of public schooling, which two decades ago would have seemed inconceivable: for-profit public schools, a burgeoning charter school movement, public vouchers for private and parochial schools. It has spurred a vast amount of new research that has challenged commonly held beliefs about what knowledge is and how it is acquired.

For the individuals leading American public schools the changes are tremendous and complex. In essence, the new K–12 landscape has redefined what good school leadership is, what it requires, how it is measured, and how it is developed. Not only must school leaders learn to reinvent their schools, many of them must also learn to reinvent themselves. Consider how one veteran principal responds when describing what the work of the principal once was:

> What a principal used to be? Boy, not what it is now. We weren't expected to know so much and do so much as we are now. People might not agree with me, but I think it was an easier job. There wasn't the pressure . . . there is all this new work—and I mean lots of new work—and none of the old work has gone away.

The job was management, it was keeping the buses running on time, the kids safe and secure, the parents happy, the superintendent happy. Teaching and learning was for teachers to worry about. You had to be able to manage, be a good disciplinarian. And someone in the district needed to like you.[3] While management skills, the nerve to discipline, and political savvy are undoubtedly qualities principals still need, improving teaching and learning has become the school leader's central concern, the essential benchmark for success.

This chapter explores three issues. First, it examines what has been learned about school leadership over the last twenty years and where some of the gaps in our understanding about instructional leadership lie. Second, it explores what effective instructional leadership requires and the implications for the work of school districts and others interested in the development of school leaders. Finally, it looks at what needs to be done if strong instructional leadership is to become the norm in American schools, not the exception.

WHAT WE HAVE LEARNED

The idea that the principal is a key actor on the school scene, with a central role to play in the drama of school improvement, is not new. In 1929, Ellwood P. Cubberley, the first dean of Stanford University's School of Education, asserted, "As is the principal, so is the school," observing that "the knowledge, insight, skill, and qualities for helpful leadership of the principal practically determines the ideals and standards of achievement of both teacher and students within the school."[4]

Since *A Nation at Risk*, a growing body of research literature has accumulated that—to varying degrees of specificity—describes effective school leadership. Two primary themes emerge from this literature. First, principals are called on to adapt to new notions of leadership. According to Joseph Murphy, president of the Principals Leadership Academy at Ohio State, principals must change "from implementers to initiators, from compliance officers to entrepreneurial risk takers, from bureaucratic managers to collaborative colleagues."[5] The school leader's primary goal is no longer "the maintenance of the organizational infrastructure, but rather the development of human resources."[6] The second theme suggests that principals must exercise instructional leadership: taking action or delegating responsibility to others to promote good teaching and growth in student learning through collaboration with teachers.

For principals, the challenge of these new demands is complicated by the fact that our understanding of what knowledge is and how it is acquired have evolved rapidly as well. Knowledge is no longer viewed as something possessed by the teacher and transmitted to students. Rather, it is seen as emergent, uncertain, and subject to revision, something mutually constructed by teachers *and* students. Further, educators are expected to understand and adapt to the ways in which social and cultural conditions affect student learning. They are encouraged to build on what students know and teach students to take responsibility for their own learning through rich discourse, extensive independent work, and hands-on activities.

The challenges principals face in making sense of and applying these new ideas are exacerbated by the research literature itself, which suffers from two quite remarkable gaps. The first gap is the absence of research that connects new conceptions about school leadership with new understandings about how students learn. A quiet assumption seems to resound through the literature—that principals who embody the new leadership skills will, de facto, improve instruction in their schools. There appears to be little, if any, evidence to support this assumption. Can we assume that a collaborative principal will somehow help teachers invest students with increased responsibility for their own learning? Will interactions between teachers and students actually change? The answers to these particular questions are not what is important here. What is important is that while *instructional leadership* is a compelling and frequently used term, the bodies of knowledge that the term encompasses—leadership and instruction—are distinct, even separate. The absence of empirical connections between these bodies of knowledge suggests that the strategies a principal should employ to improve instruction remain, in many ways, up for grabs.

A second, related gap is the lack of a clear link between what is expected of instructional leaders (improved student achievement) and the kinds of activities that would produce those results. What, specifically, are the things a principal should do to lead instruction well? To be fair, the literature is not entirely silent on this front. We're told that principals should regularly observe and provide teachers with feedback; monitor student progress by reviewing student performance on tests and other tasks; support teachers with multiple, varied opportunities for professional growth; communicate to teachers their responsibility for student achievement; and act as instructional resources by regularly discussing matters of instruction with individual teachers and at faculty meetings. However, the literature offers little about what a principal should observe, the kind of feedback to teachers that matters, or the design of professional development that may actually influence teacher practice. In sum, there is neither a great deal of specificity nor a great deal of coherence to the characterizations of what effective instructional leadership involves.

These gaps in the research leave principals who are intent on becoming instructional leaders on their own to a great extent. Some strategies they employ may have roots in research, but in general principals must rely on intuition, common sense, and their own experience. In essence, there is not nearly as much firm empirical ground on which to gain purchase as the amount of writing on school leadership might suggest. Complicating matters considerably, even *if* a principal has access to the current research about leadership, knowledge, and learning, has time to read it, and is stimulated by it, she still faces the massive challenge of figuring out how and where these ideas apply in the daily life of the schoolhouse. Ironically, new ideas, even in the hands of clever and energetic principals, do not have good landing pads in schools.

WHAT INSTRUCTIONAL LEADERSHIP REQUIRES

How then can school leaders ensure that their schools address the academic imperative facing us in the wake of *A Nation at Risk?* How can we help principals learn and employ the skills required to ensure that all children achieve at high levels? In Boston, as in other school districts across the nation, we are learning a great deal about the evolving role of the principal. What follows is a brief exploration of several important lessons about how the role of principal has changed in the last two decades, and some of the things school leaders and those charged with their development must attend to if strong instructional leadership is to flourish in American schools.

I. Principals must have a clear theory of action.

As Richard Elmore of the Harvard Graduate School of Education points out, school districts often embark on reform efforts without an explicit set of beliefs or a plan of action to achieve key goals. As a result, structural changes become ends unto themselves. Big schools break into small schools. Districts centralize and decentralize. However, these activities appear to have little, if any, effect on the core purpose of schools—student learning.[7]

There is a strong case to be made that principals must also have a theory of action for addressing the academic imperative they face. It is important for several reasons. First, having a theory of action requires that the school leader express what it is they believe the organization is and does. Absent a clear articulation of beliefs about the purpose of school and the organizational design to address them, it is difficult to motivate and generate support from the individuals responsible for doing the work. Second, a theory of action connects a school leader's vision to a particular set of activities that is focused on making those beliefs become real. For example, if a school leader believes improving academic achievement requires improving reading instruction in every classroom, the theory of action must define the specific activities that the students, teachers, principal, parents, and partners will engage in to achieve this goal. While it is not uncommon for school and district leaders to espouse beliefs like "all children can learn," it is far less common for a school or district to have a theory of action that articulates how such beliefs are made manifest. Finally, with an explicit theory of action in place there is real promise of improvement: the value of a vision can be measured, analyzed, refined, and improved. Without a clear theory of action the opposite is true: it is difficult, if not impossible, to learn from the work you do.

In Boston, our underlying theory is that (a) improved instruction will deepen student learning and improve student achievement, and that (b) the way to improve instruction is to support teachers in their schools as they learn in collaboration with one another. Boston chose to put improving literacy instruction first. Thus, principals are expected to eliminate programs and projects that distract from that focus; employ proven instructional practices in the classroom; design a coherent professional development strategy that is aligned to the literacy focus; help teachers learn new practices and work together in new ways; and align all resources—staff, time, money, parents, and partners—with the instructional focus.

The point here is not that Boston's strategy is the only strategy. These activities are not, in the word of one principal, a "theology." Rather, what is important is that *there is* a theory for improving student learning at the school level around which the district and the principals can target resources and organize effort.

2. Principals must be able to observe and analyze instruction with precision.

Principals need to know what good teaching involves and understand what they're seeing when they observe in a classroom. In essence, they must know the work to lead it. Specifically, they must be able to provide detailed feedback to teachers. Why isn't a particular lesson working? What does an effective independent reading program look like? What evidence can be used to determine whether a guided reading lesson is successful?

Equally important, school leaders must be skilled in looking at and making sense of the "artifacts" of instruction—student writing and discussion, the kinds of questions a teacher asks, work posted in classrooms and displayed in school hallways—and be able to clearly articulate what they see and whether it fits with the school's instructional vision. As one elementary principal told me, "Being good at this work [of instruction] requires a real ability to talk about the work. The problem is that school leaders have not been expected to do this. It has not, historically, been part of the job. [But] a principal can't learn this through osmosis, or from a book. She has to learn it from people who know the work inside and out. She has to observe the work. She has to talk about what she sees, unravel what she does and doesn't understand."[8]

3. Principals must be able to define clear steps for improving what they observe and analyze.

If teachers are to learn, understand, and enact new classroom practices, the school leader must be able to guide this transformation. In the words of a master principal, "A good principal must be able to give specific advice to a teacher about what to try next. That means knowing what the end result should look like and having a good sense of how to fix specific problems—be they literacy, management, or math."[9] Simply recognizing a problem is not enough. School leaders must understand what is not working, why, and what the teacher can do about it.

4. Principals must be able to analyze how a school uses resources and align those resources with improving academic achievement.

Clearly, a principal must be able to assess how well their budget supports teaching and learning, and make decisions about how best to leverage resources to support their theory of action. As 90 percent or more of a school budget goes to salaries, this requires making difficult decisions about which staff are necessary and which are not. Then, a principal must determine how existing personnel—teachers, administrators, and support staff—are deployed to support particular academic goals. An elementary school principal provides a clear example:

> We have some great schools here, where during the three-hour literacy block everyone is engaged in reading to kids. Even the custodian gets in and does it. Then you go to another school, and they have created the literacy block, but the teachers are all alone doing the work. No in-

terns, no support staff, no administrators, no parents. The thing about literacy is that the more hands on deck, in a targeted way, the better our kids perform. . . . Understanding how to employ all the adults in the building to support kids reading is part of what it takes to be a good principal. You simply can't be satisfied with the way we've used people in the past.[10]

Principals must also determine the extent to which community partnerships and parent resources are aligned with school goals. This means asking tough questions about the value of a business, higher education, or parent partnership—and the willingness to make difficult decisions about which work should continue, which should stop, and which should be refocused. Finally, school leaders must assess how time is used to achieve school goals, carefully gauging the extent to which the school schedule, common planning, and time for staff development are put to use to achieve specific instructional goals.

5. Principals must remain doggedly focused on improving instruction.

This is easier said than done. The complex social and emotional needs of students and families, operations issues, and personnel management draw principals away from the mission to improve teaching and learning. Complicating matters, school districts are seldom organized to support adult learning, so there are few opportunities for principals to learn new ideas or hone new skills. In essence, the daily life in schools and districts undermines even well-intended school leaders' efforts to address this primary goal. When I asked one successful principal about what she viewed as the most important skill for doing her work, she was unequivocal:

> I am good at saying no. If you want us to concentrate on instruction, then we must be able to say no—no to the superintendent, no to people at the district office who view us as extensions of their offices, no to the guy who wants to do a martial arts presentation at an assembly. If we are given permission to say no and we say it, we create time and space to do the work that will make a difference.[11]

In the end, the capacity of a principal to resist the inevitable creep of non-instructional demands may be as important and challenging as keeping focused on teaching and learning itself.

6. Principals must have consistent opportunities to learn together.

A well-documented culture of isolation pervades American schools. Not only do teachers usually teach in isolation, but principals lead alone as well. Opportunities to learn from colleagues or master principals are scarce. When they do occur, they often lack coherence, consistency, and focus. Principals frequently describe staff development opportunities as happening "to them"—like getting a haircut or having their brakes fixed. One elementary principal describes the experience of leading a school:

> Principals, more than anyone, are in isolated jobs. Unless they are very skilled at distributing leadership, they make daily decisions and long-term plans in isolation. They have no one to help them make sense of district directives, to share frustration and joy, to give them feedback, to problem-solve with.[12]

Like leaders in other professions, principals need the opportunity to observe and analyze their colleagues' work and to open up their own practice for comment and critique from experts in their field. Collaborative analysis of practice should become a central part of what it means to be a principal.

7. Principals must be willing to challenge district rules and cultural norms.

If part of improving schools means doing things differently, then school leaders should be predisposed to challenging the status quo. As one principal told me, "I was hired to fix an ailing system. Part of what ails the system are the traditions and the rules that govern it."[13] Another successful principal describes her role this way:

> I have been breaking the rules for years. . . . I ignore past practice and ask myself what would it really take to radically improve literacy instruction in every classroom in the school? Once I answer that question I see the obstacles in my path much more clearly. Then I can set about getting around them, ignoring them, or obliterating them. Whatever it takes.[14]

This iconoclasm seems to be a critical quality of effective school leaders. We can learn from the iconoclasts. Not only have they proven they can do the work, they know how to get it done in the face of intense pressure *not* to. Indeed, their willingness to challenge past and present practices may be an essential ingredient for accelerating improvement in teaching and student learning.

If the assertion that iconoclastic principals must lead the work to develop instructional leaders is correct, it presents school districts with a fundamental dilemma. District leaders must be willing to invite those principals who are indisputably successful, sometimes brash, and often controversial into the center of the fold, to support and mentor others. However, this presents particular risks, to which large school districts are frequently averse. Clearly, the district opens itself up to candid debate. However, more risky is the fact that iconoclastic principals are likely to challenge the very areas that help define a district's authority (e.g., policies, procedures, supervisory relationships, organizational structure) and question the extent to which these areas reinforce or undermine the focus on academic achievement. In essence, the district risks creating an organization where the very practices and policies that define it are called into question. The promise is that this will create the conditions required for constructive change, but the risks should not be overlooked. The point, after all, is not to spur revolution and lay waste to the system but to build systems where all students are learning at high levels. This requires knowing the limits of iconoclasm, identifying which expectations and practices are non-negotiable, and determining the standards by which that work should be judged.

Finally, it is worth pointing out that drawing on the expertise and passion of successful iconoclasts should only be an *interim* strategy. There should come a time when principal-as-instructional leader is the norm, not an anomaly. Districts will train and hire principals with outstanding instructional leadership skills, there will be coherent systems in place to support and refine their skills, and principals will have adequate district-based and in-school support so their time can be focused on improving teaching and learning, not other pursuits. However, until that time, district leaders cannot be afraid of taking risks when it comes to developing instructional leadership. The iconoclasts must be brought to center stage to help get the work done.

LOOKING AHEAD

Since the release of *A Nation at Risk*, the nature of the principal's job has evolved from site manager to instructional leader. But there is still considerable work to be done if strong instructional leadership is to take root. This work must take place within school districts, in institutions charged with training school leaders, and in schools themselves.

First and foremost, school districts must get and keep the right people in the job. In 2000, nearly half of all school districts reported a shortage of principal candidates. The U.S. Department of Labor estimates that by 2005 the need for school principals will increase by 20 percent.[15] Attracting good people to the job is easier said than done. As one middle school principal put it, "The problem is [that] the principalship is not viewed as a great career opportunity. Many good teachers and staff developers only see more hassles, more accountability, and far more work."[16]

District leaders must develop and invest in recruitment-screening strategies that require principal candidates to demonstrate that they understand instruction and have thought carefully about how to lead instruction across a school. Further, school districts must create the right incentives to retain strong school leaders. Certainly part of the strategy includes paying principals competitively and providing bonuses based on improved student learning. However, other incentives should be considered. Good principals want, and deserve, flexibility—flexibility over whom they hire, over how they spend their budgets, and over district policy. Finally, good principals need time for their own professional growth. Master principals must have opportunities to support and mentor others, including aspiring principals. Such opportunities should not be secondary. They should be built into the job of the principal and actively supported by districts.

School districts must also ensure that there is a rigorous supervisory process in place for principals. The process should provide all principals with feedback about their work to help deepen their understanding of instruction and refine their leadership skills. Those charged with supervising principals should be (or have been) expert principals, with a proven track record helping adults learn and enact new skills. The supervisory process should guarantee that competent principals get the recognition and support they deserve and that incompetent principals are shown the door. Removing principals may be one of the most difficult aspects of the work for district leaders, but the fundamental shift in expectations in schools makes this an essential part of the work. To do this fairly, districts must establish and communicate clear expectations for school leaders and ensure that those charged with supervising and supporting school leaders are capable of providing guidance to those who need it, and are willing to remove principals who are not capable of leading instruction well.

What can colleges, universities, and others in the business of training and certifying principals do to contribute to improving school leadership? These institutions must scrutinize the design of their programs and determine the extent to which they are providing a supply of principals equipped to address the academic imperative. Specifically, they must ask whether they are doing enough to support future principals in leading instructional improvement throughout a school, or whether they are training school leaders to perform well in a role that no longer exists. Such institutions must examine both the content of their training *and* the way the content is delivered. If there is a lesson to be learned from Boston and other districts making consistent academic gains, it is that principals must focus, and focus sharply, on improving instruction. Further, training for school leaders must take place in schools, where instructional leadership happens. It should be led by master principals, and must be differentiated, to support individuals at different levels of expertise. These lessons suggest the need for a complete overhaul of many principal training programs and demand the development of new and much closer partnerships between colleges and universities and K–12 institutions.

Even if colleges, universities, and school districts succeed in creating a pipeline of strong instructional leaders, addressing the academic imperative will likely require fundamental changes in how leadership is organized at the school level. If school leaders are expected to focus on improving instruction, then other individuals may need to perform noninstructional functions. It may be that principals should have business officers or administrative assistants to support them in their work. Or perhaps there are better models for sharing key leadership functions among the staff in a school. Can leadership for instruction be distributed more systematically among teachers? Should master teachers be responsible for the support, mentorship, and training of teachers? Indeed, it is worth asking whether there should be principals at all, or whether the principalship is a relic of a school system that was designed to fulfill social, not instructional, goals.

Across the country school districts are experimenting with alternative leadership models: high schools with chief administrative and academic officers, each with distinct roles and reporting relationships; schools without principals, led by teachers; small schools within schools, each with its own principal and support structure for students and teachers. While the jury is still out on these designs, the point is that we should experiment and research multiple leadership designs, not adhere only to one.

Finally, a word of caution about the American appetite for selecting educational leaders. At precisely a time when public expectations for schools are focused on improving teaching, learning, and student achievement, the United States seems to be leaning away from leaders who have experience or understanding of the issues we expect schools to address. There is a growing trend in large urban school districts to appoint military officers, chief executives, and politicians to the superintendency. There seem to be two main reasons for this trend. First, there is a prevailing view that professional educators created the mess of urban schooling, and therefore it will take non-educators to clean it up. Second, there is a perception that the primary problem that ails urban school districts is poor management, hence the increasing reliance on hiring expert managers.

While there may be benefits in hiring leaders with fresh perspectives and strong managerial experience, it is important to raise a few questions about this trend. Is it appropriate for someone without deep instructional knowledge to be at the helm of a school district? Is managing tanks, money, and public opinion transferable to managing improvement in instruction? Under what conditions does it work? Under what conditions does it fail? Will the view that it will take a non-educator to fix educational problems prevail? Will it trickle down to schools? What would that look like? Will generals and bankers hire captains and vice presidents as principals? Will the value of instructional knowledge be lost, or will it be distributed in new ways, to new places? If we move no closer to the notion of principal as instructional leader, will our high expectations for students be met? Or might we find ourselves further from the goal of educating American children at high levels?

The long legacy of the school leader as manager, disciplinarian, and community leader has left us with relatively well-run schools where students do not seem to learn enough, deeply enough. As we shift our expectations for students, we need school leaders who are equipped to help teachers and parents support these expectations. In essence, the shift in expectations for students must be matched by a shift in expectations for adults. Whoever the educational leaders of this generation may be, they must know enough about instruction and organizing for its improvement so the quality of what goes on in American classrooms is made more rigorous and relevant for all students. This is the work of principals themselves, the work of master principals, the work of school district leaders, and their peers in colleges and universities. It requires careful thinking, organization, effort, and risk on all fronts. Most important, it holds great promise for addressing the academic imperative facing American schools and the children they are meant to serve.

CHAPTER FOUR

A Principal Looks Back:
Standards Matter

KIM MARSHALL

After fifteen years as principal of an inner-city elementary school, I am a battle-hardened veteran with his ideals still intact. I welcome this opportunity to look at how the introduction of standards affected the day-to-day struggle to bring a first-rate education to all students.

I became principal of Boston's Mather School after three experiences that neatly framed some of the challenges of school leadership. Fresh out of college in 1969, I taught sixth graders in a Boston middle school and operated pretty much as a lone wolf, writing my own curriculum and at one point actually cutting the wires of my classroom public address speaker to silence the incessant schoolwide announcements. In my nine years in the classroom, I know that students learned a lot, but I was never held accountable to any external standards.

In 1980, intrigued by the "effective schools" research (including the work of Ron Edmonds and the British study, *Fifteen Thousand Hours*), I spent a year at the Harvard Graduate School of Education and sat at the feet of Edmonds himself.[1] I steeped myself in his research on what seemed to make some urban schools work (strong instructional leadership, high expectations, a focus on basics, effective use of test data, and a safe and humane climate) and said "Amen" to his searing comment on failing urban schools: "We can, whenever and wherever we choose, successfully teach all children whose schooling is of interest to us. We already know more than we need in order to do this. Whether we do it must finally depend on how we feel about the fact that we haven't so far."[2] I was eager to become a school leader and put these ideas to work.

But while I was in graduate school, the voters of Massachusetts passed a tax-limiting referendum that sent Boston into a budget tailspin and closed twenty-seven schools. This nixed any chance I had of being made a principal in the near future, and I prepared to return to my classroom.

Instead, I was hired as chief architect of a new citywide curriculum by Boston's Superintendent of Schools, Robert Spillane, a forceful advocate of higher student achievement and more accountable schools. This was right around the time *A Nation at Risk* came out, and I found myself in the thick of Boston's response to the "rising tide of mediocrity." Later, under Spillane's successor, Laval Wilson, I directed an ambitious systemwide strategic planning process. My colleagues and I did some useful work, but throughout my years in the central office I felt that our efforts were often like pushing a string. Without like-minded principals pulling our initiatives into the schools, we often didn't make much of a difference.

When I finally became a principal in 1987, my experiences as a teacher, graduate student, and bureaucrat had shown me three aspects of the urban school challenge: (a) talented but often cussedly independent teachers working in isolation from their colleagues and external standards; (b) provocative research theories about the key factors associated with effective urban schools; and (c) the limited power of the central office to push change into schools that had a great deal of autonomy and very little accountability. Now that I was in the principal's office, I thought I was ideally situated to make a difference for teachers and kids. Was I right?

First, the good news. Over the last fifteen years, Mather students have made significant gains. Our student attendance went from 89 percent to 95 percent and our staff attendance went from 92 percent to 98 percent. Our test scores went from rock bottom in citywide standings to about two-thirds of the way up the pack. A recent in-depth review gave us a solid B+ based on an intensive inspection of the school and standardized test scores. And in 1999, the Mather was recognized for having the biggest gains in the MCAS (the rigorous Massachusetts statewide tests) of any large elementary school in the state. I am proud of these gains and of dramatic improvements in staff skills and training, student climate, philanthropic support, and the physical plant.

But now some more sobering news. The gains we made came in agonizingly slow increments, and were accompanied by many false starts, detours, and regressions. Graphs of our students' test scores did not show the clean, linear progress I had expected. Far too many of our students score in the bottom category on standardized tests, too few are Proficient and Advanced, and our student suspension rate is too high. Serious work remains to be done.

When judging schools, everyone is an expert. If the Mather's student achievement was extraordinary, people would attribute it to certain "obvious" factors: the principal's leadership, his 78-hour workweek, recruiting great teachers, raising money and bringing in lots of resources, using the research on effective schools, and so on. But our student achievement is not extraordinary. This means that despite a lot of hard work, some key ingredients were missing.

I have a theory. I think that the absence of meaningful external standards before 1998 prevented our strenuous and thoughtful efforts from having much traction. I would like to test this theory by examining ten notorious barriers to high student achievement, our struggle with each of them before the introduction of external standards, and what changed when Massachusetts finally mandated high-stakes tests.

1. Teacher isolation. In my first months as principal, I was struck by how cut off Mather teachers were from each other and from a sense of schoolwide purpose. I understood teachers' urge to close their classroom doors and do their own thing; I had done the same thing when I was a teacher. But my reading of the effective schools research and my experience in the central office convinced me that if Mather teachers worked in isolation, there would be pockets of excellence but schoolwide performance would continue to be abysmal.

So I struggled to get the faculty working as a team. I circulated a daily newsletter (dubbed the Mather Memo) and tried to focus staff meetings on curriculum and effective teaching strategies. I encouraged staff to share their successes, publicly praised good teaching, and successfully advocated for a record-breaking number of citywide Golden Apple awards for Mather teachers. I recruited a corporate partner whose generosity made it possible, among other things, to have occasional staff luncheons and an annual Christmas party.

But morale never seemed to get out of the sub-basement. Staff meetings gravitated to student discipline problems, and as a young principal who was seen as being too "nice" to students, I was often on the defensive. We spent very little time talking about teaching and learning, and did not develop a sense of schoolwide teamwork. The result? Teachers continued to work as private artisans, sometimes masterfully, sometimes with painful mediocrity—and the overall results continued to be very disappointing.

2. Lack of teamwork. Having failed to unite the staff as one big happy family, I decided that grade-level teams were a more manageable arena in which to work on improving collegiality. I began to schedule the school so that teachers at the same grade level had the same free periods. Teams began to meet at least once a week and held occasional after-school or weekend retreats (for which they were paid). A few years later, a scheduling consultant taught me how to create once-a-week 90-minute team meetings by scheduling Art, Computer, Library, Music, and Phys Ed classes back-to-back with lunch. This gave teams even more time to meet.

After much debate, we also introduced "looping," with the entire fourth-grade team moving up to fifth grade with the same students (fifth-grade teachers looped back to fourth). Teachers found that spending two years with the same class strengthened relationships with students and parents and within their grade-level teams, and a few years later the kindergarten and first-grade teams decided to begin looping.

But despite the amount of time that teams spent together, there was a strong tendency for the agendas to be dominated by field trips, war stories about troubled students, and other management issues, with all too little attention to sharing curriculum ideas. I urged teams to use their meetings to take a hard look at student results and use the data to plan ways to improve outcomes, and I tried to bring in training and effective coaches to work with the teams, but I had limited success shifting the agendas of these meetings. In retrospect, I probably would have been more successful if I had attended team meetings and played more of a leadership role, but I was almost always downstairs managing the cafeteria at this point in the day and reasoned that teachers needed to be empowered to run their own meetings.

3. Curriculum anarchy. During my early years as principal, I was struck by the fact that most teachers resisted using a common set of grade-level standards. In the central office, I had been involved in creating Boston's citywide curriculum goals, and I was stunned by the degree to which they were simply ignored. While teachers enjoyed their "academic freedom," it caused constant problems. While teachers in one grade emphasized multiculturalism, teachers in the next grade judged students on their knowledge of traditional history facts. While one team focused on grammar and spelling, another cared deeply about style and voice. While one encouraged students to use calculators, the next wanted students to be proficient at long multiplication and division. These ragged "hand-offs" were a frequent source of unhappiness. But teachers almost never shared their feelings with the offending colleagues in the grade just below theirs. That would have risked scary confrontations on deep pedagogical disagreements, which teachers were sure would undermine staff morale. But the absence of honest discussion—culminating in an agreed-upon grade-by-grade curriculum—doomed the Mather to a deeper morale problem stemming from suppressed anger—and lousy test scores.

I saw curriculum anarchy as a major leadership challenge, and tried again and again to get teachers to buy into a coherent K–5 sequence. At one staff retreat, I asked teachers at each grade level to talk to those at the grade just below and just above theirs and agree to better curriculum hand-offs. People listened politely to each other, but made very few changes in what they were teaching. Undaunted, I brought in newly written Massachusetts curriculum frameworks and national curriculum documents, but they did not match the tests our students were required to take and could therefore be ignored with impunity. When the Boston central office produced a cumbersome new curriculum in 1996, I "translated" it into teacher-friendly packets for each grade level—but these had little impact on the private curriculums in many classrooms.

As a result, far too many of our students moved to the next grade with uneven preparation, and our fifth graders, although better prepared than most Boston elementary graduates, entered middle school with big gaps in their knowledge and skills. It was not a pretty picture, and I was intensely frustrated that I could not find a way to change it.

4. Weak alignment. As I wrestled with the curriculum issue, I saw that tests were a vital part of getting teachers on the same page. But virtually all of the standardized tests that students took were poorly aligned with the classroom curriculum (whatever that was) and were not well respected by most teachers. Boston's attempt to write citywide curriculum tests in the 1980s was not well received, and the tests quickly fell into disuse. The tests that teachers gave every Friday and at the end of each curriculum unit were of uneven quality and covered a wide variety of topics with an even wider range of expectations and criteria for excellence. The only tests that got a modicum of respect were the Metropolitan Achievement Tests, which were given in reading and math at every grade level except kindergarten, with school-by-school results published in Boston newspapers.

Sensing that teachers cared about the Metropolitan, I thought that it might be a lever for getting teachers on the same curriculum page and making predictable hand-offs of skills and knowledge to the next grade. I did a careful analysis of the Metropolitan and, without quoting specific test items, told teachers at each grade level what the test covered in reading and math. Did teachers use my pages and pages of goals? They did not. And hard as it was for me to admit it, they had a point. Teachers did not think they could improve their students' scores by teaching toward the items I had extracted from the tests—or toward Boston's curriculum, for that matter. The Metropolitans, being norm-referenced tests, were designed to spread students out on a bell-shaped curve and were not aligned to a specific set of curriculum goals or "sensitive" to good teaching (you could work hard and teach well and not have your efforts show up in improved scores). What's more, I was pushing the ethical envelope by briefing teachers on the standards that were covered by a supposedly secret test. If Mather scores had skyrocketed, there might have been a major scandal.

But I had stumbled onto an important insight. The key to turning around teachers' well-founded cynicism about the tests they were required to give and the curriculum they were supposed to teach was to make sure that tests really measured a thoughtful K–12 curriculum. We needed to find both missing elements—a clear grade-by-grade curriculum and aligned tests—at the same time. I could not persuade teachers to buy into one without the other, and without both I could not coax teachers out of the isolation of their classrooms.

5. Low expectations. Another barrier in my early years as principal was teachers' pessimism about producing significant student achievement gains. Hamstrung by the lack of aligned curriculum and tests, gun-shy about addressing their colleagues' idiosyncratic classroom goals, and discouraged by the visible results of poverty (85% of our students qualified for free and reduced-price meals and the community around the school was plagued by unemployment and violence), most teachers regarded themselves as hard-working martyrs in a hopeless cause.

Going for broke in my second month as principal, I brought in Jeff Howard, the charismatic African American social psychologist, and his "Efficacy" message hit home. Jeff spoke of combating our students' lack of achievement motivation by getting them to see that you are not just born smart—you can get smart by applying effective effort. He grabbed the faculty's attention with the notion that we could dramatically improve our results by directly confronting the downward spiral of negative beliefs about intelligence and effort. Over lunch, most of the staff buzzed with excitement.

But after lunch Jeff had to go to another school, and the consultant he left in charge was swamped by defensive and increasingly angry reactions. Was he suggesting that teachers were racist? Was he saying that teachers were making the problem worse? And what did he suggest they do on *Monday*? By late afternoon, it was clear that my gamble to unite the staff around this approach had failed.

Licking my wounds, I took a more incremental approach over the next few years, using private conversations, team meetings, the Mather Memo, and research articles to drive home the message that much higher student achievement was doable at the Mather School. I sent small groups of teachers to Efficacy training, and eventually brought in one of Jeff Howard's colleagues to train the whole staff. It was an uphill battle, but gradually Efficacy beliefs were accepted as part of the school's mission and it became taboo to express negative expectations about students' potential.

But we still did not see dramatic increases in our Metropolitan test scores. Belief was not enough. We needed something more to boost achievement in every classroom.

6. Negativism. The area in which I was least effective in my early years was dealing with some strong personalities who declared war on my goals as principal. It's been observed that inner-city schools attract and nurture strong personalities and can develop a negative culture. When a leader starts to mess around with the unspoken expectations and mores of such a culture, he is playing with fire. When I appeared on the scene preaching that "All Children Can Learn," these teachers reacted with disbelief and active resistance. A parody of the Mather Memo ridiculed my idealism: "For Sale: Rose-Colored Glasses! Buy Now! Cheap! Get that glowing feeling while all falls apart around you."

I was often aghast at the vehemence with which these teachers attacked me. Monthly confrontations with the Faculty Senate invariably got my stomach churning, and I took to quoting W. B. Yeats: "The best lack all conviction, and the worst are full of passionate intensity." I jokingly dubbed my antagonists the Gang of Six, but I could not hide my dismay when it was reported to me that on the day of the first Efficacy seminar, one of these teachers was overheard to say in the bathroom, "If I had a gun, I'd shoot Jeff Howard dead." I was continually off balance, and every mistake I made became a major crisis ("People are outraged! Morale has never been worse!"). On several occasions, I failed to set limits on outrageous and insubordinate behavior and assert my prerogatives as principal.

Over a period of years, the most negative people realized that I wasn't going anywhere and transferred out. They had understudies, and there were struggles almost every year in which I battled with them (not always very skillfully) for the hearts and minds of the silent majority, but the school gradually developed a more positive culture. However, it was only when we were confronted with a compelling external mandate that the positive folks found their voice and the remaining negative staff members fell silent.

7. A harried principal. As every busy principal knows, the hardest part of the job is making time for instructional leadership while dealing with the myriad administrative and disciplinary challenges of running a school. The limitless number of tasks that need to be done can also serve as a very plausible excuse for not dealing with the more intractable work of improving teaching and learning. After my initial setbacks with the staff, I plunged into a major campaign to raise money for a gala 350th anniversary celebration and was successful in sprucing up the aging and neglected building and garnering a great deal of publicity for the school. Although these improvements were important, I had no illusions that they were the heart of the matter.

As I got better at handling the constant stream of "over-the-transom" demands on my time, I prided myself at being able to juggle several balls at once and often quoted an intern's observation that I had two hundred separate interactions in a single day—and that did not include greeting students in the halls. I became an "intensity junkie," addicted to being frantically busy and constantly in demand. I had fallen victim to H.S.P.S.—Hyperactive Superficial Principal Syndrome—and was spending far too little time on teaching and learning.

This realization led me to devise a plan for dropping in on five teachers a day for brief, unannounced supervisory visits.[3] These visits and my follow-up conversations with teachers gave me a much better handle on what was going on in classrooms, improved my rapport with the staff, and formed the basis for much more insightful performance evaluations.

But like a recovering addict, I continued to struggle with H.S.P.S. on a daily basis. I gradually accepted that I could not (as I had naively hoped) be the school's staff developer. I began to bring in "coaches" in literacy, math, and science to work with teachers in their classrooms and team meetings. I stopped sending teachers off to isolated workshops and invested in training within the building. These changes greatly improved the quality of staff development for teachers—but test scores were still not improving as much as we hoped.

8. Not focusing on results. I became increasingly convinced that the most important reason for our disappointing scores was that we were spending too little time actually looking at what students were learning. The teachers' contract allowed me to supervise classroom teaching and inspect teachers' lesson plans, but woe betide a principal who tries to evaluate a teacher based on student learning outcomes. Resistance to evaluating teachers on results is well-founded at one level: unsophisticated administrators might use unsuitable measures like norm-referenced tests or unfairly evaluate teachers for failing to reach grade-level standards with students who were poorly taught the year before or had significant learning deficits.

But not looking at the results of teaching during the school year is part of a broader American tendency to "teach, test, and hope for the best." The headlong rush through the curriculum (whatever that might be) is rarely interrupted by a thoughtful look at how students are doing and what needs to be fixed right now or changed next year. For a principal to ask for copies of unit tests and a breakdown of student scores is profoundly counter-cultural. These private artifacts are none of the principal's business. Teacher teams don't use them much either. They rarely pause at the end of a teaching unit to look at which teaching "moves" and materials produce the best gains, which are less successful, and which students need more help. With one notable exception, I failed to get teachers to slow down, relax about the accountability bugaboo, and talk about best practices in the light of the work students actually produced.

9. Mystery grading criteria. Looking at student work, especially writing and other open-ended products, is virtually impossible without objective grading tools. In many schools, the criteria for getting an A are a secret locked up in each teacher's brain, with top grades going to students who are good mind readers. The absence of clear, public, usable guides for scoring student work prevents students from getting helpful feedback and robs teacher teams of the data they need to improve their performance.

In 1996, the Mather made a successful foray into the world of standards-based thinking. Spurred on by a summer workshop with Grant Wiggins, the author of two books on assessment, including *Assessing Student Performance*, we wrote rubrics (scoring guides) for student writing that described in a one-pager for each grade the specific criteria for getting a score of 4, 3, 2, and 1 in Mechanics/Usage, Content/Organization, and Style/Voice. It was striking how much higher our standards were once we had written these rubrics; now we knew what proficiency looked like! We could also guarantee that the same piece of student writing would get the same scores no matter who graded it. Encouraged by our success, we began to give students a "cold prompt" writing assignment (a topic they had never seen before, no help from the teacher) in

September, November, March, and June. Teachers scored the papers together and then discussed the results.

This process was a breakthrough. We had found a way to score student writing objectively; we were sharing the criteria with students and parents in advance (no surprises, no excuses); we were giving "dipstick" assessments at several points each year; teachers at each grade were working as a team to score students' work; and teachers were analyzing students' work, giving students feedback, and fine-tuning their teaching. We began to see significant improvements in our students' writing.

But after a few years of regular scoring meetings and charting of students' progress, our efforts began to flag. Finding enough time was always an issue, especially since the scoring/data analysis meetings were hard to fit into our 90-minute team meetings and many teachers had after-school family commitments. It takes very strong leadership—or another equally powerful force—to sustain this kind of work.

10. No schoolwide plan. Over the years, we eyeballed many different programs to turn around student achievement—Effective Schools, Efficacy, Success for All, Core Knowledge, Accelerated Schools, Comer, Schools Without Failure, Multiple Intelligences, Whole Language, Multicultural, and others—but none got the buy-in needed for successful implementation. As a result, we kept trying to "grow our own"—an exhausting and frustrating process. In the late 1990s, one "whole school" reform program was mandated as part of a Boston grant program. We appreciated the help (and the money!) but felt there were crucial pieces missing and drove the program administrators crazy by constantly second-guessing their model and adding components of our own. Perhaps we were asking for too much. Perhaps we should have committed to a less-than-perfect program and given it a chance to work. But we were on a constant quest for a better mousetrap.

As we continued our search, two more narrowly focused programs had a big impact. The first was Reading Recovery, a highly effective, low-tech, data-driven program for struggling first graders. What caught the attention of the whole staff was that most of the students who appeared to be doomed to school failure got back on track after twelve weeks of hard work with the highly trained Reading Recovery teachers.

After a few years of successful implementation, there was enough support to get all primary-grade teachers to buy into the Literacy Collaborative program, which was created by Irene Fountas and Gay Sue Pinnell to align the way reading and writing are taught in regular classrooms with Reading Recovery. All of our K–3 teachers bought into the program and were trained by one of their colleagues through in-class coaching and a 40-hour after-school course in which teachers looked at student work and data (using a new scale of reading proficiency) and talked constantly about best practices in a low-stakes, collegial atmosphere. The program produced significant gains in our student achievement in the lower grades, and during the 2001–2002 school year we introduced the upper-grade version of Literacy Collaborative.

But these very effective literacy programs were not part of a coherent schoolwide change plan. And this, along with all the other factors discussed above, prevented us from getting the kinds of achievement gains we knew our students could produce.

Looking over this list of ten barriers to student success, it's clear that there are powerful forces at work that tend to widen the achievement gap and create the "Matthew effect" ("To those who have, more will be given, and they will have abundance; but from those who have nothing, even what they have will be taken away." Matthew 13:12). Children who enter school with middle-class home advantages tend to do well, even if they attend ineffective schools. But disadvantaged children desperately need effective schools to teach them key life skills and launch them into success. Unless there is strong leadership pushing back, the ten factors will make things much worse for these children. If teachers work in isolation, if there isn't effective teamwork, if the curriculum is undefined and weakly aligned with tests, if there are low expectations, if a negative culture prevails, if the principal is constantly distracted by nonacademic matters, if the school does not measure and analyze student outcomes, and if the staff lacks a coherent overall improvement plan, then students' entering inequalities will be amplified and poor children will fall further and further behind, widening the achievement gap into a chasm.

This presents a tremendous professional—and moral—challenge to principals, because they are ideally situated to influence each of these factors. If the principal is an effective instructional leader, the forces will be pushed back (at least for the time being) and the gap will narrow. For vulnerable, school-dependent children, this is a godsend.

How did I measure up to this challenge? For more than a decade, I had limited success pushing back the powerful gap-widening forces. Mather students only began to make real progress when strong external standards were introduced, and that did not happen until Massachusetts introduced high-stakes tests (the MCAS) in 1998.

When we heard that 800-pound gorilla knocking on our door, the turnaround happened with amazing speed. As our fourth graders took the first round of MCAS tests, one of our most effective teachers (who taught fourth grade) burst into tears at a staff meeting and proclaimed, "No more Lone Ranger!" She pleaded with her colleagues in kindergarten, first grade, second grade, and third grade to prepare students with the necessary building blocks so that she would never again have to watch her students being humiliated by a test for which they were so poorly prepared.

Some of our colleagues joined the handwringing across Massachusetts about making students the victims of a forced march to high standards. But in a subsequent meeting, the staff sat down and actually took portions of the MCAS and came to these conclusions:

(a) although the test is hard, it really does measure the kinds of skills and knowledge students need to be successful in the twenty-first century; (b) the MCAS is a curriculum-referenced test whose items are released every year, making it possible to align the curriculum and study for the test (we are lucky to live in Massachusetts; some states use norm-referenced tests and keep their tests secret); (c) our students have a long way to go; but (d) most of our kids *can* reach the proficient level if the whole school teaches effectively over time.

The only problem was that the Massachusetts frameworks and tests were pegged to grades four, eight, and ten, leaving some uncertainty about curriculum goals for the other grades. But the grade-four tests and accompanying "bridge" documents gave us much more information than we had before. We set up committees that worked with consultants to "tease back" the standards, and we then worked as a staff (with parent input) to create booklets with clear grade-by-grade proficiency targets accompanied by rubrics and exemplars of good student work. We also set a schoolwide achievement target four years into the future (an idea suggested by Jeff Howard), and then spelled out SMART goals (Specific, Measurable, Attainable, Relevant, and Timebound) for each grade level to act as steppingstones toward the long-range target. Each year since, we have updated the SMART goals with higher and higher expectations.

I believe that the rigorous, high-stakes MCAS tests had a dramatic impact on all of the areas with which we had struggled for so long. The grade-by-grade MCAS-aligned targets put an end to curriculum anarchy and kicked off the process of locating or writing during-the-year assessments aligned with those goals. This in turn focused the curriculum and produced data that teams could sink their teeth into, giving much more substance to their meetings. The rubrics we had developed just a year before were key tools in objectively measuring student writing and displaying data in ways that encouraged effective team discussions on improving results. As teachers gave up some "academic freedom," their isolation from each other was greatly reduced and grade-level teams had a common purpose. Our staff confronted the issue of teacher expectations when we took portions of the MCAS ourselves, and there was much less negative energy as we united in a relentless push for proficiency—a term we had never used before. My work as an administrator was much more focused on student learning results, which helped in the continuing struggle with H.S.P.S. And, finally, the perennial search for the perfect school improvement program came full circle to a very straightforward mission: preparing students with the specific proficiencies needed to be successful at the next grade level and graduate from fifth grade with the skills and knowledge to get on the honor roll in any middle school. We began to focus all our energy on continuously improving each of the components of a "power cycle": clear unit goals, pretests, effective teaching, formative assessments, data analysis, feedback to students and parents, and a safety net for students who fall through the cracks.[4]

The elements for greatly improved achievement are falling into place, and there's help from the central office: Boston's citywide curriculum goals are being aligned with the MCAS and reframed in a compact format for each grade level, and additional coaching and professional time are being given to all schools. I believe that the Mather's student achievement will take off as the staff hones all the elements and captures big enough chunks of focused staff meeting time to process student work and data effectively. The most important work is hard to do within the school day, even in 90-minute meetings. Special afterschool retreats have to be in teachers' calendars well in advance, money has to be available to pay stipends, and teachers need some initial coaching on making these data analysis meetings really effective. With strong leadership and continuing staff buy-in, these ingredients ought to make it possible for virtually all students to reach at least the proficient level.

In closing, I want to return to the Ron Edmonds statement cited earlier. Edmonds often said that the existence of even *one* effective urban school (and he found a number of them) proved that we knew how to turn around failing schools—which meant that there was no excuse for any urban school to be ineffective. With these words, Edmonds laid a colossal guilt trip on urban educators who were not getting good results. His stinging rebuke may have jolted some educators out of fatalistic attitudes and gotten them thinking about ways to improve their schools. But was Edmonds right that we knew in 1978 how to turn around failing schools? Was he fair to thoughtful, hard-working school leaders? Was he a little glib about what it would take to close the gap?

From my experience as a principal, I can testify that Edmonds and his generation of researchers did not provide a detailed road map to help a failing school find its way out of the woods. Without that, success depended too much on extraordinary talent, great personal charisma, an impossibly heroic work ethic, a strong staff already in place, and luck—which allowed cynics to dismiss isolated urban successes as idiosyncratic and say they proved nothing about broader school change.

But Edmonds' much more basic contribution was in getting three key messages into the heads of people who cared about urban schools: 1) demographics are not destiny, and inner-city children can achieve at high levels; 2) some specific school characteristics are linked to beating the demographic odds; and 3) we therefore need to stop making excuses and get to work.

Turning around failing schools is extraordinarily difficult. My 15-year struggle to make one school effective has brought me face to face with my own personal and professional limitations and made me a student of school effectiveness and the key factors that get people and institutions to work more successfully. I have learned that the starting point has to be an almost religious belief that it can be done, and Edmonds served as high priest in that regard. A second necessity is an outline of what an effective school looks like, and the correlates of effective urban schools (which have held up remarkably well over the years) have given me a vision of the pieces that need to be in place for all children to learn at high levels. A third key piece is real expertise on turning around failing schools. Craft knowledge has increased by leaps and bounds. If I could go back to 1987 and start over again as principal with current knowledge about school improvement, progress would be made much more rapidly.

But student achievement would still not have reached its full potential without a fourth tool: strong external standards linked to high-stakes curriculum tests. I believe that the arrival of standards and tests in the late 1990s provided the traction needed for a principal to push back the powerful gap-widening forces that operate within all schools.

Building on the accumulated lessons of researchers and practitioners, today's principals are in a much better position to be successful. If they believe passionately that their students can achieve proficiency, if they have a clear vision of what makes a school effective, if they learn the lessons of school change, and if they take advantage of external assessments, principals should be able to lead a school staff to bring a first-rate education to every child. Ron Edmonds would have smiled about that. So should all of us.

CHAPTER FIVE

Teaching: From A Nation at Risk to a Profession at Risk?

PAM GROSSMAN

Twenty years after the publication of *A Nation at Risk*, the field of teaching stands at a crossroads. In one direction lies the course charted by organizations that have worked to raise the standards of the teaching profession, organizations such as the National Board for Professional Teaching Standards and the National Commission on Teaching and America's Future. In the other direction lies the stark reality of the numbers of uncertified and out-of-field teachers who are increasingly staffing our nation's schools, the calls for dismantling professional education for teachers, and the troubling reliance on scripted curriculum as a substitute for teachers' professional knowledge and judgment. At a time when research has begun to demonstrate the critical influence of teachers on student learning, thousands of underprepared teachers are entering the classroom.[1] At a time when standards for teacher preparation have never been higher, many teachers enter the classroom without any formal preparation, and the administration of George W. Bush is calling for the jettisoning of professional preparation for teachers. In this essay, I explore the fate of the initial recommendation of *A Nation at Risk* and the current state of the field of teaching.

WHAT THE REPORT RECOMMENDED

The recommendations of *A Nation at Risk* identify the need to raise the status, salaries, and standards for teachers. As has been true of reports before and since, the commission bemoaned the number of teachers who came from the bottom quartile of their high school or college classes and advocated the creation of incentives to attract "outstanding students" into teaching. The report also warned of shortages of teachers in math, science, foreign languages, special education, and teachers of language minority students among others, and found that "half of the newly employed mathematics, science, and English teachers are not qualified to teach these subjects."[2]

Beyond addressing the quality of individual teachers, the report focused on troubling aspects of teaching as an occupation, such as low salaries and the lack of career opportunities for experienced teachers. In addition to raising standards for entry into teaching, the commission advocated the increase of teacher salaries: "Salaries for the teaching profession should be increased and should be professionally competitive, market-sensitive, and performance-based."[3] Beyond the damaging effects of low status and low salaries, the commission also reported that "individual teachers have little influence in such critical professional decisions, as, for example, textbook selection."[4] The report urged school boards and administrators to create career ladders and increase opportunities for experienced teachers. Most surprising, at least in hindsight, was the recommendation that school boards adopt an 11-month contract for teachers to provide them with ample time to develop curriculum, to engage in professional development, and to offer specialized programs for students.

The commission's intent was clear. In order to attract and retain promising candidates into the classroom, teaching would need to become more professional. Given the complexity of the classroom, teachers would need to make professional judgments under conditions of uncertainty and to have a voice in decisions that affected their practice. The commission also believed that teachers *should* influence professional decisions such as textbook adoption and that, as professionals, they could be relied upon to do so in the best interests of students. In their report, the commission clearly opted for investing in a more professional model for teaching.

THE NATION RESPONDS

Since the publication of *A Nation at Risk*, education has remained a high priority of ordinary citizens and policymakers alike. Many of the reforms spurred by the report focused on curricular issues, including revising the curriculum and raising graduation requirements, rather than teaching. *A Nation Responds,* published a year after *A Nation at Risk,* reported that thirty-five states had enacted or approved changes in graduation requirements, while thirteen states were considering such changes. Twenty-two states had already enacted some facet of curriculum reform, while twenty-three states were considering such policies. Increased student testing and evaluation was another popular response; twenty-nine states had enacted new policies regarding student testing, while an additional thirteen states were considering such policies in 1984.

Despite the focus on improving teachers' salaries and working conditions in *A Nation at Risk,* reforms of teacher compensation and career opportunities were less popular. In 1984 only six states had enacted policies establishing master-teacher programs or career ladders, although twenty-four states were considering such policies, and only fourteen states had made efforts to raise teacher salaries. The states' initial responses focused instead on the preparation and professional development of teachers. By 1984, twenty-eight states had already enacted or approved new policies regarding teacher preparation and certification. Many of these focused on competence testing for those entering teaching or increasing subject-matter requirements and expectations for student teaching. Policymakers, at least early on, expected teachers to accomplish more in the classroom, but they did not necessarily offer better compensation or more professional opportunities in return.

The state of teaching and teacher preparation heralded in *A Nation at Risk* did, however, draw the attention of educators. The Holmes Group—a consortium of education deans from research universities—issued its report, *Tomorrow's Teachers*, followed by the Carnegie Forum on Education and the Economy's *A Nation Prepared: Teachers for the 21st Century.* Both reports supported the recommendations of *A Nation at Risk,* focusing attention on the need to better prepare teachers within the subject areas, improve the quality of student teaching, and create career ladders, with increasing responsibilities and preparation for more experienced teachers.

These reports, which focused on the "twin goals of the reform of teacher education and the reform of the teaching profession," laid the groundwork for new efforts to professionalize teaching.[5] Since a specialized knowledge base is one of the hallmarks of any profession, research began to focus on teachers' knowledge, as evidenced by documents such as *The Knowledge Base for the Beginning Teacher*, which appeared in 1987.[6] One of the clearest examples of the effort to professionalize teaching was the creation of the National Board of Professional Teaching Standards (NBPTS). Formed in 1987, the National Board was a direct outgrowth of both *A Nation at Risk* and *A Nation Prepared*. The Carnegie task force explicitly called for the creation of a national board to set standards for accomplished teaching. The decade following *A Nation at Risk* was also marked by an intensive period of reform in teacher education. Reforms were marked by a movement away from degrees in education and increased attention to subject-matter preparation. States began to require prospective teachers to major in a content area rather than in education and to raise the academic requirements for entry into teacher education.

Reforms in teacher education also focused on the quality and character of field experiences and student teaching. Teacher education programs increased the requirements for field experiences, including student teaching. Following the recommendations of both the Holmes Group and the Carnegie task force, schools of education began to create professional development schools in partnerships with local schools and districts.[7] Proclaimed as analogous to teaching hospitals for the preparation of doctors and other medical professionals, professional development schools promised greater collaboration between schools and colleges in the preparation of prospective teachers and an antidote to the uneven quality of students' field experiences.[8]

Despite the recognition of the importance of strengthening the nation's teaching force, most state policymakers focused most immediately on creating standards for student achievement and accountability systems, including high-stakes assessments. With the exception of states such as North Carolina and Connecticut, fewer states actively pursued policies that would strengthen the continuing professional development of teachers or would address the threats of teacher shortages or out-of-field teaching. While the NBPTS set new standards for accomplished teaching, states varied widely in how they recognized and made use of the experience of National Board–certified teachers. Despite the widespread recognition of impending teacher shortages, few states tackled *A Nation at Risk*'s recommendation that salaries be made professionally competitive to attract more talented individuals into teaching.

So perhaps it is not surprising that in 1996, as the standards and accountability movement swept the nation, the National Commission on Teaching and America's Future (NCTAF) echoed many of the concerns first voiced in *A Nation at Risk*. It warned that the success of the educational reforms fueled by the publication of *A Nation at Risk* would hinge on the quality of teachers and teaching in our nation's schools and highlighted the statistics on out-of-field teaching, uneven preparation for the complex work of teaching, and the unsupportive working conditions faced by teachers. The commission proposed "an audacious goal for America's future. Within a decade—by the year 2006—we will provide every student in America with what should be his or her educational birthright: access to competent, caring, qualified teaching in schools organized for success."[9] The NCTAF then called upon states to develop stronger policies regarding the preparation and support of teachers and the reorganization of schools to support both teacher and student learning. The echo of *A Nation at Risk* was unmistakable.

WHERE WE ARE NOW

Despite all of the educational reform activity over the past two decades, the teaching profession currently faces some of its most daunting challenges. These include the influx of underqualified teachers into classrooms, the potential dismantling of professional education for teachers, and the trend toward the regulation of teaching practice—regulations that may deprive teachers of the ability to make professional judgments and exercise their professional knowledge. So we face a paradox: in some areas teachers are better prepared than ever, while in schools that serve the greatest numbers of poor and minority children, more and more teachers are underqualified. Due in part to the reforms enacted in response to *A Nation at Risk*, it is harder than ever to get into a teacher education program. But in many communities, individuals can bypass these requirements altogether and enter the classroom with an emergency credential.

Teacher Shortages and Underqualified Teachers

Beginning with the publication of *A Nation at Risk*, reports began to warn of impending teacher shortages.[10] Due to increases in both student enrollment and teacher retirements, widespread shortages were predicted, particularly in the areas of special education, English as a Second Language, math, and science.

At least partly in response to the increasing demand for teachers and fears of teacher shortages, states began to issue emergency credentials and create alternate routes into teaching. In 1996, the NCTAF demonstrated the prevalence of the practice of staffing schools with teachers who did not hold full qualifications in their field. The commission's study reported that as of 1996, "more than 50,000 people who lack the training required for their jobs have entered teaching annually on emergency or substandard license."[11] These numbers have only increased since then. One recent study of California suggests that half of all first-year teachers do not have their credentials when they begin teaching.[12] A standard response to teacher shortages has always been to ease entry into the profession. Such a response diminishes the need to keep salaries competitive in order to attract promising candidates and provide an incentive for investing in professional preparation. In keeping with this tradition, the Bush administration is calling the entire enterprise of teacher education into question, citing the shortage of qualified teachers. In the 2002 report, *Meeting the Highly Qualified Teacher Challenge*, the U.S. Secretary of Education essentially calls for the abolition of professional education as it currently exists. The report concludes that states should cease requiring traditional teacher education. Instead, "states will need to streamline their certification system to focus on the few things that really matter: verbal ability, content knowledge, and, as a safety precaution, a background check of new teachers."[13]

Since one of the hallmarks of a profession is a specialized body of knowledge acquired through professional education, such a proposal strikes at the heart of the claim that teaching be considered a profession. The proposal also ignores research indicating that courses in how to teach a subject contribute more to a teacher's success than additional subject-matter courses.[14] Even James Conant, a famous critic of teacher education, recognized the need for prospective teachers to develop knowledge of how to transform their own understanding of subject matter into approaches that were developmentally appropriate for students. Without professional preparation, prospective teachers forego opportunities to develop knowledge of how to teach reading or math, knowledge of how students develop and learn—all topics that are generally covered in the professional component of the teacher education curriculum.

I recently watched a film entitled *The First Year* along with many others across the country. The film is being used to inspire college students to consider teaching as a career. It highlights the experience of five first-year teachers in Los Angeles. These teachers inspire us with their dedication to their students, and the film details their unstinting efforts to find resources for needy students and to connect with students and their families. One of the film's story lines follows a deeply committed young man as he tries to arrange for speech therapy for one of his students. The teacher is shown working individually with the student (one of the few scenes of actual instruction shown in the movie). The teacher patiently tries to get the student to sound out *two*—/t/ /wh/ /oo/. For all his good intentions, energy, and commitment, this teacher, who entered teaching through Teach for America, did not know the difference between phonetically regular words, such as cat or three, which students should be encouraged to sound out, and phonetically irregular words, like two, which are generally taught as high-frequency sight words.

Because teaching reading is complex, courses in teaching reading are required at virtually all accredited teacher education programs. One of the other committed young teachers, another Teach for America member, attended the screening of the movie. Following the film, she was asked what she wished she had known before she entered the classroom. She said she was unprepared to teach reading to the large numbers of her middle school students who were unable to read at grade level. Based on her experience, she had applied to the teacher education program at Mills College and was about to graduate soon after the screening. She proudly announced that she now felt prepared to teach reading to her future students.

A Nation at Risk recognized the need both to raise admission standards for applicants to teacher education programs and to strengthen the quality of the programs themselves. To dismantle university-based teacher education, rather than to invest in the improvement of teachers' professional education and development, would deprive prospective teachers of the opportunity to develop the understanding of how to teach challenging subject matter to all students, a key component of the reform effort. Such a direction would also undermine the effort to make teaching more professional.

Working Conditions

While proposals to ease entry into teaching have been based on claims of teacher shortages, others have argued that the problem is not a shortage of teachers, except in a few areas. Rather, high teacher turnover, particularly in challenging schools, creates the continual demand for new teachers. From this perspective, teacher retention, rather than teacher supply, is the culprit. Retention of new teachers, in turn, is directly linked to the working conditions. In an organizational analysis of teacher shortages, Richard Ingersoll argues that organizational features of schools help account for higher or lower rates of teacher turnover:

> The data show, in particular, inadequate support from the school administration, student discipline problems, limited faculty input into school decision-making, and to a lesser extent, low salaries, are all associated with higher rates of turnover, after controlling for the characteristics of both teachers and schools.[15]

Ingersoll's analysis supports the need to create more supportive working conditions for teachers, which includes allowing teachers to influence decisions that affect their classrooms—a recommendation of *A Nation at Risk* as well. He suggests that the schools with the highest turnover are least well equipped to support beginning teachers.

A key recommendation of *A Nation at Risk* was the need to create better working conditions for teachers, conditions that would attract and retain promising candidates into the profession. Such working conditions include competitive salaries, opportunities to engage in professional development, and a voice in decisions that affect their practice. How far have we come in meeting this recommendation?

While there has been some progress in raising teacher salaries over the past two decades, by and large teacher salaries nationwide have not kept up with inflation. A recent report by the National Center for Education Statistics found that, after adjusting for inflation, teachers' salaries actually declined 1 percent between 1990–1991 and 2000–2001. The pressure to raise salaries has been tempered by the political exigency of hiring teachers who are not fully certified. As John Goodlad remarked more than a decade ago:

> Temporary and emergency certificates ease the shortage in times of undersupply; while in times of oversupply, a glut of teachers removes any rising interest in providing incentives for the improvement of quality. The call for higher salaries is muted when many of those teaching have done little to be temporarily certified, just as it is muted when there are dozens of applicants for each vacancy.[16]

Partly because of the failure to raise salaries, teaching as a career option continues to compete with other much more lucrative careers that also require a college degree, while standards for entry into the profession are being lowered in response to teacher shortages.

A Nation at Risk also highlighted the need to create more challenging career opportunities for teachers, and many more opportunities for teacher leadership exist today. The NBPTS represents only one example of an organization that recognizes teachers' accomplishments. As of mid-2002, the Board had certified 16,044 teachers across the nation. These teachers work intensively to document their classroom practice and prepare portfolios that demonstrate the accomplishments and learning of their students. Across the country, Board-certified teachers have begun to take on positions of leadership in education and to participate actively in school reform, teacher education, and professional development. The Carnegie Academy for the Scholarship of Teaching and Learning, sponsored by the Carnegie Foundation for the Advancement of Teaching, is another example of an effort to highlight the accomplishments of experienced teachers and make their practice more public.

The accomplishments of these teachers represent the best of the profession, the path we could choose to take in meeting the challenge of finding highly qualified teachers. As a group, they demonstrate how investing in teachers' professional knowledge and development can pay off, not only in the classroom, but in the profession as a whole.

Unfortunately, there are indications that instead of providing teachers with greater voice in decisions, instead of investing in continuing professional development for practicing teachers, or incentives to attract these teachers to the hardest-to-staff schools, policymakers are attempting instead to regulate teaching practice more strenuously, in part through the adoption of more scripted curriculum materials.

TOWARD THE REGULATION OF TEACHING PRACTICE

Due in large part to the confluence of increased accountability measures, including high-stakes standardized assessments and the influx of both new and underqualified teachers into schools, districts around the country have begun to invest heavily in a variety of scripted curriculum materials. Many see this move as contributing to the deskilling of teachers and the deprofessionalization of teaching. Nowhere is this debate more evident than in teachers' responses to district-mandated programs such as Open Court for teaching reading.

According to a recent issue of *California Educator* devoted to this topic, the Open Court curriculum had been adopted by one in eight elementary schools in California by the year 2000.[17] While there are undoubtedly many strengths in the curriculum as originally designed, with its emphasis on phonemic awareness and support for early decoding skills among beginning readers, it is also highly prescriptive; teachers must follow a set time frame and script for instruction. Teachers have complained that the program robs them of the ability to tailor instruction to their particular group of students. One teacher in Los Angeles, a district that has invested heavily in the program, was told he must stop teaching Shakespeare to his elementary school students in order to teach Open Court, despite the success of his students on reading assessments.

On the one hand, requiring such scripted programs is a logical response to the rising numbers of new and underprepared teachers in the schools. Even well-prepared novices need well-designed curriculum materials to succeed, and new teachers who have little background in the teaching of reading would need even more guidance. But substituting programmed materials for investment in teacher knowledge and judgment is a shortsighted solution to a long-term problem. Such a solution will only further decrease the attractiveness of teaching to the kinds of individuals the Department of Education hopes to lure into the classroom with reduced entry requirements. At the other end of the career spectrum, highly accomplished teachers may find themselves increasingly stymied in their efforts to meet the needs of individual children, as was true of the Los Angeles teacher fighting to keep Shakespeare in his curriculum. As Gary Sykes noted long ago:

> Routinized instruction, and the attendant loss of autonomy, makes teaching unpalatable for bright, independent-minded college graduates

and fails to stimulate the pursuit of excellence among those who do enter. Over the long run, then, the routinization of instruction tends to deprofessionalize teaching and to further discourage capable people from entering the field.[18]

The erosion of professional autonomy and the ability to exercise professional judgment represented by such policies are ominous signs for the future of the teaching profession.

INEQUITY

An especially troubling consequence of the failure to professionalize teaching is that students in low-income and high-minority schools are much more likely to have less qualified teachers.[19] In California alone, as of 1999, 11 percent of teachers were on emergency permits or waivers, with the majority of these teachers concentrated in high-poverty districts. Another report on the status of the teaching profession in California found that in schools with the highest percentage of students qualifying for free or reduced-price lunch, 22 percent of teachers were underqualified, while in schools with the lowest percentage of such students, only 6 percent of teachers were underqualified.[20] The New York Regents' Task Force on Teaching reported that 12 percent of teachers in schools with the highest number of minority students were not certified in the field they teach, compared to only 5.4 percent in the schools with the lowest percentage of minority students.[21] In a review of standard setting in teaching, Linda Darling-Hammond concludes:

> Disparities in salaries and working conditions have re-created teacher shortages in central cities and poor rural areas. And, for a variety of reasons, many states and local governments continue to lower or eliminate standards for entry rather than to create incentives that will attract an adequate supply of teachers. As a consequence, this era is developing an even more sharply bimodal teaching force than ever before. Whereas some children are gaining access to teachers who are more qualified and well prepared than in years past, a growing number of poor and minority children are being taught by teachers who are sorely unprepared for the task they face.[22]

***

Twenty years ago, we learned from *A Nation at Risk* that we were meta-phorically at war; twenty years later, teachers are still fighting for professional recognition and respect. At a time when we have more evidence than ever that quality teaching matters enormously to children's futures, we are on the verge of forsaking the hard-won reforms that can lead to better prepared teachers for all students. The crossroad is clearly marked. We can continue to invest in the development of highly qualified and well-prepared teachers and create the incentives and working conditions to keep them in the profession. Or we can once again ease standards for entry into teaching and allow students, primarily those in high-poverty schools who are most in need of high-quality teaching, to be taught by less than qualified teachers. To pursue such a path would only increase the disparities in educational opportunity and achievement that already exist within our society. The nation, and its teaching profession, remain at risk.

CHAPTER SIX

Still at Risk: The Causes and Costs of Failure to Educate Poor and Minority Children for the Twenty-First Century

JEFF HOWARD

At the turn of the millennium there is a large group of Americans I call "those left behind." It is a population segment that comprises more than half of the African American population, as well as other minority and poor people. These are the people who are not equipped to take full advantage of opportunities afforded by the fifty years of successful social activism that culminated in the *Brown* decision of 1954 and the civil rights legislation of the 1960s. Education is, of course, the way out for the historically disadvantaged; the foundation for constructive employment, self-respect, and full citizenship. As such, the disadvantaged were a major focus of *A Nation at Risk*, the 1983 report that focused the nation's attention on the general deficiencies of our education program. I remember being excited by the publication of the report, pleased to see it so widely discussed, and generally happy with its contents. The report's simple opening statement resonated with my own experience: "Our society and its educational institutions seem to have lost sight of the basic purposes of schooling, and of the high expectations and disciplined effort needed to attain them." But successful as it was in establishing education reform as a national priority, *A Nation at*

Risk has not proven to be the catalyst for the changes many of us hoped for, especially in the cities. There is little evidence that the reform movement invigorated by its publication has made much of a difference after twenty years of effort. And a close reading, twenty years later, of the assumptions and recommendations regarding the disadvantaged in the report is surprising—and disappointing.

The clearest evidence of the continuing failure of public education, especially among minority children, is offered by the National Assessment of Educational Progress (NAEP). The NAEP is a test administered to random samples of children in each of the fifty states by the U.S. Department of Education. In four administrations of the all-important reading portion of the NAEP between 1992 and 2000, the number of African American fourth graders scoring at or above proficiency increased from 9 percent to 12 percent—meaning that in 2000, fully 88 percent failed to achieve the level of reading capability required to fully decode the increasingly complex material they will encounter in their textbooks.[1] Sixty-three percent scored in the lowest category, "below basic"—an improvement of only four percentage points since 1992. For Hispanics, the situation is almost as dismal: although the number at or above proficiency held steady at 16 percent, the percentage of students in the lowest category increased from 56 percent in 1992 to 58 percent in 2000. Scores for white children are substantially higher but still nothing to crow about: the number at or above proficiency increased from 35 percent to 40 percent in the same period, while those "below basic" dropped from 29 percent to 27 percent. (It is worth noting that six out of ten white fourth graders, the children of the most privileged population group in the United States, were reading below proficiency as the twenty-first century began.) But it is in our urban centers where the problems of public education are most acute, the most pervasive, and where the highest percentage of children are most at risk. Bad public schools destroy the only hope for those left behind. Twenty years after the publication of *A Nation at Risk*, we had a right to expect something better.

A Nation at Risk was both a ringing indictment of the failures of American education and a call to action. It ignited a vigorous school reform movement, generously funded by the philanthropic community and led by some of our most highly regarded education thinkers. That movement has generated twenty years of conferences, collaborations, models of improvement, new reading and math programs, research-based instructional strategies, and innumerable schoolwide, clusterwide, and districtwide improvement initiatives. Some of these have shown real promise, achieving, in isolated cases, real improvement. But these successes have been spotty, unreliable, and often short lived. The NAEP results tell the tale starkly: there is very little to show for all the activity and the money spent. The movement has simply failed to generate, or catalyze, real improvement in the educational outcomes of most American children. Why? More broadly, why does the wealthiest, strongest, and most vital nation in the world continue to fare so poorly at so central and future-defining a function as education? I believe the report, the reform movement it spawned, and U.S. society in general have failed to live up to improvements we had a right to expect for reasons we can specify: they all share a set of beliefs, and a basic approach to education predicated on them, that are fundamentally congruent with those of the ineffectual educational establishment so roundly criticized in 1983.

In my twenty-five years of engagement with public school educators, I have come to believe that two critical problems lie at the heart of our ongoing failures, and, I will argue, these are evident in the fabric of *A Nation at Risk*. First, there is a widespread culture of disbelief in the learning capacities of many of our children, especially children of color and the economically disadvantaged. Most educators, along with other Americans, have been socialized to believe that intelligence is innate, fixed at birth, and unequally distributed: "Some have it and some don't." Confronted with the undeniable problems and underdeveloped academic skills of many of the children of the poor in our cities, people assume that the deficits they see are caused by low intelligence.[2] Attributing poor skills to low ability leads naturally to the low expectations for future performance so clearly evident in so many classrooms—and to the tenacity with which they are held. These are low expectations with *cause*. And lack of belief in the intelligence of poor and minority children is an equal opportunity affliction; in my experience, the proportion of teachers of color who suffer from it is nearly as great as the proportion of whites.

Expressions of this disbelief take many forms, from the brutal remark of a teacher one of my colleagues encountered—"If you want better outcomes from the classrooms in this school, send us better kids"—to the more subtle statement I have heard over and over from serious, compassionate educators—"All children can learn (up to the level of their abilities)." The parenthetical second clause of this sentence, of course, negates the optimism of the first. It is a nicer way to say what the speaker really means: "What children can learn depends on the level of their abilities—and we all know those vary." Disbelief in children's capacities absolves educators (and parents) from responsibility for educating them to high standards. It creates a contagious sense of helplessness and futility among adults that easily transfers to children themselves, who quickly learn a fatalistic lack of confidence in their own abilities. And it disables the drive for professional development in many educators.

Second, and almost unbelievably, educators lack a clear consensus about the fundamental objectives of their enterprise. There is no agreement that we can bring all children up to a reasonable standard, with learning objectives aligned with the requirements of successful living in the twenty-first century. For decades, many teachers have actively resisted being pinned down to such objectives, often citing the difficulty of the conditions under which they work and the huge variation of learning capacities and previous exposure in the children they teach as obstacles to any single, aggressive standard. High standards also represent a basis for adult accountability, and there is a vocal group of educators—probably a minority but quite influential—who believe that many children are beset with disabling personal or family problems that should exempt their teachers from any responsibility for what and whether they learn. Any attempt to embrace aggressive learning objectives thus arouses suspicion; clear outcome measures strengthen the position of those who want to evaluate teachers by the learning outcomes of their students—a level of accountability many educators reject out of hand.

These two failures are closely related. It is logical for people who don't believe their students can achieve high standards to resist being held accountable for such achievement. And the easiest way to avoid accountability (without publicly admitting that you don't believe in your students) is to resist any attempt to define clear standards in the first place. As a result, we have in career educators the only professionals who share no clear, passionately held goals for which they are prepared to be held accountable—by the public or within their own councils. Disbelief and resistance to standards are two sides of the same disabling disorder, and both, I am afraid, are also clearly in evidence in *A Nation at Risk*.

The 1983 report was a creature of its time and of a culture that is still very much with us. Reading it through the lens of the two issues I have just described helps explain why its publication has triggered so little improvement in public education. In the section of the report entitled "Excellence in Education," for example, there is a strong, and to my mind rather strange, juxtaposition between the goals of excellence and equity:

> We do not believe that a public commitment to excellence and educational reform must be made at the expense of a strong public commitment to the equitable treatment of our diverse population. The twin goals of equity and high-quality schooling have profound and practical meaning for our economy and society, and we cannot permit one to yield to the other either in principle or in practice. To do so would deny young people their chance to learn and live according to their aspirations and abilities. It also would lead to a generalized accommodation to mediocrity in our society on the one hand or the creation of an undemocratic elitism on the other.

This passage seems to turn on the assumption that in a diverse society a commitment to excellence will work at cross purposes to equity, unless the balance is carefully managed. If we put too much emphasis on the drive for equity, we will be left with mediocrity. (Now, why should this be?) Reversing the priorities leads to "undemocratic elitism"—presumably because those with higher "aspirations and abilities" will far outpace the masses less endowed with those traits. What are we really saying here? Is there an underlying assumption that populations in a diverse society vary in their capacities to achieve excellence? If so, it will be difficult to achieve equity for the less able without compromising the potential for excellence among those with higher ability. In their next paragraph, the authors work to resolve this dilemma:

> Our goal must be to develop the talents of all to their fullest. Attaining that goal requires that we expect and assist all students to work to the limits of their capabilities. We should expect schools to have genuinely high standards rather than minimum ones, and parents to support and encourage their children to make the most of their talents and abilities.

The problem is to be solved by establishing as our mission "to develop the talents of all to their fullest." We do that by expecting them and assisting them "to work to the limits of their capabilities." This could be mistaken for an enlightened, liberal flexibility—a standard for each child based upon his or her own characteristics and potential. I take it to be a corruption of the principle of uniform high standards for all children, substituting what might be called case-based standards, where we encourage our students, in their diversity, to "make the most of *their* talents and abilities" (emphasis mine). This is an abdication, a resort to relative standards, motivated by lack of belief in the capacities of many of our kids. It is tantamount to no clear standards at all. The authors of *A Nation at Risk* are mired in disbelief, and as a result they are unable to advocate high standards for all children. In this, they share the defining assumptions and attitudes of the educators who operate the public school systems they rightly declared to be putting the nation at risk.

But how can any system achieve excellence without embracing clear, aggressive standards and learning objectives for all children based on them? Clear objectives represent a target, the basis of ongoing assessment, analysis, and corrective action—for students as well as their teachers. Without this clarity, people have no direction and no way of evaluating how they are doing. But proper objectives must be aggressive, too; they must specify learning outcomes, for *all* children, that are aligned to the requirements for success in the 21st-century economy. Otherwise, what is the point? What do we really accomplish when we set lower targets for some kids based on negative judgments about their "aspirations and abilities," that, even if achieved, hold no prospect for achieving the levels of proficiency required to live well and work productively? What possible value does such an education have, for them or for society? No education program can succeed without clear standards and objectives, aligned to the requirements of living and working, that are broadly understood and widely accepted. Indeed, without such objectives it is impossible even to define "success."

A Nation at Risk did not redress this problem. Quite the contrary: it implicitly endorsed a regime of relative standards and a sliding scale of expectations, based on (often negative) judgments of ability, that have bedeviled everyone trying to get educators to actually teach kids to the standards they will need to function in our world. This may seem a harsh interpretation of a venerated document. I must confess to asking myself, "am I reading too much into this?" This passage from the "Recommendations" section of the report seals the case:

We must emphasize that the variety of student aspirations, abilities, and preparation requires that appropriate content be available to satisfy diverse needs. Attention must be directed to both the nature of the content available and to the needs of particular learners. The most gifted students, for example, may need a curriculum enriched and accelerated beyond even the needs of other students of high ability. Similarly, educationally disadvantaged students may require special curriculum materials, smaller classes, or individual tutoring to help them master the material presented. Nevertheless, there remains a common expectation: We must demand the best effort and performance from all students, whether they are gifted or less able, affluent or disadvantaged, whether destined for college, the farm, or industry.

In other words, "all students can learn (up to the level of their abilities)," and they should be supplied with curriculum and instruction (and presumably "flexible" learning outcome standards) aligned to our judgments about them. With due respect to the constructive intentions of the authors of *A Nation at Risk,* this is not the basis for transforming the schools of our urban centers or of demonstrating the value of public education in the twenty-first century. To be fair, I have no way of knowing if they have changed their minds in the intervening years; whether they have or not, the belief system that underlies their 1983 rhetoric, and the approach to standards and expectations based on it, still prevail in American education—to the detriment of us all.

After years of frustration with the inability to improve our schools, the plot has thickened, or, perhaps, broadened. Ineffective schools in poor and minority communities have now become a large factor in the ongoing struggle over the role of government in education. The painful evidence of long-term decline of public education in our cities, experienced first hand by more than one generation of students and parents, has now given real impetus to the "school choice" and voucher movements, putting public education itself at risk.

Although public education has long been supported by a large majority of Americans as an essential, unquestioned element of democracy, the support has never been unanimous. Those of a political orientation hostile to any extensive role for government in our lives have always regarded free public education with a deep skepticism. The movement for "school choice" reflects this attitude. School choice is not the invention of late twentieth-century conservatives; its basic tenets were articulated nearly 150 years ago. In 1859 John Stuart Mill constructed, in "On Liberty," his famous treatise on "the limits of government interference," a template for the case against public or state-controlled education that echoes strongly across eras (and across the Atlantic). First he tells us why we ought to be suspicious:

> A general State education is a mere contrivance for molding people to be exactly like one another; and as the mold in which it casts them is that which pleases the predominant power in the government . . . in proportion as it is efficient and successful, it establishes a despotism over the mind, leading by natural tendency to one over the body. An education established and controlled by the State should exist, if it exist at all, as one among many competing experiments, carried on for the purpose of example and stimulus to keep the others up to a certain standard of excellence.

Public schools are to be limited to a role of exemplar, lest they become tools for despots. For Mill, it is the alternatives, the "competing experiments," that ought to carry the weight of educating the mass of citizens to perform functional roles in society. What are the practical implications of this? How would such a system to be financed? Mill provided a simple, practical framework for sustaining a system of schools operating outside government control:

> [I]n general, if the country contains a sufficient number of persons qualified to provide education under government auspices, the same persons would be able and willing to give an equally good education on the voluntary principle, under the assurance of remuneration afforded by a law rendering education compulsory, combined with State aid to those unable to defray the expense.

Although a free market "voluntary principle" is the philosophical driver of this approach, "remuneration" is to be assured by a compulsory education law that ensures a steady flow of customers, in conjunction with "State aid" to the poor to ensure that they come with cash in hand. If all of this sounds familiar, it should. Mill's formulation of a system of privately controlled (but publicly subsidized) schools represents a blueprint for the educational choice movement of today, with charter schools and pilot schools freed of the authority and constraints of the school bureaucracy but still funded by public school budgets, and private schools, parochial schools, and education for-profit enterprises all to be funded by vouchers.

If this conservative vision has not, so far, to be fully realized, it is because suspicion of government has not proved a strong enough motive in the United States to roll back the commitment to public education. Too many mainstream Americans benefited from public schools and hoped for the same for their children. But a real opening for the conservative vision has been provided by the failures of urban education: people are prone to become agitated, and much more open to "competing experiments," when confronted with the spectacle of too many kids who can't read or write. The realities of bad public schools in the inner cities and educators with stubbornly low expectations for their students have stimulated a hunger for alternative answers. The leaders of the school choice movement have been quick to respond. The primary venue for school choice, at least for now, seems to be urban centers with poor and minority populations, with a special focus on winning the hearts and minds of disappointed, angry parents desperate to save their kids from lives on the margins of society. It is fertile ground for anyone trying to sell wholesale change.

The strategic thrust into the inner cities has met with some real success. Voucher programs are well established in Milwaukee and Cleveland, and other urban centers are ripe for such programs as well. In its 1999 National Opinion Poll of Education, the Joint Center for Political and Economic Studies found that 60 percent of African Americans supported vouchers, compared with only 48 percent in 1996 (this compares with 53 percent of the "general population"—presumably whites—in support).[3] The 1999 plurality of supporters breaks down by subgroup in interesting ways:

> Among blacks, two-thirds of baby boomers and more than 70 percent of those younger than 35 years supported school vouchers, while a small plurality (49 to 44 percent) of those between 51 and 64 years supported vouchers, and a plurality (49 to 42 percent) of black seniors opposed them. Black Christian conservatives (68 percent in favor), persons from the lowest-income households (72 percent) and the highest-income households (71 percent), and persons from households with children (71 percent) were the black subgroups that were most favorable to vouchers.

In other words, when it comes to vouchers in the black community, those with the greatest personal stake in education—the 35-and-under group of childrearing age—along with those with the greatest financial need (and no doubt the worst schools) were the strongest supporters. In the latest (2000) survey from the Joint Center, the numbers rose even higher, with fully 75 percent of blacks under thirty-five years old supporting vouchers, compared to 60 percent of whites.[4]

Historically, the inferior education of poor and minority children was of little interest outside the communities in which they grew up because the social problems that resulted could be largely contained within the boundaries of those communities. That is no longer the case. Inner-city minority communities are now in play as highly strategic elements in an epic, long-term ideological struggle for control and definition of schooling in the United States. It is a struggle with very high stakes; according to the Department of Education, the United States spent $375 billion on K–12 public education in 2000–2001, and the prospect of diversion of even a tiny fraction of that sum into private hands is a powerful economic incentive.[5] Among the many ramifications of continuing failure to adequately prepare poor and minority children for the rigors of a global economy and society will be the erosion of an essential base of support for public education itself. Those convinced that public schools are a pillar of democracy can no longer afford to look the other way.

Why are the problems of education in our big cities, filled as they are with black and Hispanic children, so intractable? Why are the expectations of educators, after twenty years of school reform, still so low? Where (beyond the surge in support for vouchers) is the outrage? The "we're not gonna take this anymore" mobilization among parents? And where is the community leadership? And whatever has become of the school reform movement?

It is time we face up to some realities. After twenty years and billions of dollars spent, it is clear that school reform has not succeeded. As a nation, we remain ineffectual in the face of a problem that will consign an important segment of the population to, at best, the sidelines of the twenty-first century. And there is something else, something darker: the failure to educate so many minority children is rooted in a pernicious interaction between American beliefs about the distribution of intelligence and attitudes about race.

Black and brown children do poorly because we don't really expect better from them. This has everything to do with widely held, but politely repressed, attitudes about race. The burden of the notion that, when it comes to intelligence, "some have it and some don't" simply weighs harder on some kinds of people than others. African Americans in particular have long lived under the cloud of what I have elsewhere called "the rumor of inferiority"; the idea, baldly stated, that on average, black folk (and perhaps some other people of color) are *genetically* intellectually inferior to other populations.[6] This is a very old rationale for injustice, an original justification for slavery. It is still periodically aired in quasi-academic tomes, and has thoroughly infiltrated the consciousness of most Americans, including African Americans themselves.[7] The resulting general doubts about the capacities of most black children on the one hand and self-doubt on the other paralyze us all. Parents who should be angry and determined remain apathetic and passive; educators become cynical, prone to blame their own failures to teach on the limitations of their students, and resistant to change; school reformers, so optimistic at the start and full of good intentions, become demoralized and leave the field. The lack of progress we have made is testament to the power of destructive ideas to cripple our capacity for corrective action. Meanwhile, the multigenerational slow-motion train wreck continues. If this goes on much longer, you will have to count me among the advocates of "competing experiments," and perhaps vouchers to support them.

But not yet. I have spent the last twenty years in search of answers and, working with my colleagues at the Efficacy Institute, have made some promising discoveries that give me hope. There are individual classrooms in every community where teachers achieve wonderful results with children from the most disadvantaged backgrounds. Most and sometimes all of their students achieve proficiency—a very high standard of academic achievement—every year. In my speaking engagements with educators around the country I routinely ask how many know such a teacher; invariably one-third to one-half raise their hands and assure me that these are real people they could name. Working and talking with these individuals has been rewarding. We have found that there are unmistakable, replicable patterns in their beliefs and practices: they establish aggressive learning-outcome objectives for every subject they teach, and they communicate these as targets to their students; they believe *all* their students can achieve the targeted outcomes by the end of the school year, and they regularly and credibly communicate that belief. Confident in their own capacities to shape effective learning environments, they use the data from a regular schedule of assessments to drive ongoing adjustments in the curriculum they use and the instructional strategies they employ. The late Ron Edmonds, whose ideas have become gospel for many serious educators around the country, once said something to the effect that "We already have all the knowledge we need to teach our kids. We just don't use it." That we have the knowledge is certainly true, proven every day by these effective teachers. The question then becomes, "How do we make more people use it?" That is, how do we move it to scale?

Before I share my own answer to this question, I feel obliged to tell you what I think it is *not*. Professional incompetence has been widely viewed among school reformers as a leading cause of the failure of American schools. On a superficial level, this may be true; incompetent teachers rarely teach well. So for twenty years much of the energy and money of school reform went into an attempt to fix poor schools through teacher retraining and certification schemes. But the phenomenon of twenty-year veterans who have only rudimentary subject knowledge, use obviously ineffective instructional strategies, and seem not to care that most of their students don't learn much is better understood as a symptom of a much deeper problem—the sense of helplessness and futility of educators who don't believe their students have the intellectual capacity to learn. These people are neither stupid nor lazy; they are creatures of their culture, and, confronted with poorly prepared kids, they have the dispirited response typical of those indoctrinated with American beliefs about the distribution of intelligence: "What good will better instructional strategies do with kids like these?" Lack of professional competence *is* a real issue, with obvious consequences; but an exclusive or even primary focus on it takes us off the scent. It is the sense of hopelessness about the prospects of moving inner-city kids to standards that undermines the drive to become truly proficient at teaching, not the other way around. People who don't believe in their students literally knit and read newspapers when they are forced to attend staff development programs about the latest, greatest, research-based instructional approaches (which they routinely refer to as "flavors of the month," and then never use).

If not teacher retraining, what? Here is a simple, three-part prescription for what is required to reach scale—that is, achieve effective schools and school systems—building on what we have learned from our own work and from individual effective teachers.

First, we must build consensus on the mission of education. What exactly are we trying to achieve? Educators need clear targets that define success if they are to have any hope of being successful. I believe the appropriate mission for classrooms, whole schools, and school systems is *proficiency* for all students, in each subject, and at every grade level. Proficiency can be simply defined: it is the demonstration, for each subject, of possession of the appropriate *knowledge* and the *application skills* to use that knowledge in new and novel situations. This is an aggressive standard, the level of learning traditionally expected only of the "gifted and talented" in our schools. It moves considerably beyond rote memorization into the deeper realm of understanding required to actually employ knowledge to solve problems in the real world. It can also be measured. Well-designed tests can assess both knowledge and application skill—proficiency—and tell us where children are relative to the target.[8]

I must confess I am not confident that, left to their own devices, educators will adopt such an aggressive standard for all children. They have too often fought high standards and public expressions of doubt that many of our kids, especially poor and minority kids in the cities, can achieve at this level. But it is not up to educators alone to decide the mission or the standards for our children. Organized pressure from the outside is a critical element in the necessary transformation of our schools. The communities that pay for public education should organize "campaigns for proficiency," where they take the lead in determining what the standard ought to be and establish criteria for accountability for educators, who are, after all, public servants. Proficiency represents a uniform standard for all children and for the system as a whole. It is a target worthy of the actual capabilities our children, and it is aligned with the levels of knowledge and skills they will need to function in the twenty-first century.

Second, we must build belief that the mission can be accomplished. The confidence to set aggressive standards for all children only comes with the belief that they are capable of learning at this level. Acceptance of the adult accountability that will inevitably accompany clear standards is also based on confidence—in this case, confidence that adults are capable of teaching at this level. In neither case can such confidence be taken for granted. People raised in the "some have it, some don't" belief system will need to have their current understanding about the distribution of intelligence challenged and replaced by one that allows the possibility that virtually all normal kids have the intellectual capacity to achieve proficiency.[9]

Recent research shows that intelligence is not the rigid, static entity it was once believed to be. IQ scores for people of all ages have risen by about three points a decade during most of the twentieth century.[10] It has also been discovered that the longer people attend school, the higher, on average, their IQs. Interestingly, IQs have been rising for preschool children, too.[11] Better nutrition is a possible cause, but it is likely that the escalating complexities and challenges of participation in our society and economy are the most important drivers of our growing abilities.

This has critical implications for education. The most important determinant of intellectual capacity and school success is not fixed ability; it is engagement in challenging activity. *Effective effort*—which we define as effort based on tenacious engagement with a task, close attention to feedback that indicates what we must work on to improve, and continual adjustments in strategy based on that feedback—controls learning capacity. Intelligence is not a fixed asset one either has or doesn't have; children can "get smart," literally become more intelligent—if, and only if, they commit sustained effective effort at challenging new tasks. Adults who know how to engage children's effort at learning tasks can move them to proficiency. Extensive evidence supports the link between effective effort and the development of new capacities, including the highest levels of expertise and mastery in such creative, competitive activities as chess and music.[12]

This is an entirely different way of thinking about intellectual capacity and the only one I know of that will support a general commitment to proficiency. It is a belief system implicitly embraced by the great teachers who routinely move the most disadvantaged kids to the highest standards. Their successes can be used as persuasive evidence that children really can "get smart," become proficient, in the hands of a skilled educator who believes in them. People who understand that intelligence can be developed stop resisting high standards for all children, and spend their energy instead learning new instructional approaches to get them there.

Exposing educators to a new belief system about intelligence, and getting them to adopt it, will take leadership. Superintendents, principals, and opinion leaders among the teacher corps in each school must open themselves to the evidence that children can "get smart" (including the readily available evidence of local teachers who prove it by moving disadvantaged kids to proficiency). Most important, they must validate the truth of this idea in their own lives and experiences and approach others with the authenticity that comes only from personal conviction. We can transfer the "get smart" belief system to all the adults in a school system (and through them, to children) if leaders have the courage to embrace the idea themselves, and the will to learn the new leadership proficiencies required to expand the mindsets of teachers, parents, and children.

Third, we must teach people to use assessment data to drive changes in strategy. American educators have traditionally used student performance data, especially data from standardized tests, to make (often negative) judgments about children's learning capacities. In the last few years the public has turned the tables, using school and classroom performance data to make (often negative) judgments about teacher competency. These tendencies have stimulated a powerful aversion to data and resistance to its analysis. But effective, constructive use of data is an essential tool that teachers and parents can use, immediately, to realign resources, policies, and practices to move children to proficiency.

Proficiency is, by its nature, eminently measurable. That means we can use assessment tools to generate data about how our kids are doing at any given time—who is reaching the standard, who is falling short, and by how much. Useful data in a well-constructed proficiency test takes the form of detailed feedback explaining why the child got the score he or she did, and what she or he must work on to improve. An intense focus on this feedback is critical because it literally tells us what we must do to get better results in the future. It is the direct guide to corrective strategies.

For effective educators, feedback from assessments shapes curriculum and instructional strategy.[13] Curriculum is properly understood as much more than "the textbook"; it is the range of tools, including textbooks, plus a wide array of additional instructional materials and exploratory activities that educators use to transfer knowledge to learners. In an effective classroom the curriculum is neither static nor ordained by the central office; it is constantly adjusted, based on feedback, to meet the needs of a particular student or group of students in the march to proficiency.[14] The same requirement for flexibility applies to instructional strategies. The instructional approaches a good teacher uses are never set in concrete; they depend entirely on what *these* students need, *this* year, to move them to proficiency. In my experience, educators who have learned to use data are never at a loss about what to do, nor do they sit around waiting for marching orders from the central office. They are responsive and proactive. They use data to discover what their students need, then use the "knowledge base of teaching"—the compendium of documented strategies available to them—and their own inventiveness to meet the challenges.[15] These are *professional* teachers, proficient in their craft.

Ironically, the change we all want in American education requires that we—parents, leaders, and everyone with a stake in the future—demonstrate faith in the capacities of our educators to learn. We must set a high standard for them. We must expect that they will move our children to proficiency and demonstrate to us that they can do what other professionals do when confronted with problems and challenges—diagnose what is wrong and find (or invent) corrective strategies to overcome all obstacles. They will be motivated to do so if they are confronted (and supported) by communities that won't take no for an answer to the demand for high standards for all kids. And it will help a lot if we stop undercutting their initiative and inventiveness by spoonfeeding them what I have heard referred to as "teacher-proof," by-the-numbers curricula and instructional approaches developed by experts.

Can it really be that simple? I regularly hear respectable people argue that everything is terribly complicated, that the issues are so complex that they defy solution. The opposite is true. Effective organizations in every domain of activity, all over the world, employ fundamentally simple approaches, no matter how complex they look from the outside. These always involve clear objectives understood by everyone and considered mandatory, strong belief among the rank and file about their own capacities to achieve these objectives, and simple operating schemes that people can quickly learn and eventually master to solve problems and overcome obstacles. The details of particular operations and functions within an organization may be numerous and complex, but the core strategy is always simple.

This principle translates to the world of public education. We will get things right in American schools, starting in our urban centers, when we decide to hold ourselves accountable for moving all children to meet an aggressive standard, like proficiency; when we learn to believe in their capacities and our own; and when we assume a fully professional posture of defining our own strategies for improvement.

CHAPTER SEVEN

The Limits of Ideology: Curriculum and the Culture Wars

DAVID T. GORDON

Just months before she died in 1999, Jeanne Chall, a leading literacy scholar of the twentieth century, participated in a forum at the Harvard Graduate School of Education called "Beyond the Reading Wars." In the 1960s, Chall had written *Learning to Read: The Great Debate* to address the rancorous debate over whether beginning readers should learn letters and sounds before delving into books or immerse themselves in texts, picking up the sights, sounds, and meaning of words along the way. *Learning to Read* had displayed a mountain of research about the need for beginning readers to have both phonics instruction and access to interesting reading material. What more was there to say? Yet here was Chall more than thirty years later discussing a whole new round of reading debates.

In a comical exchange with the moderator, Chall was asked if a certain high-profile report issued earlier that year would settle the matter. "Well," she replied, "the basic knowledge was known for the longest time. Even the Greeks knew what kind of combination [of instruction] you needed in teaching reading. Thirty years ago I said the research showed that you do need phonics. And then you *do* need to read, you see."

"So why do we keep fighting about whole language and phonics?"

"I know many of my friends say it's a political thing," Chall replied. "The ones who like the alphabet are right-wingers, Republicans. Can you imagine? At any rate, somebody discovered along the way that you really didn't need to know all the letters. You could remember the words. That is more fun. You don't have to drill."

"And those fun people are the Democrats? The ones who don't do any work?" the moderator asked.

"Yes, the liberals," said Chall.[1]

The banter was humorous—and meant to be. But it also revealed some frustration over the tenor and substance of the disputes about reading instruction during the 1980s and 1990s. Chall, it has been said, was one to "follow the evidence fearlessly wherever it might lead."[2] Yet the curriculum debates that came after *A Nation at Risk* were often fueled not by a sober and fearless analysis of what the evidence said is best, but by ideological and political partisanship. More often than not, it led to the kind of absurd characterizations Chall was poking fun at, the oversimplifications that turned reading- and math-teaching strategies into salvos within the culture wars. Somewhere along the line phonics and arithmetic became "conservative"—the pedagogical equivalents of Reaganomics, mink coats, and Anita Bryant—while whole language and reform math became "liberal," lumped in with the progressive income tax and *Mother Jones*.

Given the sense of urgency to improve education following *A Nation at Risk*, school reform was bound to take on the look of blood sport in certain cases, particularly regarding reading and math instruction. Bitter squabbles have broken out over science and social studies instruction, high-stakes testing, and school choice. But the reading and math wars have been generally nastier and more emotional than even those conflicts. It's not hard to understand why. Reading and math are the bedrock of children's learning, the primary subjects of elementary education. Later success in school and college depends on success in those subjects during the preK–3 years.

The broad bipartisan support for the No Child Left Behind Act (NCLB) of 2001 may prove to be something of a truce, if not a peace treaty, in the curriculum wars. Conservatives and liberals, traditionalists and progressives agreed that an emphasis on "scientific," or research-based, instruction and standards was needed so that K–12 decisionmaking would be influenced less by ideology and more by practical and proven solutions to classroom dilemmas.

If the wars really are ended, what can be learned from them? One thing they teach us is the limits of ideological orthodoxy for setting educational agendas. When ideologues impose lopsided solutions, conflict is inevitable—and children are poorly served. A related lesson is about the importance of a balanced, or integrated, approach to curricular reforms—one that makes the most of what different strategies offer in order to reach the widest range of children. Not only does that usually make the most sense, but research shows that teachers seldom incorporate new materials and reform strategies whole hog. Without some evidence that proposed changes are indeed an improvement, and without a specific plan for putting those changes into practice, teachers will take it on themselves to interpret and integrate them into the practices they already know. Which suggests a third lesson: that policymakers and education researchers need to do a better job of clarifying the goals, means, and justifications for reforms. Finally, once those objectives have been clarified, teachers need to be given comprehensive training, support, and incentive if reforms are to be taken to scale.

THE PROBLEM OF IDEOLOGY

Educational ideologies are a useful starting point for discussion, for *describing* the ideal positions of different sides in a debate, but they are not very helpful for *prescribing* solutions. The post–*Nation at Risk* years have shown that reality trumps ideology time and again. California's reading and math reforms are good examples.

The state's 1987 English/Language Arts framework tried to overhaul reading instruction by installing a curriculum meant to convey "the magic of language" and "touch students' lives and stimulate their minds and hearts." It called for a radical change in instructional practice. Out was phonics: proponents of the new method argued that such skill-building exercises—"drill-and-kill"—bored students and stymied their natural excitement about reading. In came whole language, which would immerse students in texts and do away with direct instruction in letter-sound relationships, spelling, and so forth. Students would learn to read as they learned to speak—by jumping right in and doing it—and focus on the meaning of words, not their sounds or particular parts. Fundamental skills would be picked up along the way, in context. This dispute is an old story in American education—from the "alphabetic method" of Noah Webster's speller and McGuffey's readers to attacks by Horace Mann and John Dewey on phonics-based instruction to *Why Johnny Can't Read*, the 1955 bestseller that induced a public outcry for a return to direct phonics instruction.

That's where Jeanne Chall comes in. In 1961, the Carnegie Corporation of New York asked Chall, then at the City University of New York, to determine what the evidence said. She analyzed dozens of studies published from 1910 to 1967, reviewed the most widely used reading textbooks and their teachers manuals, talked with authors and editors of beginning reading programs, and visited hundreds of classrooms in the United States and the United Kingdom. She published her results in 1967 in *Learning to Read*.

The verdict? A combination of phonics for beginners and good literature for all was best. "To read, one needs to be able to use *both* the alphabetic principle and the meaning of words," she wrote. "What distinguished the more effective beginning reading instruction was its early emphasis on learning the code. Instruction that focused, at the beginning, on meaning tended to produce less favorable results." Early phonics instruction in which children learn letter-sound relationships by sounding out words as they read was especially beneficial to children of low socioeconomic status who did not come from language-rich or literacy-rich homes.[3]

In the 1970s and 1980s, when education research was exploring new territory in beginning reading through the lenses of psychology and neurology, evidence continued to mount showing the efficacy of early phonics instruction combined with exposure to high-quality reading material. Later editions of *Learning to Read*, published in 1983 and 1996, reported even stronger support of the advantages of "code emphasis over meaning emphasis" for beginning readers.[4]

But whole language, the latest incarnation of the whole-word method, was winning the ideological battle. It got the approval of teachers unions, schools of education, and others sympathetic to its progressive underpinnings. Its idealized view of children as self-motivated, joyful learners who, with the right encouragement, could construct meaning out of texts without having to know a bunch of rules had a highly romantic appeal.[5]

Whatever its merits, whole language was done a disservice by those adherents who presented it in increasingly strident ways, turning the reading debate into a conflict between good and evil rather than what it should have been: a difference of opinion between people of good will. In California, the discussion took on an almost "theological" character, as journalist Nicholas Lemann puts it, shaped by the crusading, absolutist fervor of its participants.[6]

California's education leaders bought into an ideology rather than a proven, research-based instructional plan. Consulting with whole-language advocates, they were presented with a "choice": (a) provide beginning readers with a humane, nurturing whole-language environment in which their natural interest and love for rich reading material would flourish, or (b) offer them mind-numbing phonics-based instruction. Bill Honig, California's superintendent of public instruction at the time, would later claim, "We thought we were pushing literature. We were neutral on phonics. Then the whole-language movement hijacked what we were doing."[7] The new framework didn't mention whole language directly, but it was full of the theory's romantic language, as its references to the "magic" of language and efforts to "stimulate hearts and minds" suggest.

A similar theological good-versus-evil hue colored the state's math reforms, which included the introduction of new frameworks in 1985 and 1992. Familiar themes emerged, pitting a child-centered ideology emphasizing "real-life" problem-solving against the boring, factory-floor experience of arithmetic drills and pencil-and-paper computation. With reform math, students would use calculators and manipulatives—objects such as beans, sticks, or blocks—to understand numeric relationships. They would read about math problems and discuss them in an effort to understand not just computational value but how such knowledge applies in life. They would work in small groups, tackling together the sorts of problems one encounters in everyday life. Basic skills would—like phonics in the reading reforms—get picked up by students along the way in an informal or indirect manner. This same departure from a basic-skills emphasis characterized the 1989 standards issued by the National Council of Teachers of Mathematics (NCTM). To reformers, traditional instruction was "mindless mimicry mathematics."[8]

Of course, ideological excess was not limited to reformers. By the early 1990s, grassroots opposition to both the math and reading frameworks in California had swelled into a statewide movement. Helped by the relatively new technologies of the World Wide Web and email, parents and mathematicians founded Mathematically Correct, an advocacy group that became a powerful opponent of what was now being called "fuzzy math" after the reform's endorsement of estimation rather than computation. Meanwhile, the media began seeking and finding extreme examples of the new methods in action. In one memorable anecdote, *Time* magazine reporter Margot Hornblower visited a fifth-grade class in Sun Valley, California, where the teacher began class by asking, "What if everybody here had to shake hands with everyone else? How many handshakes would that take?" The kids split into small groups and puzzled over the activity for some time—the reporter said for an hour, the teacher later said twenty minutes. Regardless, none of the children could arrive at an answer, and the class tried it again the next day.[9]

Such stories were often exaggerated by opponents of the reforms as representative of the depth and scope of reforms. This was unfair. But they had a potent political effect. In 1997, California revised its framework again to blend traditional instruction with reform methods, putting a greater emphasis on arithmetic, computation, and paper-and-pencil algorithms such as long division. In 2000, the NCTM did the same. But the NCTM also made a point of spelling out more clearly how the standards should be applied, especially in the elementary and middle grades. In some ways, the NCTM saw the math wars as a great misunderstanding and suggested that the revised standards were a clarification, not a correction, of the 1989 framework.[10]

A similar uprising took place over reading. Years after overseeing the 1987 reform, California's former superintendent of public instruction Bill Honig would say, "The best antidote to a zealous philosophy is reality."[11] The coup de grace for whole language in his state came with the publication of the 1994 National Assessment of Educational Progress (NAEP) reading scores. In just eight years, California had fallen from first among states to dead last, tied with Louisiana. Fifty-nine percent of fourth graders could not read at the fourth-grade level, compared to a national average of 44 percent reading below grade level. African American and Hispanic children fared worst, with 71 percent and 81 percent, respectively, lacking necessary reading skills, compared with 44 percent of white students.

Whole-language proponents cited a number of factors to explain the change, such as larger class size, a new surge of immigration, the high percentage of students from families of low socioeconomic status, and poor training of teachers in whole-language teaching. They pointed out that other states using whole language, such as New Hampshire, had improved test scores significantly.[12] But those arguments fell on deaf ears, especially the arguments about immigration and poverty, given that 49 percent of those who read below basic levels had college graduates for parents. Nowhere else in the nation did the children of college-educated parents score lower than in California.[13]

Something was clearly wrong with California reading instruction, and conservatives had a field day promoting an image of a huge state bureaucracy imposing illiteracy on its children with its politically correct theory. Even before the NAEP scores came out, Republicans had held up whole language from coast to coast in 1994, when they won their first congressional majority in half a century, as a symbol of failed "liberal" ideas. They were not above their own ideological excesses: fundamentalist Christians suggested that whole language's goal of helping students make meaning out of texts was an effort to undermine a literal, or fundamentalist, reading of anything, but especially the Bible.[14]

After the NAEP embarrassment, California amended its reading framework in 1996, calling for a "balanced, comprehensive approach" to reading instruction in its schools that would provide direct instruction in phonics, vocabulary, and spelling while acknowledging whole-language advocates' concern that, of course, "the best instruction provides a strong relationship between what children learn in phonics and what they read."[15] It was a point Jeanne Chall had made in *Learning to Read* twenty-nine years earlier.

THE NEED FOR BALANCE

Chall had warned against taking phonics to an extreme. Early phonics instruction was a necessary tool that should be replaced with reading good stories as quickly as possible. But she had also criticized education professionals for ignoring half a century of research evidence because of their ideological bias against skills-based phonics instruction—the belief that phonics was incompatible with progressive education.[16]

Even as research continued in the 1990s to demonstrate the need for a balanced reading approach, whole-language theorists attacked advocates of balance in baldly political terms. A founding theorist of whole language bizarrely accused Jeanne Chall of doing the bidding of "right-wing" groups bent on destroying public education because she had unmasked the potential harm of a radical application of his theory.[17]

At this time, the federal government did what the Carnegie Corporation had tried to do in supporting Chall's work in the 1960s: get beyond the ideological squabbles to determine what reading research actually said. The National Research Council (NRC), the research arm of the National Academy of Sciences, took up the task. Three shifts in thinking during the 1980s made the project compelling, according to Catherine Snow, the Harvard literacy expert who directed the study. First, a large body of new research increased our understanding of the importance of preschool experiences in the development of literacy—that during those years, children are not just getting ready for reading instruction but actively developing literacy skills. Second, research conducted in the previous two decades about the nature of the reading process had resolved many of the issues phonics and whole-language advocates were fighting about, demolishing some theoretical underpinnings of what Snow calls "radical whole-language practice"—research that had yet to filter down to the trenches. Third, given this consensus on instructional matters, prevention of reading problems rather than reading instruction per se became more of a concern.

In 1998, the NRC issued its verdict: both sides in the reading wars were right—and both were wrong. "The reading wars are over," the panel declared. The findings, published in a book titled *Preventing Reading Difficulties in Young Children*, emphasized the need for reading instruction that balanced and integrated what phonics and whole-language proponents were advocating. Good readers accomplish three things, said the report: "They understand the alphabetic system of English to identify printed works; they have and use background knowledge and strategies to obtain meaning from print; and they read fluently." In other words, they understand and appreciate both the sounds and the meanings of words. The report placed special emphasis on the impact of the preschool years. What kinds of experiences do children need *before* they get to school and formal reading instruction begins?[18]

In a later edition of the book, the authors expressed concern about the use of the term *balance*, a metaphor that, they said, could imply "a little of this and a little of that" or suggest evenly dividing classroom time between phonics and comprehension activities. Instead, they clarified their findings as a call for *integrating* these strategies so that "the opportunities to learn these two aspects of skilled reading should be going on at the same time, in the context of the same activities, and that the choice of instructional activities should be part of an overall, coherent approach to supporting literacy development, not a haphazard selection from unrelated, though varied, activities."[19]

Mathematicians opposed to radical reforms made similar arguments in favor of balanced math instruction that teaches basic skills but also links them to real-life contexts. They argued that having a rich understanding of the abstract concepts and basic facts of mathematics is essential to being able to adapt that knowledge to a variety of plausible and authentic circumstances. Since there is inevitably an abstract or theoretical aspect to any principle, separating the conceptual from the actual is counterproductive and confusing.

TEACHERS TAKE MATTERS INTO THEIR OWN HANDS

While researchers and policymakers have come to the realization that balanced instruction works best, school practitioners seem to have known that all along. Their natural gravitation toward balanced instruction is typical of how school reform works, according to historians David Tyack and William Tobin: "Reformers believe their innovations will transform schools, but it is important to recognize that schools change reforms. Over and over again teachers have selectively implemented and altered reforms."[20]

For example, in one 1995 study, researchers found that children in classes identified as "whole language" made greater gains in reading comprehension than those in classes tagged "basic skills." They also became independent readers more quickly. But when the researchers took a closer look, they found that those whole-language classrooms actually provided abundant instruction in basic skills.[21]

Meanwhile, in their decade-long study of California math reform, researchers David K. Cohen and Heather C. Hill found that teachers by and large reported using a mix of methods, taking parts of the curriculum that made sense and ignoring those that didn't:

> What reformers and opponents packaged tidily, teachers disaggregated and reassembled. Their logic was different from and more complex than both the logic put forward by reformers in the frameworks, who saw what we call "conventional" and "reform" ideas about teaching and student learning as opposed to each other, and to the critics of reform, whose view of these matters was at least as black and white as that of the reformers. Though many teachers expressed strong allegiance to the principal reform ideas, most did not discard the corresponding conventional ideas.[22]

A 1999 report by the *Harvard Education Letter* found a similar pattern among teachers in Massachusetts, where teachers and curriculum coordinators using materials based on the 1989 NCTM reform math standards began supplementing materials that focused heavily on problem-solving with paper-and-pencil, skills-building worksheets. For example, the math curriculum coordinator for public schools in Braintree, William Kendall, told education journalist Andreae Downs, "It's often good to blend curricula. Kids need practice. It's not enough just to get the big idea and move on, you need practice before you get it right."[23]

Why do practitioners take matters into their own hands? Cohen and Hill ventured a few guesses. First, school practitioners often get conflicting messages from policymakers at various levels about whether, for example, to teach basic skills or discard them. State directives may be contradicted by district-level directives or by leaders in schools—principals, teacher leaders, or the strong lobbying of local parents' groups that are at odds with state policy. So many different messages may make teachers feel that the best thing to do is keep on keeping on until the problem is sorted out.

Another explanation cited by Cohen and Hill is that "teachers learn things from experience that reformers, critics, and policymakers can never know because they lack the experience and rarely inquire of teachers." When math reforms didn't work in California, policymakers accused teachers of not committing to the framework or of implementing the reforms ineffectively by mixing innovative practices and content with traditional ones. But teachers often told researchers that their professional experience might require them to adjust on the fly to help certain students or classes build essential skills. Like lawyers, doctors, architects, or other professionals, teachers knew that what is drawn up on the board rarely translates easily into practice.

In their analysis of the California math reforms, Cohen and Hill found a great gap between what was prescribed as policy and what took place in practice.[24] This complicated the effort to try to evaluate reforms and assign blame or credit for failure or success—a point California whole-language advocates also made when trying to explain the state's miserable showing in reading in 1994. The interpretation and implementation of standards can vary in each district, school, and classroom. New standards-based curriculum materials often have errors, and the commitment of time and resources to preparing teachers to use such new materials also varies widely.

Because reform efforts often produce glass-half-full and glass-half-empty results, the conclusions we draw from those results must be carefully weighed so that, to paraphrase Bill Honig, reality maintains the upper hand over ideology. For example, researchers at Northwestern University and the University of Chicago compared international math scores to determine how fifth-grade students who had been enrolled in the K–4 reform program Everyday Mathematics matched up with their U.S. and foreign counterparts. The researchers found that the Taiwanese and Japanese fifth graders performed better than all of the American students. Students in Everyday Mathematics outperformed U.S. students from traditional math classes, scored higher than the Taiwanese in some cases, and, on average, scored only slightly lower than Japanese students. Is this good news or bad news? Do we see progress being made through the reform program and should we build on these apparent gains? Or do we just see continued failure—Americans languishing behind the world *again*—and scrap the program?

The value of education research to practice and policymaking naturally depends on the quality or the trustworthiness of the research itself. In 2000, the *Christian Science Monitor* reported that two math reform programs—Core-Plus and the Connected Math Project—got favorable reviews from the U.S. Department of Education based on research conducted by people affiliated with the curricula's developers. Core-Plus was evaluated by an education researcher from the University of Iowa who was a co-director of the program—and in line to receive royalties from sales of its textbooks. "Nobody, including research ethicists, argues that [the Core-Plus study is] invalid," wrote reporter Mark Clayton. Many observers noted that the study would probably provide useful data and analysis about the program. But without a truly independent review, the DOE's recommendation is suspect—and gives ample fodder to skeptics of reforms.[25]

Concerns about skewed research have also been raised by whole-language proponents about recent reports on reading instruction. They note, for example, that the study *Teaching Children to Read*, commissioned by the National Institute of Child Health and Human Development and published in 2000, clearly favored an increased emphasis on phonics instruction. The report, which laid the groundwork for the "Reading First" initiative passed into law as part of the No Child Left Behind Act, focused on quantitative research—that is, studies connecting teaching strategies to test scores. By ignoring qualitative research studies—such as case studies, small-group studies, and in-school observation—the report gave an incomplete picture of the role of classroom instruction in improved reading scores, critics said. In 2002, a new panel went back to the drawing board, looking at qualitative research as well.[26]

New York Times education columnist Richard Rothstein suggests that the current emphasis in federal legislation on "scientifically based research"—the language used in the Reading Excellence Act of 1998 and repeated numerous times in No Child Left Behind—may undermine the balanced approach by tilting policy in favor of phonics because "scientific study is easier for phonics than whole language." He writes: "Researchers can teach about phonemes, then test if children they know get 'car' by removing a sound from 'cart.' It is harder to design experiments to see if storytelling spurs a desire to read." Rothstein also points out that "[s]cientific studies of separate parts of a reading program exist, but there is no well-established science that precisely balances phonemic awareness, phonics, vocabulary lessons and storytelling. The balance differs for each child. Teachers fluent in both skill- and literature-based techniques are needed."[27]

HELPING TEACHERS SUPPORT REFORMS

The past twenty years of reform have also shown that getting teachers to change their practice has been more difficult than expected. The teaching profession is by nature a conservative one. For example, Cohen and Hill report that the math-reform ideas that got the most teacher approval were those that did little to challenge conventional practice and required only modest effort to implement—a little more time here, a change in activities there. Anything that appeared to subvert or challenge what they considered to be essential math teaching and learning got only reluctant attention, if any. "All of this suggests one final explanation," write Cohen and Hill. "[L]earning is often slow and painful, and even when rapid, it attaches to inherited ideas, intellectual structures, and familiar practices."[28]

A comparative study of math teaching in the United States and China demonstrates the importance of teacher knowledge. In an effort to learn why Americans did more poorly, researcher Liping Ma, senior scholar at the Carnegie Foundation for the Advancement of Teaching, found that a high percentage of U.S. teachers had a weak grasp of basic math concepts, particularly at the elementary school level. Teachers lacked a fundamental understanding of standard algorithms, as well as alternative means of problem-solving and why the standard ones have been determined most efficient. A teacher "should know these various solutions of the problem, know how and why students came up with them, know the relationship between the nonstandard ways and the standard way, and know the single conception underlying all the different ways," she writes in her influential book, *Knowing and Teaching Elementary Mathematics*. Ma suggests that to improve mathematics instruction in the United States, more attention must be paid to fundamental math knowledge in preservice teacher training, teacher preparation time, and professional development.[29]

But knowing how to teach math involves more than simply knowing mathematics, and attention to content knowledge alone won't improve teaching and learning. According to the research of Stanford University's Linda Darling-Hammond, students learn best from teachers who have university-level courses in math education as well as a fundamentally sound math knowledge. "Sometimes very bright people who are not taught to teach are very poor teachers because they don't know what it is to struggle to learn, and haven't thought much about how people learn. Content is important, but it isn't enough," she told the *Harvard Education Letter*. Teachers' ability to adapt curricula to the needs of each student is crucial to improved instruction in any curriculum, she says.[30] Critics of education programs who say that teacher training should focus primarily on content, not pedagogy, fail to appreciate the special skills required for good teaching. Katherine K. Merseth, director of teacher education at Harvard and a former math teacher, says fundamental content knowledge is of course essential. But teachers also need techniques in their teaching repertoire that reflect how children learn and make sense of things:

> Can you explain to me why one-half divided by two-thirds is three-fourths? Don't tell me how to do it, because that's what many people will do. Give me an example. Tell me a story that represents that equation. We all know you invert and multiply. But why? Or as a kid once said, "If x equals five, why did you call it x? Why didn't you just call it five?" You need to be able to draw on the content knowledge itself. But simply having the content background will not make you an effective teacher. To be an effective teacher, you must understand your audience.[31]

In their study, Cohen and Hill found that efforts were successful "only when teachers had significant opportunities to learn how to improve mathematics teaching. When teachers had extended opportunities to study and learn the new mathematics curriculum that their students would use, they were more likely to report practices similar to the aims of the state policy. These opportunities, which often lasted for three days or more, were not typical of professional education in U.S. schools." Having the opportunity to examine student work with colleagues and discuss it in the context of what reforms were trying to achieve was crucial to making classroom improvements.[32]

That same lesson is true of reading. Both preservice and inservice training of teachers is essential to improving reading instruction. John Goodlad, a founder of the Center for Educational Renewal at the University of Washington, Seattle, has argued that the paltry preparation of most primary-grade teachers—the average teacher takes one university-level course in reading instruction—makes intervention to help poor readers almost impossible: "Diagnosis and remediation of the non-readers lie largely outside the repertoire of teachers whose brief pedagogical preparation provided little more than an overview."[33] Meanwhile, the NRC found that "[p]rofessional development of teachers, teachers aides, and professional or volunteer tutors [was] integral to each program—there is an important relationship between the skill of the teacher and the response of the children to early intervention. Effective intervention programs pay close attention to the preparation and supervision of the teachers or tutors."[34]

At the twentieth anniversary of *A Nation at Risk,* that is a recurring theme, not only in discussions about curriculum reform but also about reform in general. Improving the work of teachers must be central; that is, proposed solutions should be practice based and not simply responses to ideological braying in the public arena. Although it often takes partisan firebrands to get the attention of policymakers, the ideas and prescriptions of ideologues are usually too simplistic and unbending to be helpful in shaping effective reform practices. They make good conversation starters but poor plans for action. The curriculum battles of the post–*Nation at Risk* period have long since demonstrated their limits.

Only a sober assessment of what works on the classroom level— which requires a complex, intensive, and ongoing discussion of the work schools and teachers do, both generally and in very specific, on-the-scene ways—can bring about the kinds of improvements and reforms the writers of *A Nation at Risk* hoped to inspire with their rhetorical alarms. In its 1998 report calling for an end to the reading wars, the NRC committee noted, "The knowledge base is now large enough that the controversies that have dominated discussions of reading development and reading instruction have given way to a widely honored *pax lectura,* the conditions of which include a shared focus on the needs and rights of all children to learn to read."[35] One can only hope that such a peace will pervade future discussions about how best to educate children, giving sobriety and reason the upper hand over the ideological excesses that Jeanne Chall laid bare in 1999. To do so, we, like Chall, must be willing to go fearlessly wherever the evidence leads.

CHAPTER EIGHT

Missed Opportunities:
Why the Federal Response to
A Nation at Risk Was Inadequate

MARIS A. VINOVSKIS

Throughout American history, state and local political leaders as well as the public have periodically discovered crises in education that inspired immediate interventions. For example, in antebellum America, concerns that the poor condition of public schools would undermine democratic institutions inspired Horace Mann to spearhead the Massachusetts common school movement, while John Pierce led a comparable effort in Michigan.

More than a century later, the Soviet Union's success at putting the first space satellite into orbit in 1958 raised nationwide concerns about math, science, and foreign-language learning, though federal funds for curriculum improvements were targeted at higher education rather than public schools.

It was not until the 1960s, when Washington began to play a significant role in K–12 education policy under president Lyndon Johnson (a former schoolteacher), that concerns about the quality of U.S. education gained significant attention on a national level, culminating in the creation of a federal Department of Education (DOE) in 1979, during the administration of Jimmy Carter.

The DOE didn't appear to have much of a future following Ronald Reagan's landslide election as president in 1980. The Reagan White House highlighted the shortcomings in federal education programs and called for abolishing the DOE. It survived, though funds for federal compensatory education programs were slashed.

Meanwhile, the National Commission on Excellence in Education (NCEE) was created to reassess the state of U.S. schools. The commission's 1983 report, *A Nation at Risk*, helped to stimulate widespread educational reforms and offered a blueprint for immediate ways to reform American education.

However, that work was built in part on the false assumption that we already knew how best to improve our public schools. The NCEE did not call for additional education research or development, and the Reagan White House and Congress even reduced the small amount of funds allocated for these activities. In doing so, we sacrificed long-term gains in education research and programming for short-term solutions that would satisfy the demands of policymakers and the voting public for immediate action.

The process of identifying promising educational practices, rigorously testing their effectiveness in model programs, and then trying them out in different settings often can take fifteen to twenty years. Yet since *A Nation at Risk*, few in federal policymaking—and perhaps just as few in K–12 schools—have demonstrated the patience for rigorous and sustained efforts at finding solutions. As a result, federal education policy has evolved in fits and starts.

As we reconsider the contributions of *A Nation at Risk* after two decades, it is an appropriate time to assess the report's short-term contributions and speculate on what might have happened if the participants at the time had simultaneously invested in a more rigorous, large-scale education research and development program.

At the same time, it is worth glancing back at the 1970s and early 1980s, when federal education research and development, still in its infancy, was repeatedly undercut by a lack of funding and political commitment. Only by doing so can we understand why *A Nation at Risk* and subsequent major national reform initiatives were not as successful as they should have been.

AMERICAN EDUCATION IN THE LATE 1970s
AND EARLY 1980s

The decade of the 1970s presented serious challenges for educators and policymakers. Federal compensatory education programs such as Head Start and Title I of the Elementary and Secondary Education Act (ESEA), which aimed to redress social inequities, had not lived up to earlier expectations. A series of national and local evaluations raised questions about the success of these programs.[1] At the same time, much of the public's concern about education focused upon the renewed attempts to desegregate schools in the North through the judicial system.[2]

While public concerns about the efficacy of federal education initiatives grew, the Carter administration sought to reward the growing involvement of the National Education Association (NEA) in national politics by creating the U.S. Department of Education. The controversial decision to create a separate, cabinet-level office, which was opposed by the American Federation of Teachers (AFT) and others, survived a close vote in the House of Representatives and further angered conservatives who feared even more federal intrusion into state and local education affairs.[3]

Whether the nation really was at risk educationally was heatedly debated at the time. Student achievement and parental perceptions of the quality of education presented a mixed picture during the late 1970s and early 1980s. There were no major overall changes in the quality of student achievement. According to trend data from the National Assessment of Educational Progress (NAEP), the performance of K–12 students on science, math, and reading tests varied for different cohorts—it rose slightly for a few student age groups, stayed the same for many, and declined slightly for others.[4]

Yet while many parents continued to view their own child's school favorably, there were increasing public doubts about the quality of education outside of their own communities.[5] Worries about the inadequacy of American schools were fueled by fear that the United States was becoming less competitive economically than its global trading partners. The high inflation and slow economic growth of the 1970s led many economists, educators, and policymakers to blame the deterioration in U.S. economic productivity on the poor quality of our education system.[6]

These concerns were particularly evident in the South, which continued to trail the rest of the nation in economic and education development.[7] Southern governors in the early 1980s, such as Lamar Alexander (R-TN), Bill Clinton (D-AR), Bob Graham (D-FL), James Hunt (D-NC), and Richard Riley (D-SC), led the call for improving schools in order to bolster the economic well-being of their states.[8] They were joined by influential outside organizations such as the Committee for Economic Development, an independent research and educational organization of business executives and educators, which warned that the nation's economic competitiveness was being undermined by our weak school systems.[9]

Despite such concerns, education was not a particularly important issue in the 1980 presidential election. President Jimmy Carter praised the federal role in education and defended the newly created Department of Education. His opponent, former California Governor Ronald Reagan, opposed federal intrusion into state and local education and vowed to abolish the DOE. Yet the electorate was more concerned about the weak economy, the setbacks in foreign policy, and highly symbolic issues such as legalized abortion and crime.[10]

CREATING A NATION AT RISK

The Reagan administration focused on reducing the size of the federal government and cutting taxes.[11] While the Omnibus Budget Reconciliation Act of 1981 made substantial cuts in the federal education budget, the Department of Education survived due in large part to a coalition of moderate Republicans and Democrats in Congress.[12] Secretary of Education Terrel Bell, considered by many Reagan supporters as too moderate, proposed the creation of a presidential commission to study the problems facing education and suggest some solutions. Bell, who was sympathetic to federal education research based on his experiences as Nixon's commissioner of education in the early 1970s, hoped that such an independent panel would provide a more balanced and positive picture of American education than the increasingly hostile comments in the media.

When the White House rejected Bell's request, he created the 18-member National Commission on Excellence in Education as a cabinet-level initiative on August 26, 1981, under the leadership of David P. Gardner, president of the University of Utah.[13] The charge to the panel was to examine the quality of learning and teaching in American education with particular attention to teenagers and high schools. The commission was to define the problems facing schools as well as identify any barriers to attaining excellence in education. The NCEE panel was to report to the nation within eighteen months of its first meeting and make practical recommendations for improving American schooling.[14]

The NCEE panel worked diligently and produced a unanimous and influential report, *A Nation at Risk: The Imperative for Educational Reform*. In its open letter of transmittal to Secretary Bell and the public on April 26, 1983, the commission issued its now classic warning about the deplorable state of American education and its dire consequences for the economy:

> Our Nation is at risk. Our once unchallenged preeminence in commerce, industry, science, and technological innovation is being overtaken by competitors throughout the world. This report is concerned with only one of the many causes and dimensions of the problem, but it is one that undergirds American prosperity, security, and civility . . .
>
> If an unfriendly foreign power had attempted to impose on America the mediocre educational performance that exists today, we might well have viewed it as an act of war. As it stands, we have allowed this to happen to ourselves. We have even squandered the gains in student achievement made in the wake of the Sputnik challenge. Moreover, we have dismantled essential support systems that helped make those gains possible. We have, in effect, been committing an act of unthinking, unilateral educational disarmament.[15]

Overall, the report portrayed the quality of education as deteriorating and cited selected education statistics and other information about the poor performance of American students. The commission did acknowledge briefly that the average citizen today was better educated than their counterparts a generation earlier, but the panel quickly returned to its alarmist tone and message. Nevertheless, the panel felt that the declines in the quality of education could be reversed if there were dedicated leadership and sufficient public will to do so.[16]

One crucial, implicit assumption was that we already knew what had to be done to improve education. As they put it, "The essential raw materials needed to reform our educational system are waiting to be mobilized through effective leadership."[17] Among the "raw materials" that they counted on mobilizing were the commitment of the American people to improving education and the dedication of teachers. Moreover, the NCEE panel praised "our better understanding of learning and teaching and the implications of this knowledge for school practice, and the numerous examples of local success as a result of superior effort and effective dissemination."[18]

The commission issued a set of recommendations it felt could be implemented over the next few years. The panel believed that "there is little mystery about what we believe must be done."[19] They called for strengthening state and local high school graduation requirements, including establishing a minimum number of basic courses for all students as well as a slightly more ambitious curriculum for college-bound ones. In addition, they called for schools, colleges, and universities to "adopt more rigorous and measurable standards, and higher expectations, for academic performance and student conduct, and that four-year colleges and universities raise their requirements for admission."[20] The panel also advocated "more time be devoted to learning the New Basics" as well as improving the preparation and compensation of teachers.[21] Finally, the NCEE recommended that citizens hold educators and elected officials responsible for providing the necessary leadership and endorse the fiscal support needed to enact the proposed reforms.[22]

Some scholars criticized *A Nation at Risk* for creating a misleading sense of doom rather than providing a balanced assessment of American schooling in the early 1980s.[23] But the public and most policymakers heralded the report and embraced many of its recommendations. More than a half-million copies of *A Nation at Risk* were distributed, and the report received notice in more than seven hundred articles in forty-five newspapers within the first four months.[24]

Along with several other reports on education that appeared in the mid-1980s, *A Nation at Risk* helped to launch the first wave of education reform that called for expanding high school graduation requirements, establishing minimum competency tests, and providing merit pay for extraordinary teachers.[25]

FEDERAL EDUCATION RESEARCH AND DEVELOPMENT

But was the commission right that we knew what to do to fix U.S. schools? If so, were such "answers" supported by rigorous, large-scale research? The federal government has been involved in collecting, analyzing, and disseminating education statistics since 1867.[26] Yet it was not until the mid-1960s that an effort was made to design and test educational programs through the newly created research and development (R&D) centers and the regional educational laboratories.[27]

Moreover, larger federally funded demonstration programs such as Follow Through in the late 1960s and early 1970s pointed to the importance of more systematic development to improve American education.[28] The Nixon administration responded to calls for better education research by creating the National Institute of Education (NIE) in 1972. The following year, a conference sponsored by the Brookings Panel on Social Experimentation suggested a five-stage process of development, which, from the initial experiment to the dissemination of the field-test results, would require about 10–12 years to complete:

> The experiment would begin as a highly controlled investigation at a single site involving random assignment to control and treatment groups and careful observations of inputs and outcomes. If the intervention appeared to have appreciable positive effects under these conditions, a couple of years would then be devoted to developing it further, creating a training program for teachers and instruments for measuring the program's implementation and outcomes. The intervention would next be tried out under natural conditions in a small number of sites, close enough to the sponsor's home base to be supervised without great travel and communication costs, and curriculum, training procedures, and measuring instruments would be revised in light of this experience. Not until after all of this development, small-scale testing, and revision had been successfully completed would a large-scale field test be undertaken to find out how the intervention works under a variety of conditions and with a variety of populations. In the final stage, full results of the field testing and training would be disseminated to those who wanted to adopt the intervention in their own school.[29]

Yet any optimism for federal education research was undercut from the start. Congress so severely underfunded the NIE that it only began to function effectively in the mid-1970s.[30] The quality of the education research on some issues like reading did improve, but the work at many of the R&D centers and regional educational laboratories was too fragmented and small to provide the type of large-scale research and development that had been recommended by the Brookings panel.[31]

Federal education research and development suffered additional set-backs during the early 1980s. The Reagan administration was suspicious of NIE's staff and apparent liberal agenda, which the White House believed emphasized educational equity at the expense of excellence. The White House appointed Edward Curran to direct NIE, which had just been incorporated into the new Office of Educational Research and Improvement (OERI). Curran and his allies promptly fired much of NIE's staff and unsuccessfully tried to eliminate the agency altogether. NIE survived because Secretary Bell and the agency's friends on Capitol Hill managed to thwart the efforts to abolish it, but its funding was drastically cut. Even some long-time congressional supporters of education research such as Senator Robert Stafford (R-VT) were willing to accept the elimination of what they regarded as non-essential agencies such as NIE in order to preserve more monies for compensatory education services.[32] As a result, while overall Department of Education monies fell by 11 percent in real dollars between FY1981 and FY1988, NIE lost 70 percent of its funding during those years.[33]

Not only was funding for education research and development deeply cut, but the ability of NIE to allocate the remaining monies flexibly was severely curtailed by Congress. Using the political influence of their lobby group, the Council for Educational Redevelopment and Research (CEDaR), the R&D centers, and the regional educational laboratories persuaded a few members of Congress to earmark funds for them at the expense of other projects. There was a near halt in the early 1980s to NIE's funding of most activities besides the centers and labs.[34]

So while *A Nation at Risk* called for a mobilization of educational resources to improve schools and prepare the United States for global competition in the twenty-first century, it was clear that federal education research was not going to get the funding or direction it would need in order to play an effective part in this national effort. The policy of fits and starts would continue.

LIMITED IMPACT

As mentioned above, the public response to *A Nation at Risk* generally was very positive. Many of the report's specific recommendations for reforms such as additional required high school courses, minimum competency testing, and more time spent in school were widely praised and often implemented. As Arkansas Governor Bill Clinton put it in 1990: "When *A Nation at Risk* burst on the national scene like a firestorm in early 1983, feelings about public education and its problems that a large majority of Americans had held for some time began to surface."

All over the United States, and especially in the South, the poorest and least educated part of the country, people began to respond. Even before *A Nation at Risk*, Florida and Mississippi had enacted major reform programs supported by tax increases for schools.

Since then, there has been a substantial effort to upgrade education in almost every state: to increase the number of courses schools have to offer and the number students must take; to reduce class size in the early grades; to increase opportunities for gifted students; to provide more computers; to test students more; to evaluate teachers more effectively; and, in many states, to reward outstanding performance by schools, students, and teachers.[35]

Scholars and policymakers used the release of the report as a stimulus for debating American education policies and practices.[36] Yet there was almost no attention paid to the need for any additional education research or development. Instead, much of the focus was on assembling indicators of educational progress for the Department of Education's controversial but widely publicized "wall chart." The annual wall chart presented comparative state data using such crude measures of academic achievement as ACT and SAT scores (which measured only the achievement of college-bound high school students).[37]

Rather than investing more in systematic research and development, the Reagan administration chose to focus on augmenting diagnostic capabilities by improving the National Assessment of Educational Progress and revamping the National Center for Education Statistics (NCES) into a first-class statistical data organization. The expanded state-level NAEP scores provided more accurate and relevant indicators of K–12 student achievement than previously had been available. These indicators of relative state-level student achievement were a welcome improvement and helped to spur state and local school reforms.[38]

Despite the time and monies spent on implementing the recommendations from *A Nation at Risk*, as well as those from other similar Washington-based education organizations, there was little, if any, overall progress in student achievement.[39] Most analysts acknowledged the disappointing results. For example, Chester E. Finn, Jr., who directed OERI during Reagan's second term, noted in 1991:

> Reformers carrying the banner of the excellence movement have made valiant efforts during the past decade to upgrade educational performance. Nearly all of these have been well intentioned, hard fought, and compatible with the diagnoses rendered by innumerable studies, experts, panels, and task forces.
>
> The problem is that they do not seem to have done much good, at least when gauged in terms of student learning. The average pupil continues to emerge from the typical school in possession of mediocre skills and skimpy knowledge. Most of the trend lines are flat. The patient is in more-or-less stable condition but still gravely ill.[40]

Similarly, education journalist Thomas Toch concluded that "despite a plethora of significant reforms in public education, national and international assessments suggest that attainment of advanced academic skills continues to elude the vast majority of students. After nearly a decade of reform, educational excellence remains a scarce commodity in the public schools."[41]

What might have happened if the federal government had not settled for playing the diagnostic technician and instead had invested in more rigorous, large-scale research and development projects that eventually might have suggested better ways of improving student academic achievement? As it stands, while *A Nation at Risk* encouraged some useful and immediate education improvements, they were not sufficient by themselves to increase student performance, as had been expected.

THE NATIONAL EDUCATION GOALS, AMERICA 2000, AND GOALS 2000

As the impetus from *A Nation at Risk* was fading in the late 1980s, education reform received a boost from other initiatives such as the historic meeting of President George H. Bush and the nation's governors at Charlottesville, Virginia, in September 1989 and the subsequent drafting of the National Education Goals.[42] Also, growing GOP skepticism of existing federal education programs, such as Chapter 1 (later called Title I) of the Elementary and Secondary Education Act (ESEA) of 1965, led to the proposed package of reforms labeled as America 2000. While America 2000—which centered on six national education goals, school choice, voluntary national testing, and partnership with America 2000 communities—did not pass, it signaled the beginning of more comprehensive packages of federal education reforms and dissatisfaction with existing initiatives.[43]

Interestingly, the America 2000 package included a proposal for creating, testing, and disseminating "break the mold" models of schools through the New American Schools Development Corporation.[44] At the same time, however, while OERI made some modest advances in trying to improve education research and statistics, the Department of Education did not undertake any large-scale education development projects. Most of the R&D centers and the regional educational laboratories, for example, continued to produce numerous small, fragmented research projects rather than initiate more systemic, rigorous development programs.[45]

The election of Bill Clinton as president brought new changes to federal compensatory education policies. Rather than simply reauthorizing Chapter 1 and providing more funds for it, the Clinton administration unveiled its Goals 2000 proposal for systemic or standards-based reforms. Under the leadership of Secretary of Education Richard Riley and Undersecretary Marshall "Mike" Smith, Goals 2000 called for the drafting of ambitious state content standards, development of the related academic curriculum, and creation of rigorous student assessments. The alignment of these standards, curriculum, and evaluations at the state level provided the framework not only for Goals 2000, but also for the reauthorization of Title I in 1994. The emphasis now was on ensuring that all students reach the high standards rather than just focusing on at-risk children.[46]

The idea of systemic reform had been developed by policy researchers, such as Mike Smith and Jennifer O'Day, as part of the OERI-funded Consortium for Policy Research in Education (CPRE) in the late 1980s and early 1990s. It was a plausible but untested concept that grew out of the state-level standards movements of the 1980s, as well as some of the America 2000 proposals. While systemic reform was, in practice, often defined in a number of different ways during the 1990s, it stimulated widespread policy debates about state-level content standards, the curriculum, and student assessments.[47] Goals 2000 also triggered an intense, divisive debate in the U.S. House of Representatives in 1993 and 1994 about the need to institute "opportunity-to-learn" standards to ensure that adequate resources were available to all students.[48]

One might have expected that the Clinton administration, in particular, would have devoted more resources to large-scale research and development. Systemic reform was a relatively new approach that had been built on the little existing empirical research, and now it could be tested further as it was being implemented throughout the nation. The new administration had also recruited key personnel and advisers who were experienced researchers. Undersecretary Mike Smith, for example, was not only a distinguished researcher and former NIE employee, but also participated in the 1973 Brookings panel that called for more rigorous, large-scale development projects.

Surprisingly, the Clinton administration paid relatively little attention to either improving OERI or funding large-scale development projects. Most of OERI's assistant secretaries during those years were not prominent or experienced researchers themselves and they did not hire such individuals even when there were opportunities to do so. Rather than trying to build up the research agency, the Clinton administration actually reduced OERI's staff by more than 25 percent. The OERI structure was changed as the 1994 authorizing legislation created five Research Institutes, but the operation of the agency was not altered much in practice.

Thus, while the Clinton administration called for and implemented a bold new approach to improving American education, it repeated the approach taken by the Reagan administration by not backing up that effort with major large-scale research and development projects. Ten years after *A Nation at Risk*, federally sponsored education research was still spinning its wheels.

NO CHILD LEFT BEHIND

By the late 1990s, both political parties, for different reasons, were content to allow the Goals 2000 legislation to lapse. And neither the Democrats nor the Republicans highlighted the failure of the nation to reach any of the eight ambitious National Education Goals in the target year of 2000.

Democratic policymakers and many educators argued that systemic reform had not been fully implemented and that now it was just beginning to improve student outcomes; therefore, they urged that the Department of Education should "stay the course" and reauthorize Title I of ESEA with only some modest adjustments.[49]

On the other hand, House and Senate Republicans complained that K–12 student achievement scores continued to be stagnant in the 1990s and therefore the current reforms were not effective. Many conservatives reiterated their call for more flexibility in using federal monies at the state and local levels; some GOP members of Congress also called for a voucher program to enable parents more choice in whether to send their children to a public or private school.[50]

During the exceedingly close 2000 presidential election, education was one of the top domestic issues. The Republican candidate, George W. Bush, questioned the effectiveness of federal education programs and highlighted his successes in education reform as the governor of Texas. Vice president Al Gore, the Democratic nominee, defended the Clinton administration's policies and challenged Bush's claim of having improved Texas schooling. By putting forth his own No Child Left Behind initiative, Bush succeeded in blunting the traditional Democratic advantage on education among the voters.[51]

Once in office, the Bush administration made education reform one of its top legislative priorities, advocating yet another major initiative to address the ongoing crisis in American education. After a series of compromises by both sides, the No Child Left Behind Act was passed and signed into law on January 8, 2002. The legislation called for more federal funding for Title I, as well as for more strict state and local accountability for improving education—including penalties for failing schools and new options for students attending them. Particular attention was paid to improving early reading skills.[52]

"Scientifically based research" was mentioned more than one hundred times in the No Child Left Behind legislation.[53] This reflected the increasing calls in Congress during the late 1990s for more scientifically based education programs as well as more rigorous and objective program evaluations. Particularly persistent were demands for the use of more randomized trials in education research.[54] But there was considerable confusion about what constituted scientific work.[55] Frustrated by the continued poor quality of educational research and evaluation, GOP and Democratic members of the House Subcommittee on Early Childhood, Youth, and Families unanimously agreed to include a detailed but highly controversial set of characteristics in their 2000 OERI reauthorization bill.

No Child Left Behind proposed a substantial revamping of federal education research and program evaluations—restructuring OERI into a more independent agency within the Department of Education and placing more emphasis on rigorous research and evaluations. The House unanimously passed the Education Sciences Reform Act (H.R. 3801) on March 20, 2002, and the Senate was considering its own version of that legislation as this book went to press.[56]

The simultaneous emphasis today on yet another new federal compensatory education initiative, as well as enhanced and more scientifically oriented education research and evaluation, is certainly welcome. Yet it is not clear exactly how much emphasis will be placed on the kind of large-scale research and development education projects recommended by the Brookings panel three decades ago. Two decades after *A Nation at Risk*, the role of research and development in education reform remains ambiguous.

CONCLUSION

A Nation at Risk was a clarion call for immediate action to improve our deteriorating school systems. While the National Commission on Excellence in Education portrayed a rather one-sided, alarmist picture of the crisis in American education, it rightly drew attention to the need for education improvements. Since then, educators and policymakers continue to point to the persistent problems. As a result, rather than discovering a new "crisis" in education in the early 1980s, the NCEE panel actually identified more chronic problems in many state and local education systems that warranted additional interventions in order to meet the mounting economic and social challenges of the last quarter of the twentieth century.

The report of the NCEE panel, as well as those of numerous other education commissions in the 1980s, reflected the growing post–World

War II tendency not only to see education problems as national ones, but also to explore what role the federal government could play in making improvements. As dissatisfaction with American education in general, and the effectiveness of federal compensatory education programs in particular, rose after the early 1980s, both Democratic and Republican leaders sought to devise and promote comprehensive school reform efforts. And, as with *A Nation at Risk*, most federal initiatives rested on the assumption that we already knew enough to address the problems.

Yet the presumed scientifically based knowledge supporting the recommendations of *A Nation at Risk*, America 2000, Goals 2000, and No Child Left Behind generally was non-existent or weak—reflecting the relatively underdeveloped state of educational research and development.

Proponents of the reforms simply assumed that we already knew enough to resolve the immediate crisis, if only we had the political will to implement their recommendations and provide the necessary resources. Some of these reform proponents also had a low opinion of the quality of the existing research and development; therefore, they saw little value in funding more of the same. Finally, as the reformers usually saw themselves responding to an immediate crisis rather than addressing a more long-term, chronic weakness in American education, they were less interested in investing in large-scale research and development initiatives that would not provide useful guidance for another ten to fifteen years.

That's not to say that a better appreciation of the weak conceptual and scientific underpinning of the various proposed education reform initiatives should have deterred educators and policymakers from trying to institute needed reforms. But such an understanding might have encouraged them to make fewer grandiose claims about the likely effectiveness of their proposed interventions and to refrain from being too narrowly prescriptive in their advice in areas where we lacked adequate knowledge.

While policymakers and the public can and should set appropriate goals for education improvements, the relatively weak state of our education research and development suggests the need to allow for considerable flexibility and experimentation in the implementation of these reforms at the state and local levels—while holding the policymakers, schools, teachers, students, and parents accountable, in varying degrees, for reaching realistic but ambitious goals for student outcomes.

The 1973 Brookings panel provided a thoughtful approach for thinking about long-term, large-scale education research and development. The specific tasks are challenging and expensive to put into operation over a long period. But if the National Commission on Excellence in Education had included among its recommendations such a proposal, and the Reagan administration and the 98th Congress had supported them, perhaps today, as we attempt "to leave no child behind," we would have much better information about how to achieve this laudable goal.

CHAPTER NINE

The Emerging State Leadership Role in Education Reform: Notes of a Participant-Observer

ROBERT B. SCHWARTZ

In his strikingly candid memoir of his service as Ronald Reagan's first secretary of education, T. H. Bell describes the behind-the-scenes struggle within the administration to control the president's message at the White House event celebrating the release of *A Nation at Risk*. Despite the best efforts of Bell and Reagan's chief of staff, James Baker, to keep Reagan's speech focused on the themes of the report—higher standards, more rigorous high school graduation requirements, better teacher preparation and compensation, more instructional time, etc.— the president used the occasion to reiterate his favorite education themes: restore prayer in the schools, provide tuition tax credits for private and parochial school parents, expand school choice.[1]

Despite the president's attempt to change the subject by introducing topics not touched on in the report, the message of *A Nation at Risk* was sufficiently clear and compelling to carry on its own. The report struck a nerve, and within days of its release its apocalyptic language and vivid call to arms were repeated and endorsed in editorial pages and opinion columns in nearly every major newspaper and news magazine in the country.

Although the report called for action at every level of government and from every sector of society, it was clear from the president's remarks and from his education track record that an administration that had campaigned on a pledge to abolish the Department of Education was an unlikely candidate to provide national leadership in responding to the conditions so graphically outlined in the Commission's report.

It was in this environment that the states stepped forward to assert their leadership role in education reform, a role that has grown steadily stronger and more sophisticated over the ensuing twenty years. This is not to suggest that there weren't states with a strong tradition of state-level leadership on education issues pre-1983 (New York and California come immediately to mind) or that the blizzard of state-level reform initiatives launched in the 1980s were all undertaken in response to *A Nation at Risk*. But the major education reform movements of the 1960s and 1970s emanated from the courts (e.g., school desegregation, school finance equity) or from Washington (e.g., compensatory education, bilingual education), with the states as reactors rather than initiators. In the 1960s and 1970s the education agenda was heavily focused on equity, and the civil rights movement taught us that the educational needs of poor and minority children (and, later, limited-English-speaking children and children with special needs) could best be protected through federal programs rather than being left to each state. As the reform agenda moved to include an increasingly expansive view of equity in the present era, with that term now encompassing the "right" of all students to be taught a rich and rigorous curriculum well aligned with state standards and tests, the federal role, especially in the Clinton era, was redesigned to reinforce and support a reform agenda that was in large measure set by the states.

A key factor in this redefinition of the relationship between the federal and state roles in education over this period has been the emerging leadership role of governors. Indeed, prior to *A Nation at Risk,* discussion of the state role in education was usually focused primarily on the activities of state boards and departments of education. Of course governors and legislators were sometimes the central players in the creation of state reform initiatives, but education was rarely *the* issue on which a governor built a reputation. I'm not certain when the term *education governor* first came into use, but I can only think of one pre-1980s governor to whom the term might apply, Terry Sanford of North Carolina, cofounder with Harvard's James Conant of the Education Commission of the States (ECS).

In the 1980s a whole new generation of governors emerged, mostly in the South, for whom education reform was the key to economic growth and development. For governors like Lamar Alexander (TN), Bill Clinton (AK), Bob Graham (FL), Jim Hunt (NC), Dick Riley (SC), and Bill Winter (MS), the release of A Nation at Risk only reinforced their own understanding that the single most important thing states could do to secure their economic future was to improve the quality of their schools. By the end of the decade the number of state leaders who could legitimately lay claim to the title of "education governor" had swelled considerably, and such leaders could now be found in all regions, not just the South.

It is difficult to overstate the sheer volume of education reform activity unleashed in the states in the immediate aftermath of A Nation at Risk. In a document issued only fifteen months after the Commission's report, ECS reported that over 250 state task forces had been created to study virtually every aspect of education. In that short period forty-four states raised graduation requirements, forty-five strengthened teacher certification and evaluation requirements, and twenty-seven states adopted measures to increase instructional time.[2] The scorecard issued by the Department of Education a year later reported additional initiatives enacted or proposed by twenty or more states to create state-supported specialized schools, provide academic enrichment, tighten academic requirements for participation in athletics and other extracurricular activities, adopt performance-based teacher incentives, initiate state-sponsored professional development programs for teachers and administrators, etc., etc. If there had been a contest for the most active legislature, Arkansas would in all likelihood have won, having passed 122 separate education bills in a 12-month period![3] It was no wonder that by 1986 the reaction had begun to set in, and a more nuanced and sophisticated state reform strategy began to emerge.

In July 1986 my interest in the emerging state role in education reform, and especially the leadership role of governors, became more than academic, for that month I became education policy advisor to Massachusetts Governor Michael Dukakis. As it happens, one of my very first assignments was to accompany the governor to the annual summer meeting of the National Governors' Association (NGA) in Hilton Head,

South Carolina, where the entire three-day agenda revolved around the release of a major education report developed over the previous year by the governors, entitled *Time for Results*. The report was in reality a compilation of seven short reports, each the product of a task force of governors, focused on such topics as school readiness, leadership, teaching, technology, parental involvement, and choice. Although the task force reports themselves weren't especially memorable, NGA chair Lamar Alexander's summary captured substantial media attention, especially this formulation:

> To sum it up: the Governors are ready for some old-fashioned horse-trading. We'll regulate less, if schools and school districts will produce better results. The kind of horse trading we're talking about will change dramatically the way most American schools work. First, the governors want to help establish clear goals and better report cards, ways to measure what students know and can do. Then we're ready to give up a lot of state regulation or control—even to fight for changes in the law to make that happen—*if* schools and school districts will be accountable for the results. . . . These changes will require more rewards for success and consequences for failure for teachers, school leaders, schools, and school districts.[4]

Implicit in *Time for Results* is an acknowledgement that the legislative response most governors had fashioned to *A Nation at Risk* leaned too heavily on mandates and not enough on incentives. The governors Alexander had appointed to cochair the report—Clinton and Kean—were especially thoughtful and eloquent on the need for governors and other state policymakers to understand that, without a strategy to engage teachers and principals and to address their concerns, additional mandates and exhortations from on high were likely to be counterproductive. As Governor Kean stated in his summary of the teaching task force recommendations:

> There have been many successes, but we don't give enough attention to what motivates people to teach when we design recruitment programs. Teachers care about the intrinsic rewards of teaching and the professional environment of the school. If we want to attract more able teachers, and keep the ones we have, we have to respond to what they care about.[5]

As someone new to state government but with substantial prior experience working with elected officials in Boston and Washington, what impressed and astonished me at Hilton Head was the number of governors who could speak off-the-cuff with in-depth knowledge and passion about education policy issues. The format of the meeting was a series of roundtable discussions with invited guests like Albert Shanker of the American Federation of Teachers and U.S. Education Secretary William Bennett, and it quickly became apparent to this observer that governors like Riley, Alexander, Kean, and Clinton had developed a very sophisticated understanding of the challenge of bringing about large-scale improvements in the performance of their schools.

Shanker and Kean had both served on a task force established in 1985 by the Carnegie Forum on Education and the Economy to examine the conditions of teaching, and the report of that task force came in for considerable discussion at Hilton Head. *A Nation Prepared: Teachers for the 21st Century* was, as its title suggests, at least in part a response to *A Nation at Risk*. Its message was that without a highly qualified, highly motivated teaching force, the call for higher standards, tougher graduation requirements, and more instructional time would be unlikely to yield significant gains in student achievement. The Carnegie report argued both for restructuring the teaching profession and restructuring schools. Its thesis was that two significant reforms were essential if talented young people were to be recruited and retained in teaching. First, the profession had to become more stratified, with new leadership roles for the most accomplished teachers that would extend their influence in the school and justify a more sharply differentiated compensation system. The key recommendation to accomplish this goal was to create a National Board for Professional Teaching Standards that would assess and certify accomplished teachers, analogous to the role national certification boards play in medicine and other professions. Thanks to the Carnegie Corporation and other national foundations, a National Board was in fact created and remains the principal legacy of *A Nation Prepared*.[6]

The argument for creating a more stratified teaching force spoke to the perception that the relative flatness of the profession was a major disincentive for ambitious young people to choose teaching careers, and for the exodus of nearly a third of those entering the classroom within their first five years. But unless schools were restructured to give teachers substantially more autonomy and control over their working environment, the task force argued, creating a more differentiated set of roles for teachers would not solve the recruitment and retention problem.

These two reports—*Time for Results* and *A Nation Prepared*— touched off what was to become the second wave of reform. For those policymakers who understood the limitations of a strategy that in too many places could be summarized as "raise the bar and exhort them to jump higher," the Carnegie Task Force report came as a breath of fresh air. One morning in 1987, Nick Paleologos, newly elected House chair of the Massachusetts Legislative Committee on Education, heard that the Carnegie Task Force was meeting in a Boston suburb that same afternoon. He immediately drafted a resolution endorsing the report and offering Massachusetts as a test site for its recommendations, rushed it through the House, and drove out to the meeting to present it to the task force. A year later the Massachusetts legislature enacted a package of school reform measures, the most radical of which was a grants program to encourage schools to adopt bold restructuring plans, in response to which the state would agree to waive inhibiting laws and regulations. The schools selected were dubbed Carnegie Schools to acknowledge the intellectual origins of the program.

Massachusetts was hardly alone in the late 1980s in enacting a school reform agenda that put more emphasis on supporting bottom-up innovation than top-down mandates, and on building a stronger teaching corps. Several states, including Lamar Alexander's Tennessee, pressed ahead with the creation of career ladders for teachers, while others, like New Jersey under Tom Kean's leadership, focused on the creation of alternative certification pathways. But in the annual gatherings of governors' education policy aides during those years, and in the annual follow-up reports to *Time for Results* that we helped NGA staff prepare, there was an increasing recognition that to formulate the reform choices as mandates vs. incentives, or top down vs. bottom up, was to create a false dichotomy. The real question was how to strike the right balance between the two, and which policy levers were most effective at each level of the system. At the very same time that states were strengthening the capacity of districts and schools to innovate from the bottom, governors were also beginning to focus on the necessary prerequisites for holding schools accountable for results.

If the "horse trade" proposed in *Time for Results* were to be meaning-ful, there would have to be some agreed-upon way for governors to be able to measure progress. This implied not only agreement around indi-cators, but, more fundamentally, agreement on goals. As the NGA put it in *Time for Results, 1987*, its first-year follow-up report:

> Governors should lead the way in defining targets the nation as a whole should aim for. The data we have now on education results is not good enough. . . . What do we actually know about how well we are doing? Let's invite the American people to think with us about the results we *should* be getting.[7]

As Maris Vinovskis observes in his excellent monograph, *The Road to Charlottesville*, the idea of national education goals did not originate at the Charlottesville Summit in 1989. As far back as the Eisenhower era there had been calls for national education goals by various national bodies, but none of these proposals had gained political traction.[8] My introduction to the concept of national education goals came at a week-long meeting of the Aspen Institute's Education for a Changing Society program in July 1988. Chaired by the late Frank Keppel, former dean of the Harvard Graduate School of Education and ranking education offi-cial in the Kennedy and Johnson administrations, the meeting was de-signed to craft a proposed federal education agenda for the next admin-istration.

At the opening session of the Aspen meeting, Keppel went around the table, asking participants to name the single most important thing a next president could do to support educational improvement. One of the first people to speak was Bill Honig, chief of California schools, who had already launched what was arguably the nation's most sys-temic state reform agenda. Honig made a passionate plea for the impor-tance of a coherent national reform strategy anchored by national goals, arguing that in our highly mobile society and increasing global economy it made little sense not to have national goals and some way of measuring state progress against those goals. Honig pointed out that his colleagues in the Council of Chief State School Officers had, a few years earlier, approved the use of the National Assessment of Educational Progress (NAEP) for cross-state comparisons, and that Congress had re-cently authorized state-level participation in NAEP. His point was that the politics around the issue of the federal role were changing, and that state education leaders as well as governors were ready for a more national reform strategy.

As other state and local education leaders and analysts around the table supported Honig's position, I thought with some embarrassment of the rather timid education position paper I had helped draft for the Dukakis campaign, which had studiously steered clear of anything so bold as national goals and tests. As it turned out, the Bush campaign was equally cautious in its education proposals, with the consequence that education hardly surfaced as a significant issue in the fall campaign.

On our last day in Aspen, Keppel asked Richard Mills, Governor Kean's education advisor, and me to join him for breakfast. Keppel knew that Bush leaned on Kean for education advice, and confessed that his rationale for inviting Mills and me to the meeting was his belief that one of us was likely to be part of the next president's transition team. He urged us to see that the idea of national education goals didn't get lost.

As it happens, the idea didn't need our advocacy to move forward, for it had already surfaced in a much more important and influential venue, the Southern Regional Education Board (SREB). Once again it was the southern governors, this time under the chairmanship of Dick Riley, who led the way. In October 1988, SREB's Commission for Education Quality released a report entitled *Goals for Education: Challenge 2000*, which called on its member states "to meet or exceed national standards in education by the year 2000." The report then enumerated a dozen goals, among them some that would resurface a year later at Charlottesville (e.g., all children ready for the first grade, 90 percent high school graduation rate).[9]

The story of the Charlottesville Summit has been well told elsewhere and does not need repeating. Vinovskis is especially good on the back and forth between the Bush administration and the NGA during the planning process that led up to the event.[10] At the summit itself, the most dramatic moments took place in the final plenary session, which was closed to the press and therefore went unreported. The session took place in a cafeteria (we were on the campus of the University of Virginia), with the president and his advisors seated at a table in the front and the governors and staff in long rows of tables before him. The mood was upbeat; the final language of the summit statement had been negotiated in a late-night session by top White House and NGA staff; the press was waiting expectantly outside. Just as the president was launched into his final round of ceremonial comments and thank yous, Governor Clinton asked to be recognized. He and Governor Campbell of South Carolina (Riley's successor) had been the lead governors for the NGA on the planning process, and he had worked tirelessly to forge bipartisan consensus around the proposed national goals. The issue of resources had been kept almost entirely off the table in the discussions and summit policy statement, but Clinton wanted to make sure that the president understood that these ambitious goals could not be accomplished without a significant infusion of money. Interestingly, he did not use the occasion to plead for more federal funds, acknowledging that what happened in Washington was between the president and Congress. Rather, he was seeking President Bush's assurance that his "Read my lips, no new taxes" campaign pledge would not be used in *state* campaigns against governors who advocated increased taxes to fund education reform. His argument was that if the administration erected a political environment in which governors were not free to raise revenues to pay for these reforms, then the act of establishing these goals would turn out to be a hollow political exercise and a great opportunity to move our whole education system forward would have been lost. After Clinton spoke, a half dozen other governors, Republicans as well as Democrats, jumped up to support Clinton, arguing that they had put themselves on the line politically to raise state taxes to support education reform and they were prepared to do it again, but only if they could be assured that the president would stand behind them. Not wanting his boss to be cornered, John Sununu, Bush's chief of staff, immediately began gathering up the president's papers and stage whispering to him that the press was waiting and that they couldn't fall behind schedule. At that point Governor Kean stepped in and calmed the waters, calling on his colleagues not to allow a division over what was essentially a political issue to cloud what had been a genuinely historic set of policy agreements on the future direction of American education.

One of the most striking features of the policy statement adopted at Charlottesville is how little was expected of, or promised by, the federal government. The governors were seeking regulatory relief and a "we're in this together" declaration of partnership and support. The governors had learned over the previous nine years that conservative Republican administrations wanted to reduce or eliminate the federal role in education, not expand it, so there were no expectations of new federal funds to support the implementation of the national goals. So just as they had done after the release of *A Nation at Risk* six years earlier, the governors returned home from Charlottesville and began working with education leaders and others in their states to fashion state-specific strategies to fulfill the aspirations embodied in the proposed national goals.

Although the goals were not formally adopted by the governors until their winter meeting early in 1990, the political momentum from Charlottesville was sufficiently powerful to trigger a third wave of reform in the states, a wave that ultimately became a movement. The standards movement obviously had several different sources, and it would be a gross oversimplification to credit (or blame!) the adoption of a set of education goals by the nation's governors for the creation of what has now, with the most recent reauthorization of the Elementary and Secondary Education Act, become our de jure as well as de facto national education policy. Education researchers and analysts, especially those who had studied the organization and governance of education in high-performing European and Asian nations, were arguing for a more rigorous, coherent, focused national education strategy during this same late 1980s and early 1990s time period, among them Harold Stevenson, James Stigler, David Cohen, Marshall Smith, and Jennifer O'Day. Well before Charlottesville, the National Council of Teachers of Mathematics had launched an ambitious set of publications aimed at defining the kind of mathematical knowledge and skills that all American students should be expected to master at each level of schooling, and the kinds of support teachers would need to enable their students to do this. The American Association for the Advancement of Science had initiated a parallel effort focused on science. And, as mentioned earlier, Bill Honig in California was already well into the design of a comprehensive state strategy to create an aligned system of curriculum frameworks in the core academic subjects, matching assessments, and a statewide network of content-based professional development centers to help teachers acquire the knowledge and skills to teach to these frameworks.

The adoption of national goals, especially Goal 3, with its promise that by the year 2000 all students would be able to demonstrate proficiency in English, math, science, history, and geography, brought the question of a more national strategy around educational goals and measurement out from the relative shadows of professional societies and research journals fully into the public arena. How could students demonstrate proficiency in history, for example, unless there was agreement on what historical concepts and events students should know at each level of schooling, and on how to assess student mastery of the agreed-upon content? And how, in a nation in which education is by virtue of statutory authority, tradition, and funding principally a responsibility of state and local government, could we move toward the creation of national standards and tests?

Marian Robinson and I have elsewhere chronicled the attempts of the National Education Goals Panel (created to monitor progress toward the national goals), the National Council on Education Standards and Testing (created to advise the government on the wisdom and feasibility of national standards and tests), successive Congresses, and the Bush and Clinton administrations to work their way through these thorny issues of education policy and intergovernmental division of labor during the years 1990 to 1995.[11] For our purposes here, suffice it to say that because of the very substantial controversy that developed over federally funded projects to create proposed national standards in history and English, the responsibility for academic standard-setting remained with the states. In 1994 Congress authorized the creation of a federally appointed council to conduct voluntary reviews of state standards, but even that level of federal involvement proved politically untenable, and the National Education Standards and Improvement Council (NESIC) was repealed before its initial members were ever appointed.

The issue raised at the tail end of the Charlottesville Summit by then-Governor Clinton about the relationship between goals and resources and the need for political leaders to acknowledge that educational improvement costs money reappeared front and center in the early 1990s policy debates, this time in the form of and argument over opportunity-to-learn standards. Liberal Democrats argued that learning standards for students must be accompanied by standards to measure whether or not schools were providing equitable opportunities for all youngsters to meet those standards; conservative Republicans argued that schools would improve only when educators were held accountable for results, and that measuring inputs would simply trigger the same old excuses for failure.

While these policy debates were raging back and forth in Washington, states were moving ahead on their own to begin to put in place the building blocks for a more systemic, standards-based reform strategy. In

1994–1995, researchers at the Consortium for Policy Research in Education (CPRE) initiated a multiyear study of the progress of systemic, standards-based reform in nine states and twenty-five districts within those states. In a report published two years later, the researchers were struck by the degree to which these states had moved forward in a steady, incremental fashion to develop or revise academic standards, to begin to align their assessment systems with these standards, and to start to address the daunting challenge of strengthening the capacity of the teaching force to teach to the standards. While the political debate raged in Washington and advocates for charters, vouchers, and more market-based solutions became more vocal and visible, these states continued to refine and strengthen their systemic policies. Some of these states faced serious attacks from the Religious Right and consequently made significant modifications in their standards or assessment systems in response to their critics, but none was knocked off course. Rather, they responded by seeking a better balance between newer and older approaches, deleting objectionable non-academic learning goals, for example, or restoring multiple-choice items to their state tests to balance more performance-oriented tasks.[12]

Although the states in the CPRE study were for the most part acknowledged leaders in education reform during this period (e.g., California, Connecticut, Florida, Kentucky, South Carolina, Texas), they were by no means the only states moving down the standards-based reform track. Because this movement was playing out state by state, it was for the most part off the screen of national commentators. The national press corps, especially those whose interest was mostly in the politics of education, thought the status of standards-based reform could be tracked by following the congressional fate of Goals 2000. Thus, when control of Congress changed hands in 1995 and the assault on Goals 2000 from Speaker Gingrich and his allies heated up, casual observers were led to believe that the standards movement was about to become history.

It was in this context that a bipartisan group of governors led by Tommy Thompson of Wisconsin, the chair of the NGA, and a small group of corporate chief executive officers led by Lou Gerstner of IBM convened a second national education summit in March 1996. Several months earlier, Thompson had invited Gerstner to address the governors at their annual summer meeting. His subject ostensibly was technology, but he used the occasion to challenge the governors to become much more aggressive about the pace of education reform. He reminded them that we were already halfway through the decade during which we were supposed to, among other ambitious goals, become the first in the world in mathematics and science, and that on this and the other goals we seemed to be stuck in the water. His theme was that if business leaders had responded with as little urgency to the threat of international competition, the American economy would now be in very deep trouble. If we couldn't make significantly greater progress in improving our education performance relative to other nations in the next five years, he warned, it would have dire consequences for our long-term social and economic health. Thompson agreed that governors needed to pick up the pace of reform. In return, Gerstner offered to bring together other national business leaders to meet with governors to develop an action plan.

The 1996 summit was strikingly different on at least two counts from the 1989 event. First, it was held on corporate turf (IBM's Executive Conference Center at Palisades, New York), and the presence of the leaders of many of the nation's largest firms sent a very powerful signal to the governors that education reform was a major priority for corporate America. In the inevitable behind-the-scenes skirmishing over the wording of the summit policy statement—conservative governors, led by Allen of Virginia and Ridge of Pennsylvania, wanted to broaden the agenda to include school choice—the firmness of Gerstner and his colleagues strengthened Thompson's hand enormously.

A second difference, reflecting the ascendancy of the new Republican majority in Congress and its continuing attack on Goals 2000, was the near total absence of any reference to the importance of federal-state partnership in education. Standard-setting was a state-level responsibility; national standards were off the table.[13] After the controversies that had surrounded the Bush administration's efforts to support the development of national standards in history and English language arts, and the congressional repeal of NESIC, the summit planners decided to behave as if the ups and downs of federal policy on this issue were irrelevant to the responsibilities of governors. President Clinton was invited as a guest (he gave a luncheon talk), not as a co-convener, and his education secretary was one of forty "resource people" (essentially, glorified observers invited to provide the education community token representation in response to intensive lobbying from the various education associations).

A major goal of the 1996 summit was to convince an overwhelmingly Republican cohort of new governors that standards-based reform was nonpartisan, commanded strong support from business, was a crucial state-level responsibility, and therefore required their active attention and leadership. The summit policy statement committed the governors to "the development and establishment of internationally competitive education standards, assessments to measure academic achievement, and accountability systems in our states, according to each state's governing structure, within in the next two years." To support that effort, business leaders committed to launch a campaign to persuade employers to take high school transcripts more seriously in the hiring process for entry-level workers, and to consider the quality of a state's academic standards and its level of student achievement in plant location and expansion decisions. Together, governors and business leaders agreed to "designate an external, independent, non-governmental entity" to provide advice and assistance to states on the standards agenda.[14] To fulfill this commitment, the six governors and six corporate chief executives who planned the summit incorporated Achieve, with themselves as directors, and in early 1997 they hired me to be the organization's first president.

Although I had no prior history with Lou Gerstner or the other corporate leaders on the Achieve board, from 1990 to 1996 I had directed the education program at the Pew Charitable Trusts. In that role I had worked with several key governors and their staffs, most notably Jim Hunt and Roy Romer. Because I had come to the foundation fresh from the Charlottesville Summit, with a mandate from the Pew board to build a more national K–12 strategy, much of our grant-making focused on supporting organizations that were addressing key issues in standards-based reform. The National Center on Education and the Economy, co-developers of the New Standards project, was one such grantee; the National Board for Professional Teaching Standards was another. Both organizations benefited greatly from Governor Hunt's leadership role on their boards. A third example was the National Education Goals panel, cochaired by Governor Romer. Because the panel was a governmental entity, Pew did not fund it directly, but at Romer's request we commissioned a public opinion survey, released to coincide with the Goals panel's first annual report, highlighting the gap in perception about the academic preparation of high school graduates between employers and college officials on the one hand, and parents and students on the other.

Because so much of the focus of Pew's grant-making was on strengthening the network of national organizations that could collectively provide technical and political support for this state-based reform movement, I was invited to join some of the planning meetings for the 1996 summit and to attend as a resource person. I therefore came to Achieve with some understanding of the context in which the organization was created, and with a conviction, shared by the board, that national leadership and direction for this movement could best come from the bottom up (i.e., from the governors and other state leaders) rather than from the federal government.

My work at Achieve over these past five years has provided an extraordinary vantage point from which to observe the way standards-based reform is playing out in a substantial cross-section of states. My observations can be summarized into three broad generalizations. First, the standards-based reform mantra—rigorous standards, aligned assessments, accountability for results—is vastly oversimplified, and getting the right policies in place at the state level to support this reform strategy is much more difficult than it looks. Just take the first two pieces of the puzzle, for example: clear, rigorous, measurable academic standards, and rich assessments carefully aligned to measure progress against those standards. Achieve's core business is benchmarking state standards. At the request of state leaders we conduct a close analysis of their English and math standards, using panels of subject-matter experts to compare the standards against national and international exemplars, and then we conduct a close item-by-item alignment analysis of the state's tests against those standards, looking for such things as the content match, the performance level expected from students, the range of difficulty of the items, and the degree to which the test as a whole measures the full depth and breadth of the standards. A dozen states have now asked us to conduct benchmarking studies for them, and so far we have found only one state—Massachusetts—that in our judgment has clear, rigorous standards and high-quality tests that are well aligned with those standards.[15]

My point here is not to tout Achieve's work or the rigor of our own standards, but to underline the enormous challenge states face in simply getting the right foundation stones in place to support the rest of the reform agenda. In some states the standards are so broad and general that virtually any test could be said to be aligned with their standards, an argument that commercial test companies are only too happy to make as they sell states off-the-shelf tests. In other states the standards may be appropriately specific and measurable, but the tests are designed only to measure the low end of the standards, with too many fact and recall items and too few questions that require students to analyze or explain. The good news here is that states are asking independent outside organizations like Achieve to give them a candid critique of their standards and tests, and in the best cases—most notably Indiana and Ohio—have acted on the results of these studies to strengthen the foundation of their reform programs.

A second generalization I can make from our work is that, despite the enormous challenges in creating a state policy framework to support standards-based reform, several states are well along in meeting these challenges and are beginning to see slow but steady gains in student performance as a result. An important corollary here is that, although one can point to some common elements in the strategies of high-reform states, there is no single prescription for success. States are highly diverse in their political cultures, reform history, governance structures, financing systems, and demographics, and policies that work well in one setting may not fly at all elsewhere.

This point was brought home most forcefully to me in the summer of 2001, when in the space of several weeks I chaired policy review teams for Achieve in three states, Maryland, Massachusetts, and Texas. Achieve policy reviews, like our benchmarking studies, take place at the request of states, but they are less technical and much broader in their focus. States ask us to look not only at their standards and tests, but also at their policies and strategies for strengthening the organizational capacity of districts and schools and the professional capacity of teachers and principals to implement standards-based reform. States also invite us to review their accountability policies and systems and their strategies for engaging the public and sustaining support for their reforms. Our methodology for conducting these reviews is to assemble a four- to six-person review team with appropriate expertise; work with the state education agency to assemble a voluminous briefing book with all relevant legislation, policy, and research documents; spend two or three days on the ground interviewing a broad cross-section of policymakers, practitioners, and stakeholders; and then issue a short report outlining our findings and recommendations.[16]

The most important commonality across these three very different states was that each had started down the standards path at least eight years earlier, and had managed to stay on course despite changes in political or educational leadership. The Texas story is the best known, with a sustained reform trajectory that dates back to the work of the Perot Commission in the mid-1980s. The governorship has passed back and forth between the parties over that time, from White (D) to Clements (R) to Richards (D) to Bush (R) and Perry (R), and there have been several education commissioners during this period, but there has been remarkable consistency at the policy level. Most observers credit the Texas business community for creating a political environment in which elected leaders from both parties have had a stake in ensuring the stability and continuity of the reform agenda. This is not to say that there haven't been mid-course corrections, but the spirit has been one of continuous refinement and improvement, not fits and starts and sudden changes in direction.

In Maryland the standards-based reform movement can also be traced back to the recommendations of a commission chaired by a prominent business leader, Walter Sondheim, whose 1989 report created the framework for Maryland's next decade of reform. Unlike Texas, however, Maryland has enjoyed extraordinary stability of educational leadership, with its state superintendent, Nancy Grasmick, now in her eleventh year in office. One of Maryland's unusual governance features is that its school districts are organized by county, which means that Grasmick can and does meet monthly with all twenty-four district superintendents around a conference table. The Texas commissioner, by contrast, would need a good-sized auditorium to meet with his 1,000-plus district leaders, and in any event the sheer size of Texas does not encourage such meetings. This combination of continuity of educational leadership and a manageable number of local districts has enabled Maryland to create much more of a working partnership between state and local educators than any other state we have visited. This is especially true in Baltimore, where, under a unique court-approved agreement, the local school board is a joint city-state creation.

Despite their huge differences in size and political culture, the reform strategies of Maryland and Texas have more in common with each other than either has with Massachusetts. The Massachusetts reform program springs from a single piece of comprehensive reform legislation, the Massachusetts Education Reform Act of 1993, that in one stroke changed the entire state policy landscape in education: funding, local governance, teacher certification, tenure, a dozen other issues. At its heart was a proposed bargain between the state's political leaders, backed by business, and its education leaders, a bargain reminiscent of Lamar Alexander's mid-1980s horse trade: more money (roughly $7 billion over seven years) in return for more accountability. Accountability was to revolve around school and student performance on the Massachusetts Comprehensive Assessment System (MCAS), an ambitious new set of state tests designed to measure performance against an ambitious set of state standards. Unlike Texas, which deliberately designed a relatively low-level test and set the initial proficiency bar quite low, Massachusetts followed what some have called the "big-bang" theory, creating a test that represents a substantial stretch for many schools, especially those serving substantial concentrations of low-income and minority children.

These different choices about the initial degree of rigor of state tests and where to set the bar for proficiency are mirrored in the different approaches to accountability taken by these states. For Texas the principal unit of accountability is the school. Schools are placed in four different categories based principally on the proportion of their students who meet the state's academic proficiency targets, and the power of the public searchlight is strong enough in Texas to motivate schools to work hard to become "recognized" or "exemplary" (the top two categories). The particular genius of the Texas accountability system lies in the requirement for schools to report data disaggregated by race and income, and to demonstrate that all groups are meeting the state's targets. Schoolwide averages can no longer mask significant inequities in performance among groups.

The weight of the Massachusetts accountability system, by contrast, has to this point fallen disproportionately on students. Although Texas high school students have for several years been required to pass the tenth-grade Texas Assessment of Academic Skills, or TAAS, tests as a condition of graduation, pass rates have been sufficiently high so that this requirement has not been a significant political issue, and this policy has already been challenged and upheld in the courts. Although no one in Massachusetts has yet been denied a diploma because of the testing requirement, at this writing 19 percent of the class of 2003 (the first class for whom the requirement applies) is at risk of not graduating, and those students are disproportionately concentrated in Boston and other urban centers. Because the Commonwealth has been slow to put in place any school- or district-level accountability policies, the public perception in Massachusetts is that the only at-risk parties here are students.

Maryland's approach to assessment and accountability is somewhere between the other two states. Like Texas, Maryland's focus has been on the school, and to date its assessment system has yielded only school-level scores, not individual student scores. This has been a matter of some controversy, but its assessment program (MSPAP) was entirely performance based (meaning no multiple-choice items) and designed as much to guide instructional improvement as to furnish information useful for accountability purposes. Maryland is the only state we visited where teachers and principals cited the state's assessment program as a powerful positive influence on teaching. Unfortunately, because of a combination of declining political support at home and the new federal requirement for annual tests in grades three to eight that can provide individual scores, Maryland will be replacing the MSPAP in 2002–2003. Maryland is also in the process of implementing a set of end-of-course tests, passage of several of which will be required for high school graduation beginning in 2007.

Although this comparative analysis of the reform strategies of these states has focused principally on their assessment and accountability systems, all these states have in recent years paid significant attention to the capacity-building agenda as well, although none would say that it has yet done enough. Texas has been especially aggressive in mounting statewide professional development programs on early literacy and mathematics designed to reach thousands of teachers. All three states have beefed up the academic content requirements of the teacher certification programs and developed or expanded alternative routes to certification. All three states have websites designed to help educators learn from the practices of higher performing schools and districts. In Texas and Massachusetts, these programs, run by independent nonprofit organizations, have attracted sufficient national attention to warrant expansion to other states. Despite the different reform pathways these states have chosen, choices that reflect significant differences in the prior conditions of their education systems as well as the other differences referred to earlier, all three states have made substantial progress in raising student performance. In each case, gains on their own state tests have been corroborated by gains on other measures independent of the state reforms, principally the National Assessment of Educational Progress (NAEP). Had we been invited to look at other high-reform states (e.g., Connecticut, Kentucky, North Carolina), we would probably be reporting a similar picture: different reform pathways, consistency and continuity of effort, promising initial results. There are, of course, many other states that no one would characterize as "high reform," and the jury is still out on whether "high reform" becomes the norm or the exception.

This leads me to my final generalization, which is that, despite the understandable backlash that has arisen in some communities because of perceived overemphasis on testing and underinvestment in instructional improvement, there continues to be strong public and political support for the core propositions of this movement. When the Public Agenda asks parents and other key stakeholders whether they want to continue with standards-based reform or the path they are on, make midcourse corrections, or go back to a prestandards world, only 2 percent say "turn back."[17] For all of the enormous implementation challenges states, districts, and schools face as they move forward with this ambitious agenda, it is simply not an option to return to an era in which we had no clear academic learning goals for students, no statewide way of measuring student and school progress against these goals, and in which it was perfectly acceptable to hold very different expectations for schools serving low-income and minority kids than for those serving middle-class kids.

As we head into the first year of implementation of the most prescriptive piece of federal education legislation since the Elementary and Secondary Education Act (ESEA) was originally enacted in 1965, many states will face a new set of major challenges, especially states whose reform strategies differ most from the Texas model that underpins the 2001 No Child Left Behind Act (NCLB). Unlike Goals 2000 and the 1994 reauthorization of ESEA, which by design respected the diversity of state reform strategies, NCLB imposes a uniform testing regimen in all states. It is more than a little ironic that a movement that has been state led and state driven, in large part because of the desire of conservative Republican presidents and congressional leaders over the past two decades to reduce or eliminate the federal role in education, should now run the risk of being smothered in the warm embrace of a conservative Republican administration. Whether NCLB's one-size-fits-all assessment and accountability requirements will strengthen or sink this movement is an open question. Will the next generation of governors, state education chiefs, and business leaders have the knowledge, commitment, and political skills to keep their state reform programs on course, even if that course conflicts with the requirements of NCLB? Stay tuned.

I would like to thank two long-time colleagues, Michael Cohen and Marshall Smith, for their helpful comments on an earlier draft of this paper. They participated in some of these same events, but their perspective as senior education officials in the Clinton administration naturally leads them to place more emphasis on the federal leadership role than I have done.

CHAPTER TEN

The American Way of School Reform

NATHAN GLAZER

The "American way of school reform" is shaped by the structure of American public education. That structure differs from the way other nations go about organizing their public education and leads to a unique pattern in undertaking reform, one we have experienced in full force since the 1983 report decrying the condition of American public education, though it was not unfamiliar before. Let me describe a few features of that pattern.

First, we find a great dependence on and faith in research to guide us to the best ways to improve our schools. Research on school improvement is indeed extensive, more extensive and possibly more influential than anywhere else in the world. That research supports various paths to reform, and so we find a diversity of possible paths.

Second, we find a deep reluctance to mandate those approaches that from time to time come to be thought of as the best ways to improve schools. They are always plural—no "one best way" has emerged in recent decades to achieve universal acceptance, whether at the national level or the state level. An energetic superintendent may mandate a best way for a school system, but it is doubtful that it gets implemented in every school. An energetic principal may mandate a best way for his school, but it is doubtful it gets implemented in every class.

Third, we see great dependence on extra-governmental institutions, individuals, and funds to implement the best ways. Without foundations, businesses, parents, and reform leaders willing to pitch in to shore up or improve what is ostensibly a public function, American education might remain as placid, immoveable, and resistant to reform and change as education systems in most other countries.

Fourth, perhaps a necessary consequence of the above, even changes that are widely accepted, admired, hoped for, filter at varying rates through the school system or school systems, never becoming universal, and even at their most successful remaining limited in their penetration.

Fifth, school leaders, particularly of large-city school systems, have short spans of leadership, generally interspersed with stays in the varying institutions we have available as less stressful time-out spots for those wounded in public service—colleges and universities, foundations, consultantships. This phenomenon of short spells of leadership only became evident in the 1960s or 1970s: school leaders could have very long terms before that, when we enjoyed a long period of stability and wide approval of American education.

Sixth, as a consequence of all the above, the half-life of even the reforms that arouse the most admiration and are best supported by research are relatively short: enthusiasm flags, leaders change, new research leads to new enthusiasms, new ideas come up, new parties may enter the fray with new interests.

And, finally, as a result of all this, education regularly falls back into a "default" condition, not very different from what existed before the wave of reform had introduced its partial changes.

One could spell out other characteristics, but the above is sufficient to give a general picture that will not be unfamiliar to all those engaged in school reform. What is remarkable is the enthusiasm and vigor with which points of view on reform will be maintained over many years in view of the common experience, outlined above, as to what is likely to happen. One can explain this commitment in the face of always very partial and limited success as owing to the importance of education in the minds of parents and employers and politicians: they know that having greater literacy, numeracy, learnability is better for their children, employees, citizens. Dealing with an enterprise of this significance, one cannot simply sit aside and analyze it objectively: professors in schools of education can do so, but those involved in a more hands-on manner have to keep going. They are sustained by deeply rooted interests, not likely to change, in having better-educated children, employees, citizens—interests indeed we all share and cannot put aside.

Underlying all the above is the distinctive organization of American public education, which does not change much, and which all realize it would be hopelessly quixotic to try to order or systematize in the pattern of the French or Japanese (though our view of these as nationally ordered and systematized may be somewhat idealized—at least the French system responds to some degree to the growing diversity of its students and the strength of separatist feeling in some regions). American public education is based on the building block of the thousands of school systems, and the fifty states, alongside which are hundreds of independent teacher-training institutions, textbook and test-materials and other educational-product producers, associations of teachers and administrators and educational specialists, influential foundations, public oversight and reform groups, and on and on. The diversity is astonishing when viewed in an international context—the differences in salaries teachers receive from district to district, or the amount of money available to educate children from district to district, would be inconceivable in Japan, France, Germany (despite its formally federal organization), and we know that will not change much—scores of lawsuits have not basically affected the pattern of support of schools on the basis of local taxation of variable local taxable property.

This variousness means that we have a system that fosters and responds to diversity, but these same characteristics mean that it is also resistant to centralization, and that very different levels of resources from district to district are available to implement change. The resistance to centralization is sustained by powerful ideologies, of the Right and Left, that decry centralization, and powerful interests, in the form of parents who understandably seek the best (and best-funded) local school system for their child. If there were a "one best system," who would have the power to implement it? (The phrase is David Tyack's, and it refers to the centralized and bureaucratized big-city school systems that emerged around the beginning of the last century, and which are the "default" condition for big-city schools, a system unchallenged until the 1950s or 1960s.)

Even the formally all-powerful states, which could if they wished (according to their constitutions and the national constitution) probably create a Japanese-style centralized system, do not dare to go that far. Local resistance would be too great. Increasingly, the states do adopt state standards, but these tend to be vague and are fought vigorously if they become specific and directive. (This is the situation in Massachusetts today.) They are in any case, whether vague or specific, subject to great individual variation by schools and teachers. There are after all no state school inspectors to check. These newly mandated tests are required for high school graduation or some other important "high-stakes" use, but they get rapidly modified when it is discovered, as could have been known before, that certain groups of students will be penalized as a result of failure. The federal government's increasing involvement in education stops short of anything like meaningful national curricula or meaningful national tests—these are left to the states or to nongovernmental organizations. We can celebrate this diversity, or mourn it, but it is not likely to change.

This diversity always introduces anomalies in any effort at major reform. So the new federal legislation that requires that students be given the opportunity to leave failing schools can do little to change the fact that the definition of "failing" will vary greatly from state to state, so that the "failing" schools of New York may be better than the "succeeding" schools of Arkansas.[1]

These generalizations come from some personal experience in efforts at school reform, as well as from the wide range of literature examining school reform. As indicated in point one above, the United States leads the world in education research, and much of this research is a rich examination of efforts of reform and why they fail. We also have a somewhat lesser body of research in reforms that succeed—there are fewer clearly successful efforts, and the accounts of success are more likely to be journalistic than scholarly. But the kind of research that explains failure is extensive and indeed may be considered a specialty of American educational research.

Many of the characteristics of American school reform are displayed in the experience of the New American Schools Development Corporation (NASDC), which sought to find, fund, and expand school models that would "break the mold." That term, widely used in the last ten or fifteen years, is itself of interest, expressing the sense among school reformers and those professionally involved in the schools that there is something wrong with the existing mold, that it is indeed rigid and needs to be broken, rather than modified, embellished, or treated in a variety of other less extreme ways.

The experience of NASDC exemplifies the experience of many other reform efforts of the last forty-five years. It resembles a series of raids into a large, soft, and permeable but not easily transformed mass. It is a story that has been repeated many times during the present age of school reform, which we can date back to the shock of Sputnik in 1957 and the impact of racial desegregation and the civil rights movement of the 1960s. The great effort to change the teaching of science and math after Sputnik shows the same model: government and nongovernmental funds, designated not for total transformation but for penetration, supported reforms that it was hoped would produce so much better results that they would be adopted voluntarily. When it came to math and science, the chief areas of interest after Sputnik, it is my impression and there is some data that shows considerable success in changing curricula. Whether the overall effect has been to increase numeracy and scientific knowledge is more doubtful. The attempts to spread the consensus of the leaders of the disciplines in social science to the lower schools in the form of new curricula were less successful and aroused controversy even forty years ago. NASDC, in its larger efforts to "break the mold" of public education, was more ambitious, and its experience better represents the power of resistance to presumably superior models.

The experience of NASDC has been admirably summarized in an article by Jeffrey Mirel that bears the title "Unrequited Promise," not unfamiliar in its thrust from other studies of failed school reform enterprises.[2] NASDC was one of the many efforts launched in the wake of the 1983 report. It was established by CEOs from major corporations in 1991, responding to President George H. W. Bush's education summit, one of the rare occasions on which an American president met with all the governors of the states. Mirel tells us: "NASDC's founders envisioned a complete overhaul of American education stimulated by the spread of innovative designs . . ." NASDC and the federal government would fund these innovative designs: "Initially, the plan for NASDC was to complement the creation of 535 federally funded 'break the mold' schools by 1996. Each of the 435 congressional districts would be home to one of these schools; two more schools per state would be funded as well. Each school would receive a one-time Federal grant of $1 million in start-up funds. The privately funded NASDC would support R&D teams tasked with designing innovative reform models to be implemented in these schools."

This overall design was responsive to American political realities (the political imperative that every congressional district should have a chance at getting greater federal funds) but it was never implemented. NASDC instead asked educators to provide models that could be implemented in some schools, as the basis for a wider effort to "break the mold," and funds were made available to the educational researchers and reformers that responded to this call. Eleven winning designs were funded, and they variously had access to other funds from foundations for evaluative research on their effectiveness and the like.

The range of winning designs did cover a gamut of educational philosophies, though the progressive tradition was dominant. The choice of designs was responsive to the political reality that a range of different approaches to school reform have wide support. Despite early enthusiasm, those more familiar with the history of educational reform were skeptical and ready to place the enterprise in the all-too-familiar framework of early enthusiasm and relatively early demise that I have outlined above. And so, David Tyack and Larry Cuban, quoted by Mirel, asserted that such efforts "often resembled shooting stars that spurted across the pedagogical heavens, leaving a meteoric trail in the media but burning up and disappearing in the everyday atmosphere of the schools."

One of the winning designs, ATLAS, was a product of four major organizations working in the field of educational reform, three of which are identified with charismatic educational leaders. The four organizations are the Educational Development Center, which had pioneered the new curricula in science and mathematics that were developed and spread widely in schools during the late 1950s and 1960s; James Comer's School Development Program at Yale, which is oriented to the inner-city school and its problems; Theodore Sizer's Coalition of Effective Schools, which is oriented more toward high schools; and Howard Gardner and David Perkins' Project Zero at Harvard, whose origin is in arts education. All had extensive experience working in schools, with administrators, teachers, curriculum specialists. ATLAS may have been unique among the funded models in the amount of research it commissioned to describe its processes and to evaluate its effectiveness, particularly in the form of ethnographic accounts of its work. It may have been unique too in sponsoring an associated seminar involving participants from all four participating organizations, from the schools in which these organizations were working, as well as some outside participants. I was one of them. Despite my involvement, I can scarcely speak as an expert on how ATLAS worked, and I wonder if anyone has the comprehensive knowledge of its various interventions that a well-based overall judgment would require. When one reads the excellent ethnographic accounts of ATLAS' work in the schools and realizes how partial and limited they are—for example, a study of how a single teacher, over a period of time, tried to respond to new curricular approaches—one despairs at being able to give a coherent and balanced account of even such a limited enterprise in school life.

So ATLAS has been well studied, but possibly not studied enough, if one wants to make a reliable and comprehensive assessment. Only one of its research products, *School Reform Behind the Scenes*, numbers six authors who were involved in ATLAS (Joseph P. McDonald, Thomas Hatch, Edward Carbo, Nancy Ames, Norris M. Haines, and Edward T. Joyner) and four afterwords by the principles of the four organizations that joined to make ATLAS.[3] We learn a great deal about ATLAS from this effort, but we scarcely learn enough. This book concentrates on the variations in philosophy and approach of the four partner organizations. These would all be considered, from a distance, to have a similar approach to education, and indeed did consider themselves to have similar approaches—otherwise why would they have joined together in making their proposal to NASDC? But they discovered while trying to work together how different even similar organizations can be in their approach to education. Much of the work of ATLAS and of the associated seminar seems to have consisted of efforts to define the various educational philosophies and how they did or did not come together.

But while they debated these issues, the actual reform program, funded by "soft money" (though ATLAS in some form exists years after the initial funding was to run out), had to be launched in the cooperating schools and could not wait for the harmonization of the various approaches that were trying to work together. The overall ATLAS philosophy or approach had to be "implemented," even though much was unsettled. As McDonald et al. write, "Much energy went into the production and distribution of newsletters, articles, teleconferences, support materials, and training institutes. Soon, however, the organization faced up to the predictable dilemma of implementation. Putting good ideas into practice is much harder than putting them into currency." That is well put, so well put that one is tempted to ask, if it is so hard to put good ideas into currency, should we ask how good the ideas were to begin with?

In the absence of an authoritative command structure, linking ideas and philosophies to schools, which ATLAS (or NASDC) of course did not have, reform meant selling ideas and practices to administrators, principals, teachers. That was the point—or one point—of the newsletters, teleconferences, institutes, etc. ATLAS was to operate not at random in appreciative and accepting schools—which is the way the four organizations had worked before their coming together in ATLAS, and the way other educational reform efforts operate—but by creating "pathways" linking elementary and secondary schools within a single school system. There was much to commend this model. One of the great problems in all education is articulation, some mechanism so that what is learned in one grade or school connects with what is learned in the next. Many schools never solve this problem. The "pathways" approach would ensure that ATLAS' innovations would not fade out as students moved from one school to an unconnected one (though of course the mobility of American students means that, regardless of the commitment of a school district to maintaining the pathway, many students will move away from the pathway or the district).

The autonomy of school districts meant that ATLAS had to sell itself to a superintendent of schools to permit it to operate, but then the selling had to continue, as one reads the reports, to principals and even individual teachers. ATLAS wanted to ensure before it entered a school that it had a mass of support among the teachers—it would not enter on the basis of higher authority alone. Here it resembles many efforts at action in various fields in the modern democratic world, in which increasingly one must operate by persuasion rather than authority, whether one is putting up a new building or introducing a new curriculum. Of course schools are to some extent authoritative structures, and new procedures and curricula can be introduced by fiat, but it is generally agreed that unless teachers are also persuaded, things will not work out well. One way ATLAS operated was in effect to run school fairs in which the products and approaches of the allied organizations were available and on view and teachers could opt for them.

The original NASDC conception called for "whole school reform." That was certainly the ambition of ATLAS too—the aim was transformation, not simply the insertion of a new curricular idea or program here, a teacher improvement seminar there, and the like. But whole school reform, despite the attractiveness of the idea and the slogan, came up against the reality of the democratic principle of willing participation, which even when it was extensive was far from complete among teachers and principals. It also came up against the reality that—to quote from a RAND survey of principals in schools with a NASDC presence which Mirel cites—"standardized multiple-choice tests are misaligned with the classroom practices of reforming schools." This was a particular problem for ATLAS, with its orientation toward project-based curricula, to learner-centered education, to the role of teacher as coach or guide. Almost all the NASDC school models followed this dominant progressive paradigm. The ATLAS schools had to face the reality of the parents' (and also principals' and teachers') concern: How will my child or student subject to these reforming efforts do in standardized tests, those required for promotion, or graduation, or admissions to colleges?

ATLAS may have solved—or attempted to solve—through its "pathways" approach the problem of alignment between schools, itself a noteworthy effort and achievement, but how could it solve the problem of alignment with the larger school system and, indeed, with the larger society and economy? That would require reform on a scale far beyond the reach of ATLAS or NASDC. Mirel reports from another study of a NASDC model (not ATLAS) that "parents were bothered by the lack of course grades and college prep courses. They saw Odyssey [the model in question] as an attempt to shift the curriculum to a more vocation-oriented track that would ensure a 'compliant, trained workforce' for local industry." Project-based education will of course try to be responsive to and will build on local characteristics—social, economic, geographic. The parents may have been responsive to the reality that college education was a necessary base for economic advancement, and were willing to eschew a better project-based education for college-entry opportunity.

For the models to influence and transform a school, a pathway, a district, a degree of continuity in personnel was required that it was difficult to achieve. Oddly enough, the attractiveness of the reform effort itself could undermine that necessary continuity. A teacher or principal who was particularly responsive to the ATLAS efforts, very likely a superior principal or teacher, might be taken up by the ATLAS enterprise, employed by ATLAS in one capacity or another, and would leave the post by which continuity of application of the ATLAS innovation was best ensured. But independent of the opportunities reform enterprises themselves made available to upwardly mobile teachers and principals, there was the constant change, at the superintendent level, that characterizes our school systems, so that the support at the top that was necessary in maintaining the ATLAS presence might simply disappear. One of the districts in which NASDC operated most extensively was Memphis. In the late 1990s, Mirel reports, the superintendent mandated "that *all* of Memphis's more than 160 schools adopt a reform model, a policy that angered and alienated many teachers." A number of NASDC models were made use of, one of which was ATLAS. But then in 2000 a new superintendent came in, and as a result "the district's six-year experiment in whole-school reform" was abandoned.

"Whole school reform" in the end escaped the reach of ATLAS and other NASDC models. The NASDC effort became another example of the American model of school reform, which so often consists of raids and experiments and examples in various schools with uneven penetration and short lives. A recent report on Chicago's reform effort characterizes the situation well: principals and teachers "find themselves faced with a large and fragmented array of school improvement grants, programs, and partnerships that rarely afford them the time or support to adopt and master practices that may improve student learning."[4] "Whole school reform" may have been its intention; in implementation it was rather more partial and limited.

One conclusion that followed from the ATLAS experience was, paradoxically, that "whole school reform" might require the creation of new schools rather than the effort to reshape existing schools. Reforms in existing schools, with their set practices and distinctive school cultures, become in practice too partial and short-lived. Matters are different if one creates new schools, and examples of effective change and reform lasting over a long period of time are more evident in new than existing schools.

The Waldorf school, the Montessori school, the Catholic parochial school, the Christian school, the Edison school, and many other examples better realize a sustained reform program. Home schooling is also an example of successful "whole school reform." These are all examples of whole school reform that have shown some staying power and considerable success in maintaining their original thrust and intention. Part of their staying power is based on an ability to satisfy parents. Part is owing to their ability to attract teachers committed to the intentions, objectives, practices of the schools. In view of the difficulty of comparisons, one must hesitate to say that they necessarily achieve better academic results than public schools.

The American public school has evolved into a distinctive pattern that is not easy to change. Public law, strong teacher organizations, parent interests, and diversity shape it in a way that satisfies enough constituencies so that it is not easily reshaped to better suit the ideals of school reformers, even though one or another reform might well be able to show general superiority. Outside interventions, even when they dispose of apparently great sums of money—think of Walter Annenberg's munificent gifts to reform efforts, sums that will now be surpassed by those of the Gates Foundation—pale beside the huge sums that maintain the existing school systems. What is a one-time injection of $50 million or $100 million in reform efforts in a school budget (as in New York City) that annually expends $10 billion?

That is one reason reform efforts affect only some schools for a limited period of time. But another is that on the whole Americans are satisfied with their schools, whatever case can be made that they could be so much better. Those dissatisfied do have the opportunity to either move to the district with the schools that better match their desires, or to attend private schools, or to create new schools, and all these forms of exit are practiced on a large scale.

The one great dissatisfied element that has the least opportunity to move to the districts whose schools would satisfy them, to attend well-funded private schools, or to create new schools are inner-city and urban blacks—which is one reason why choice programs and voucher programs are popular among them. This large dissatisfied constituency is also on the whole more satisfied with conservative schools (stronger discipline, traditional modes of learning) than the progressive efforts that attract reformers. The recent U.S. Supreme Court decision upholding the constitutionality of including religious schools (that is, primarily Catholic schools) among the schools that parents who are granted public vouchers may select will go far toward satisfying this group.

Meanwhile, the field for educational innovation remains wide, and foundation funds will, we can be sure, be available to implement interesting new approaches to some degree. While no reform effort can deceive itself into thinking it has a good chance to transform American education in view of the characteristics of our school system, any one might well make substantial inroads into affecting the practices of a good number of schools and districts, and exhibiting what it can achieve to the others.

Editor's note: This abridged version of A Nation at Risk *excludes only certain appendices containing procedural information about the making of the report and a few lines from the introduction describing those appendices. The main body of the report is otherwise fully intact.*

A Nation at Risk: The Imperative for Educational Reform

THE NATIONAL COMMISSION ON EXCELLENCE IN EDUCATION
APRIL 26, 1983

INTRODUCTION

Secretary of Education T. H. Bell created the National Commission on Excellence in Education on August 26, 1981, directing it to examine the quality of education in the United States and to make a report to the Nation and to him within 18 months of its first meeting. In accordance with the Secretary's instructions, this report contains practical recommendations for educational improvement and fulfills the Commission's responsibilities under the terms of its charter.

The Commission was created as a result of the Secretary's concern about "the widespread public perception that something is seriously remiss in our educational system." Soliciting the "support of all who care about our future," the Secretary noted that he was establishing the Commission based on his "responsibility to provide leadership, constructive criticism, and effective assistance to schools and universities."

The Commission's charter contained several specific charges to which we have given particular attention. These included:

- assessing the quality of teaching and learning in our Nation's public and private schools, colleges, and universities;

- comparing American schools and colleges with those of other advanced nations;
- studying the relationship between college admissions requirements and student achievement in high school;
- identifying educational programs which result in notable student success in college;
- assessing the degree to which major social and educational changes in the last quarter century have affected student achievement; and
- defining problems which must be faced and overcome if we are successfully to pursue the course of excellence in education.

The Commission's charter directed it to pay particular attention to teenage youth, and we have done so largely by focusing on high schools. Selective attention was given to the formative years spent in elementary schools, to higher education, and to vocational and technical programs. We refer those interested in the need for similar reform in higher education to the recent report of the American Council on Education, *To Strengthen the Quality of Higher Education.*

In going about its work the Commission has relied in the main upon five sources of information:

- papers commissioned from experts on a variety of educational issues;
- administrators, teachers, students, representatives of professional and public groups, parents, business leaders, public officials, and scholars who testified at eight meetings of the full Commission, six public hearings, two panel discussions, a symposium, and a series of meetings organized by the Department of Education's Regional Offices;
- existing analyses of problems in education;
- letters from concerned citizens, teachers, and administrators who volunteered extensive comments on problems and possibilities in American education; and
- descriptions of notable programs and promising approaches in education.

To these public-minded citizens who took the trouble to share their concerns with us—frequently at their own expense in time, money, and effort—we extend our thanks. In all cases, we have benefited from their advice and taken their views into account; how we have treated their suggestions is, of course, our responsibility alone. In addition, we are grateful to the individuals in schools, universities, foundations, business, government, and communities throughout the United States who provided the facilities and staff so necessary to the success of our many public functions.

The Commission was impressed during the course of its activities by the diversity of opinion it received regarding the condition of American education and by conflicting views about what should be done. In many ways, the membership of the Commission itself reflected that diversity and difference of opinion during the course of its work. This report, nevertheless, gives evidence that men and women of good will can agree on common goals and on ways to pursue them. . . .

A Nation at Risk

Our Nation is at risk. Our once unchallenged preeminence in commerce, industry, science, and technological innovation is being overtaken by competitors throughout the world. This report is concerned with only one of the many causes and dimensions of the problem, but it is the one that undergirds American prosperity, security, and civility. We report to the American people that while we can take justifiable pride in what our schools and colleges have historically accomplished and contributed to the United States and the well-being of its people, the educational foundations of our society are presently being eroded by a rising tide of mediocrity that threatens our very future as a Nation and a people. What was unimaginable a generation ago has begun to occur—others are matching and surpassing our educational attainments.

If an unfriendly foreign power had attempted to impose on America the mediocre educational performance that exists today, we might well have viewed it as an act of war. As it stands, we have allowed this to happen to ourselves. We have even squandered the gains in student achievement made in the wake of the Sputnik challenge. Moreover, we have dismantled essential support systems which helped make those gains possible. We have, in effect, been committing an act of unthinking, unilateral educational disarmament.

Our society and its educational institutions seem to have lost sight of the basic purposes of schooling, and of the high expectations and disciplined effort needed to attain them. This report, the result of 18 months of study, seeks to generate reform of our educational system in fundamental ways and to renew the Nation's commitment to schools and colleges of high quality throughout the length and breadth of our land.

That we have compromised this commitment is, upon reflection, hardly surprising, given the multitude of often conflicting demands we have placed on our Nation's schools and colleges. They are routinely called on to provide solutions to personal, social, and political problems that the home and other institutions either will not or cannot resolve. We must understand that these demands on our schools and colleges often exact an educational cost as well as a financial one.

On the occasion of the Commission's first meeting, President Reagan noted the central importance of education in American life when he said: "Certainly there are few areas of American life as important to our society, to our people, and to our families as our schools and colleges." This report, therefore, is as much an open letter to the American people as it is a report to the Secretary of Education. We are confident that the American people, properly informed, will do what is right for their children and for the generations to come.

The Risk

History is not kind to idlers. The time is long past when America's destiny was assured simply by an abundance of natural resources and inexhaustible human enthusiasm, and by our relative isolation from the malignant problems of older civilizations. The world is indeed one global village. We live among determined, well-educated, and strongly motivated competitors. We compete with them for international standing and markets, not only with products but also with the ideas of our laboratories and neighborhood workshops. America's position in the world may once have been reasonably secure with only a few exceptionally well-trained men and women. It is no longer.

The risk is not only that the Japanese make automobiles more efficiently than Americans and have government subsidies for development and export. It is not just that the South Koreans recently built the world's most efficient steel mill, or that American machine tools, once the pride of the world, are being displaced by German products. It is also that these developments signify a redistribution of trained capability throughout the globe. Knowledge, learning, information, and skilled intelligence are the new raw materials of international commerce and are today spreading throughout the world as vigorously as miracle drugs, synthetic fertilizers, and blue jeans did earlier. If only to keep and improve on the slim competitive edge we still retain in world markets, we must dedicate ourselves to the reform of our educational system for the benefit of all—old and young alike, affluent and poor, majority and minority. Learning is the indispensable investment required for success in the "information age" we are entering.

Our concern, however, goes well beyond matters such as industry and commerce. It also includes the intellectual, moral, and spiritual strengths of our people which knit together the very fabric of our society. The people of the United States need to know that individuals in our society who do not possess the levels of skill, literacy, and training essential to this new era will be effectively disenfranchised, not simply from the material rewards that accompany competent performance, but also from the chance to participate fully in our national life. A high level of shared education is essential to a free, democratic society and to the fostering of a common culture, especially in a country that prides itself on pluralism and individual freedom.

For our country to function, citizens must be able to reach some common understandings on complex issues, often on short notice and on the basis of conflicting or incomplete evidence. Education helps form these common understandings, a point Thomas Jefferson made long ago in his justly famous dictum:

> I know no safe depository of the ultimate powers of the society but the people themselves; and if we think them not enlightened enough to exercise their control with a wholesome discretion, the remedy is not to take it from them but to inform their discretion.

Part of what is at risk is the promise first made on this continent: All, regardless of race or class or economic status, are entitled to a fair chance and to the tools for developing their individual powers of mind and spirit to the utmost. This promise means that all children by virtue of their own efforts, competently guided, can hope to attain the mature and informed judgment needed to secure gainful employment, and to manage their own lives, thereby serving not only their own interests but also the progress of society itself.

Indicators of the Risk

The educational dimensions of the risk before us have been amply documented in testimony received by the Commission. For example:

- International comparisons of student achievement, completed a decade ago, reveal that on 19 academic tests American students were never first or second and, in comparison with other industrialized nations, were last seven times.
- Some 23 million American adults are functionally illiterate by the simplest tests of everyday reading, writing, and comprehension.
- About 13 percent of all 17-year-olds in the United States can be considered functionally illiterate. Functional illiteracy among minority youth may run as high as 40 percent.
- Average achievement of high school students on most standardized tests is now lower than 26 years ago when Sputnik was launched.
- Over half the population of gifted students do not match their tested ability with comparable achievement in school.
- The College Board's Scholastic Aptitude Tests (SAT) demonstrate a virtually unbroken decline from 1963 to 1980. Average verbal scores fell over 50 points and average mathematics scores dropped nearly 40 points. College Board achievement tests also reveal consistent declines in recent years in such subjects as physics and English.
- Both the number and proportion of students demonstrating superior achievement on the SATs (i.e., those with scores of 650 or higher) have also dramatically declined.
- Many 17-year-olds do not possess the "higher order" intellectual skills we should expect of them. Nearly 40 percent cannot draw inferences from written material; only one-fifth can write a persuasive essay; and only one-third can solve a mathematics problem requiring several steps.
- There was a steady decline in science achievement scores of U.S. 17-year-olds as measured by national assessments of science in 1969, 1973, and 1977.

- Between 1975 and 1980, remedial mathematics courses in public 4-year colleges increased by 72 percent and now constitute one-quarter of all mathematics courses taught in those institutions.
- Average tested achievement of students graduating from college is also lower.
- Business and military leaders complain that they are required to spend millions of dollars on costly remedial education and training programs in such basic skills as reading, writing, spelling, and computation. The Department of the Navy, for example, reported to the Commission that one-quarter of its recent recruits cannot read at the ninth grade level, the minimum needed simply to understand written safety instructions. Without remedial work they cannot even begin, much less complete, the sophisticated training essential in much of the modern military.

These deficiencies come at a time when the demand for highly skilled workers in new fields is accelerating rapidly. For example:

- Computers and computer-controlled equipment are penetrating every aspect of our lives—homes, factories, and offices.
- One estimate indicates that by the turn of the century millions of jobs will involve laser technology and robotics.
- Technology is radically transforming a host of other occupations. They include health care, medical science, energy production, food processing, construction, and the building, repair, and maintenance of sophisticated scientific, educational, military, and industrial equipment.

Analysts examining these indicators of student performance and the demands for new skills have made some chilling observations. Educational researcher Paul Hurd concluded at the end of a thorough national survey of student achievement that within the context of the modern scientific revolution, "We are raising a new generation of Americans that is scientifically and technologically illiterate." In a similar vein, John Slaughter, a former Director of the National Science Foundation, warned of "a growing chasm between a small scientific and technological elite and a citizenry ill-informed, indeed uninformed, on issues with a science component."

But the problem does not stop there, nor do all observers see it the same way. Some worry that schools may emphasize such rudiments as reading and computation at the expense of other essential skills such as comprehension, analysis, solving problems, and drawing conclusions. Still others are concerned that an over-emphasis on technical and occupational skills will leave little time for studying the arts and humanities that so enrich daily life, help maintain civility, and develop a sense of community. Knowledge of the humanities, they maintain, must be harnessed to science and technology if the latter are to remain creative and humane, just as the humanities need to be informed by science and technology if they are to remain relevant to the human condition. Another analyst, Paul Copperman, has drawn a sobering conclusion. Until now, he has noted:

> Each generation of Americans has outstripped its parents in education, in literacy, and in economic attainment. For the first time in the history of our country, the educational skills of one generation will not surpass, will not equal, will not even approach, those of their parents.

It is important, of course, to recognize that *the average citizen* today is better educated and more knowledgeable than the average citizen of a generation ago—more literate, and exposed to more mathematics, literature, and science. The positive impact of this fact on the well-being of our country and the lives of our people cannot be overstated. Nevertheless, *the average graduate* of our schools and colleges today is not as well-educated as the average graduate of 25 or 35 years ago, when a much smaller proportion of our population completed high school and college. The negative impact of this fact likewise cannot be overstated.

Hope and Frustration

Statistics and their interpretation by experts show only the surface dimension of the difficulties we face. Beneath them lies a tension between hope and frustration that characterizes current attitudes about education at every level.

We have heard the voices of high school and college students, school board members, and teachers; of leaders of industry, minority groups, and higher education; of parents and State officials. We could hear the hope evident in their commitment to quality education and in their descriptions of outstanding programs and schools. We could also hear the intensity of their frustration, a growing impatience with shoddiness in many walks of American life, and the complaint that this shoddiness is too often reflected in our schools and colleges. Their frustration threatens to overwhelm their hope.

What lies behind this emerging national sense of frustration can be described as both a dimming of personal expectations and the fear of losing a shared vision for America.

On the personal level the student, the parent, and the caring teacher all perceive that a basic promise is not being kept. More and more young people emerge from high school ready neither for college nor for work. This predicament becomes more acute as the knowledge base continues its rapid expansion, the number of traditional jobs shrinks, and new jobs demand greater sophistication and preparation.

On a broader scale, we sense that this undertone of frustration has significant political implications, for it cuts across ages, generations, races, and political and economic groups. We have come to understand that the public will demand that educational and political leaders act forcefully and effectively on these issues. Indeed, such demands have already appeared and could well become a unifying national preoccupation. This unity, however, can be achieved only if we avoid the unproductive tendency of some to search for scapegoats among the victims, such as the beleaguered teachers.

On the positive side is the significant movement by political and educational leaders to search for solutions—so far centering largely on the nearly desperate need for increased support for the teaching of mathematics and science. This movement is but a start on what we believe is a larger and more educationally encompassing need to improve teaching and learning in fields such as English, history, geography, economics, and foreign languages. We believe this movement must be broadened and directed toward reform and excellence throughout education.

Excellence in Education

We define "excellence" to mean several related things. At the level of the *individual learner,* it means performing on the boundary of individual ability in ways that test and push back personal limits, in school and in the workplace. Excellence characterizes a *school or college* that sets high expectations and goals for all learners, then tries in every way possible to help students reach them. Excellence characterizes a *society* that has adopted these policies, for it will then be prepared through the education and skill of its people to respond to the challenges of a rapidly changing world. Our Nation's people and its schools and colleges must be committed to achieving excellence in all these senses.

We do not believe that a public commitment to excellence and educational reform must be made at the expense of a strong public commitment to the equitable treatment of our diverse population. The twin goals of equity and high-quality schooling have profound and practical meaning for our economy and society, and we cannot permit one to yield to the other either in principle or in practice. To do so would deny young people their chance to learn and live according to their aspirations and abilities. It also would lead to a generalized accommodation to mediocrity in our society on the one hand or the creation of an undemocratic elitism on the other.

Our goal must be to develop the talents of all to their fullest. Attaining that goal requires that we expect and assist all students to work to the limits of their capabilities. We should expect schools to have genuinely high standards rather than minimum ones, and parents to support and encourage their children to make the most of their talents and abilities.

The search for solutions to our educational problems must also include a commitment to life-long learning. The task of rebuilding our system of learning is enormous and must be properly understood and taken seriously: Although a million and a half new workers enter the economy each year from our schools and colleges, the adults working today will still make up about 75 percent of the workforce in the year 2000. These workers, and new entrants into the workforce, will need further education and retraining if they—and we as a Nation—are to thrive and prosper.

The Learning Society

In a world of ever-accelerating competition and change in the conditions of the workplace, of ever-greater danger, and of ever-larger opportunities for those prepared to meet them, educational reform should focus on the goal of creating a Learning Society. At the heart of such a society is the commitment to a set of values and to a system of education that affords all members the opportunity to stretch their minds to full capacity, from early childhood through adulthood, learning more as the world itself changes. Such a society has as a basic foundation the idea that education is important not only because of what it contributes to one's career goals but also because of the value it adds to the general quality of one's life. Also at the heart of the Learning Society are educational opportunities extending far beyond the traditional institutions of learning, our schools and colleges. They extend into homes and workplaces; into libraries, art galleries, museums, and science centers; indeed, into every place where the individual can develop and mature in work and life. In our view, formal schooling in youth is the essential foundation for learning throughout one's life. But without life-long learning, one's skills will become rapidly dated.

In contrast to the ideal of the Learning Society, however, we find that for too many people education means doing the minimum work necessary for the moment, then coasting through life on what may have been learned in its first quarter. But this should not surprise us because we tend to express our educational standards and expectations largely in terms of "minimum requirements." And where there should be a coherent continuum of learning, we have none, but instead an often incoherent, outdated patchwork quilt. Many individual, sometimes heroic, examples of schools and colleges of great merit do exist. Our findings and testimony confirm the vitality of a number of notable schools and programs, but their very distinction stands out against a vast mass shaped by tensions and pressures that inhibit systematic academic and vocational achievement for the majority of students. In some metropolitan areas basic literacy has become the goal rather than the starting point. In some colleges maintaining enrollments is of greater day-to-day concern than maintaining rigorous academic standards. And the ideal of academic excellence as the primary goal of schooling seems to be fading across the board in American education.

Thus, we issue this call to all who care about America and its future: to parents and students; to teachers, administrators, and school board members; to colleges and industry; to union members and military leaders; to governors and State legislators; to the President; to members of Congress and other public officials; to members of learned and scientific societies; to the print and electronic media; to concerned citizens everywhere. America is at risk.

We are confident that America can address this risk. If the tasks we set forth are initiated now and our recommendations are fully realized over the next several years, we can expect reform of our Nation's schools, colleges, and universities. This would also reverse the current declining trend—a trend that stems more from weakness of purpose, confusion of vision, underuse of talent, and lack of leadership, than from conditions beyond our control.

The Tools at Hand

It is our conviction that the essential raw materials needed to reform our educational system are waiting to be mobilized through effective leadership:

- the natural abilities of the young that cry out to be developed and the undiminished concern of parents for the well-being of their children;
- the commitment of the Nation to high retention rates in schools and colleges and to full access to education for all;
- the persistent and authentic American dream that superior performance can raise one's state in life and shape one's own future;
- the dedication, against all odds, that keeps teachers serving in schools and colleges, even as the rewards diminish;
- our better understanding of learning and teaching and the implications of this knowledge for school practice, and the numerous examples of local success as a result of superior effort and effective dissemination;
- the ingenuity of our policymakers, scientists, State and local educators, and scholars in formulating solutions once problems are better understood;
- the traditional belief that paying for education is an investment in ever-renewable human resources that are more durable and flexible than capital plant and equipment, and the availability in this country of sufficient financial means to invest in education;
- the equally sound tradition, from the Northwest Ordinance of 1787 until today, that the Federal Government should supplement State, local, and other resources to foster key national educational goals; and
- the voluntary efforts of individuals, businesses, and parent and civic groups to cooperate in strengthening educational programs.

These raw materials, combined with the unparalleled array of educational organizations in America, offer us the possibility to create a Learning Society, in which public, private, and parochial schools; colleges and universities; vocational and technical schools and institutes; libraries; science centers, museums, and other cultural institutions; and corporate training and retraining programs offer opportunities and choices for all to learn throughout life.

The Public's Commitment

Of all the tools at hand, the public's support for education is the most powerful. In a message to a National Academy of Sciences meeting in May 1982, President Reagan commented on this fact when he said:

> This public awareness—and I hope public action—is long overdue. . . .
> This country was built on American respect for education. . . . Our
> challenge now is to create a resurgence of that thirst for education that
> typifies our Nation's history.

The most recent (1982) Gallup Poll of the *Public's Attitudes Toward the Public Schools* strongly supported a theme heard during our hearings: People are steadfast in their belief that education is the major foundation for the future strength of this country. They even considered education more important than developing the best industrial system or the strongest military force, perhaps because they understood education as the cornerstone of both. They also held that education is "extremely important" to one's future success, and that public education should be the top priority for additional Federal funds. Education occupied first place among 12 funding categories considered in the survey—above health care, welfare, and military defense, with 55 percent selecting public education as one of their first three choices. Very clearly, the public understands the primary importance of education as the foundation for a satisfying life, an enlightened and civil society, a strong economy, and a secure Nation.

At the same time, the public has no patience with undemanding and superfluous high school offerings. In another survey, more than 75 percent of all those questioned believed every student planning to go to college should take 4 years of mathematics, English, history/U.S. government, and science, with more than 50 percent adding 2 years each of a foreign language and economics or business. The public even supports requiring much of this curriculum for students who do not plan to go to college. These standards far exceed the strictest high school graduation requirements of any State today, and they also exceed the admission standards of all but a handful of our most selective colleges and universities.

Another dimension of the public's support offers the prospect of constructive reform. The best term to characterize it may simply be the honorable word "patriotism." Citizens know intuitively what some of the best economists have shown in their research, that education is one of the chief engines of a society's material well-being. They know, too, that education is the common bond of a pluralistic society and helps tie us to other cultures around the globe. Citizens also know in their bones that the safety of the United States depends principally on the wit, skill, and spirit of a self-confident people, today and tomorrow. It is, therefore, essential—especially in a period of long-term decline in educational achievement—for government at all levels to affirm its responsibility for nurturing the Nation's intellectual capital.

And perhaps most important, citizens know and believe that the meaning of America to the rest of the world must be something better than it seems to many today. Americans like to think of this Nation as the preeminent country for generating the great ideas and material benefits for all mankind. The citizen is dismayed at a steady 15-year decline in industrial productivity, as one great American industry after another falls to world competition. The citizen wants the country to act on the belief, expressed in our hearings and by the large majority in the Gallup Poll, that education should be at the top of the Nation's agenda.

FINDINGS

We conclude that declines in educational performance are in large part the result of disturbing inadequacies in the way the educational process itself is often conducted. The findings that follow, culled from a much more extensive list, reflect four important aspects of the educational process: content, expectations, time, and teaching.

Findings Regarding Content

By content we mean the very "stuff" of education, the curriculum. Because of our concern about the curriculum, the Commission examined patterns of courses high school students took in 1964–69 compared with course patterns in 1976–81. On the basis of these analyses we conclude:

- Secondary school curricula have been homogenized, diluted, and diffused to the point that they no longer have a central purpose. In effect, we have a cafeteria style curriculum in which the appetizers and desserts can easily be mistaken for the main courses. Students have migrated from vocational and college preparatory programs to "general track" courses in large numbers. The proportion of students taking a general program of study has increased from 12 percent in 1964 to 42 percent in 1979.
- This curricular smorgasbord, combined with extensive student choice, explains a great deal about where we find ourselves today. We offer intermediate algebra, but only 31 percent of our recent high school graduates complete it; we offer French I, but only 13 percent complete it; and we offer geography, but only 16 percent complete it. Calculus is available in schools enrolling about 60 percent of all students, but only 6 percent of all students complete it.
- Twenty-five percent of the credits earned by general track high school students are in physical and health education, work experience outside the school, remedial English and mathematics, and personal service and development courses, such as training for adulthood and marriage.

Findings Regarding Expectations

We define expectations in terms of the level of knowledge, abilities, and skills school and college graduates should possess. They also refer to the time, hard work, behavior, self-discipline, and motivation that are essential for high student achievement. Such expectations are expressed to students in several different ways:

- by grades, which reflect the degree to which students demonstrate their mastery of subject matter;
- through high school and college graduation requirements, which tell students which subjects are most important;
- by the presence or absence of rigorous examinations requiring students to demonstrate their mastery of content and skill before receiving a diploma or a degree;

- by college admissions requirements, which reinforce high school standards; and
- by the difficulty of the subject matter students confront in their texts and assigned readings.

Our analyses in each of these areas indicate notable deficiencies:

- The amount of homework for high school seniors has decreased (two-thirds report less than 1 hour a night) and grades have risen as average student achievement has been declining.
- In many other industrialized nations, courses in mathematics (other than arithmetic or general mathematics), biology, chemistry, physics, and geography start in grade 6 and are required of *all* students. The time spent on these subjects, based on class hours, is about three times that spent by even the most science-oriented U.S. students, i.e., those who select 4 years of science and mathematics in secondary school.
- A 1980 State-by-State survey of high school diploma requirements reveals that only eight States require high schools to offer foreign language instruction, but none requires students to take the courses. Thirty-five States require only 1 year of mathematics, and 36 require only 1 year of science for a diploma.
- In 13 States, 50 percent or more of the units required for high school graduation may be electives chosen by the student. Given this freedom to choose the substance of half or more of their education, many students opt for less demanding personal service courses, such as bachelor living.
- "Minimum competency" examinations (now required in 37 States) fall short of what is needed, as the "minimum" tends to become the "maximum," thus lowering educational standards for all.
- One-fifth of all 4-year public colleges in the United States must accept every high school graduate within the State regardless of program followed or grades, thereby serving notice to high school students that they can expect to attend college even if they do not follow a demanding course of study in high school or perform well.
- About 23 percent of our more selective colleges and universities reported that their general level of selectivity declined during the

1970s, and 29 percent reported reducing the number of specific high school courses required for admission (usually by dropping foreign language requirements, which are now specified as a condition for admission by only one-fifth of our institutions of higher education).

- Too few experienced teachers and scholars are involved in writing textbooks. During the past decade or so a large number of texts have been "written down" by their publishers to ever-lower reading levels in response to perceived market demands.

- A recent study by Education Products Information Exchange revealed that a majority of students were able to master 80 percent of the material in some of their subject-matter texts before they had even opened the books. Many books do not challenge the students to whom they are assigned.

- Expenditures for textbooks and other instructional materials have declined by 50 percent over the past 17 years. While some recommend a level of spending on texts of between 5 and 10 percent of the operating costs of schools, the budgets for basal texts and related materials have been dropping during the past decade and a half to only 0.7 percent today.

Findings Regarding Time

Evidence presented to the Commission demonstrates three disturbing facts about the use that American schools and students make of time: (1) compared to other nations, American students spend much less time on school work; (2) time spent in the classroom and on homework is often used ineffectively; and (3) schools are not doing enough to help students develop either the study skills required to use time well or the willingness to spend more time on school work.

- In England and other industrialized countries, it is not unusual for academic high school students to spend 8 hours a day at school, 220 days per year. In the United States, by contrast, the typical school day lasts 6 hours and the school year is 180 days.

- In many schools, the time spent learning how to cook and drive counts as much toward a high school diploma as the time spent studying mathematics, English, chemistry, U.S. history, or biology.

- A study of the school week in the United States found that some schools provided students only 17 hours of academic instruction during the week, and the average school provided about 22.
- A California study of individual classrooms found that because of poor management of classroom time, some elementary students received only one-fifth of the instruction others received in reading comprehension.
- In most schools, the teaching of study skills is haphazard and unplanned. Consequently, many students complete high school and enter college without disciplined and systematic study habits.

Findings Regarding Teaching

The Commission found that not enough of the academically able students are being attracted to teaching; that teacher preparation programs need substantial improvement; that the professional working life of teachers is on the whole unacceptable; and that a serious shortage of teachers exists in key fields.

- Too many teachers are being drawn from the bottom quarter of graduating high school and college students.
- The teacher preparation curriculum is weighted heavily with courses in "educational methods" at the expense of courses in subjects to be taught. A survey of 1,350 institutions training teachers indicated that 41 percent of the time of elementary school teacher candidates is spent in education courses, which reduces the amount of time available for subject matter courses.
- The average salary after 12 years of teaching is only $17,000 per year, and many teachers are required to supplement their income with part-time and summer employment. In addition, individual teachers have little influence in such critical professional decisions as, for example, textbook selection.
- Despite widespread publicity about an overpopulation of teachers, severe shortages of certain kinds of teachers exist: in the fields of mathematics, science, and foreign languages; and among specialists in education for gifted and talented, language minority, and handicapped students.
- The shortage of teachers in mathematics and science is particularly severe. A 1981 survey of 45 States revealed shortages of mathemat-

ics teachers in 43 States, critical shortages of earth sciences teachers in 33 States, and of physics teachers everywhere.
- Half of the newly employed mathematics, science, and English teachers are not qualified to teach these subjects; fewer than one-third of U. S. high schools offer physics taught by qualified teachers.

RECOMMENDATIONS

In light of the urgent need for improvement, both immediate and long term, this Commission has agreed on a set of recommendations that the American people can begin to act on now, that can be implemented over the next several years, and that promise lasting reform. The topics are familiar; there is little mystery about what we believe must be done. Many schools, districts, and States are already giving serious and constructive attention to these matters, even though their plans may differ from our recommendations in some details.

We wish to note that we refer to public, private, and parochial schools and colleges alike. All are valuable national resources. Examples of actions similar to those recommended below can be found in each of them.

We must emphasize that the variety of student aspirations, abilities, and preparation requires that appropriate content be available to satisfy diverse needs. Attention must be directed to both the nature of the content available and to the needs of particular learners. The most gifted students, for example, may need a curriculum enriched and accelerated beyond even the needs of other students of high ability. Similarly, educationally disadvantaged students may require special curriculum materials, smaller classes, or individual tutoring to help them master the material presented. Nevertheless, there remains a common expectation: We must demand the best effort and performance from all students, whether they are gifted or less able, affluent or disadvantaged, whether destined for college, the farm, or industry.

Our recommendations are based on the beliefs that everyone can learn, that everyone is born with an urge to learn which can be nurtured, that a solid high school education is within the reach of virtually all, and that life-long learning will equip people with the skills required for new careers and for citizenship.

Recommendation A: Content

We recommend *that State and local high school graduation require-*
ments be strengthened and that, at a minimum, all students seeking a di-
ploma be required to lay the foundations in the Five New Basics by tak-
ing the following curriculum during their 4 years of high school: (a) 4
years of English; (b) 3 years of mathematics; (c) 3 years of science; (d) 3
years of social studies; and (e) one-half year of computer science. For the
college-bound, 2 years of foreign language in high school are strongly
recommended in addition to those taken earlier.

Whatever the student's educational or work objectives, knowledge of
the New Basics is the foundation of success for the after-school years
and, therefore, forms the core of the modern curriculum. A high level of
shared education in these Basics, together with work in the fine and performing arts and foreign languages, constitutes the mind and spirit of
our culture. The following Implementing Recommendations are intended as illustrative descriptions. They are included here to clarify what
we mean by the essentials of a strong curriculum.

Implementing Recommendations

1. The teaching of *English* in high school should equip graduates to:
   (a) comprehend, interpret, evaluate, and use what they read; (b) write
   well-organized, effective papers; (c) listen effectively and discuss ideas
   intelligently; and (d) know our literary heritage and how it enhances
   imagination and ethical understanding, and how it relates to the cus-
   toms, ideas, and values of today's life and culture.
2. The teaching of *mathematics* in high school should equip graduates to:
   (a) understand geometric and algebraic concepts; (b) understand elementary probability and statistics; (c) apply mathematics in everyday
   situations; and (d) estimate, approximate, measure, and test the accu-
   racy of their calculations. In addition to the traditional sequence of
   studies available for college-bound students, new, equally demanding
   mathematics curricula need to be developed for those who do not plan
   to continue their formal education immediately.
3. The teaching of *science* in high school should provide graduates with
   an introduction to: (a) the concepts, laws, and processes of the physical and biological sciences; (b) the methods of scientific inquiry and
   reasoning; (c) the application of scientific knowledge to everyday life;
   and (d) the social and environmental implications of scientific and

technological development. Science courses must be revised and updated for both the college-bound and those not intending to go to college. An example of such work is the American Chemical Society's "Chemistry in the Community" program.

4. The teaching of *social studies* in high school should be designed to: (a) enable students to fix their places and possibilities within the larger social and cultural structure; (b) understand the broad sweep of both ancient and contemporary ideas that have shaped our world; and (c) understand the fundamentals of how our economic system works and how our political system functions; and (d) grasp the difference between free and repressive societies. An understanding of each of these areas is requisite to the informed and committed exercise of citizenship in our free society.

5. The teaching of *computer science* in high school should equip graduates to: (a) understand the computer as an information, computation, and communication device; (b) use the computer in the study of the other Basics and for personal and work-related purposes; and (c) understand the world of computers, electronics, and related technologies.

In addition to the New Basics, other important curriculum matters must be addressed:

6. Achieving proficiency in a *foreign language* ordinarily requires from 4 to 6 years of study and should, therefore, be started in the elementary grades. We believe it is desirable that students achieve such proficiency because study of a foreign language introduces students to non-English-speaking cultures, heightens awareness and comprehension of one's native tongue, and serves the Nation's needs in commerce, diplomacy, defense, and education.

7. The high school curriculum should also provide students with programs requiring rigorous effort in subjects that advance students' personal, educational, and occupational goals, such as the fine and performing arts and vocational education. These areas complement the New Basics, and they should demand the same level of performance as the Basics.

8. The curriculum in the crucial eight grades leading to the high school years should be specifically designed to provide a sound base for study in those and later years in such areas as English language development and writing, computational and problem solving skills, science, social

studies, foreign language, and the arts. These years should foster an enthusiasm for learning and the development of the individual's gifts and talents.

We encourage the continuation of efforts by groups such as the American Chemical Society, the American Association for the Advancement of Science, the Modern Language Association, and the National Councils of Teachers of English and Teachers of Mathematics, to revise, update, improve, and make available new and more diverse curricular materials. We applaud the consortia of educators and scientific, industrial, and scholarly societies that cooperate to improve the school curriculum.

Recommendation B: Standards and Expectations

We recommend *that schools, colleges, and universities adopt more rigorous and measurable standards, and higher expectations, for academic performance and student conduct, and that 4-year colleges and universities raise their requirements for admission. This will help students do their best educationally with challenging materials in an environment that supports learning and authentic accomplishment.*

Implementing Recommendations

1. Grades should be indicators of academic achievement so they can be relied on as evidence of a student's readiness for further study.
2. Four-year colleges and universities should raise their admissions requirements and advise all potential applicants of the standards for admission in terms of specific courses required, performance in these areas, and levels of achievement on standardized achievement tests in each of the five Basics and, where applicable, foreign languages.
3. Standardized tests of achievement (not to be confused with aptitude tests) should be administered at major transition points from one level of schooling to another and particularly from high school to college or work. The purposes of these tests would be to: (a) certify the student's credentials; (b) identify the need for remedial intervention; and (c) identify the opportunity for advanced or accelerated work. The tests should be administered as part of a nationwide (but not Federal) system of State and local standardized tests. This system should include other diagnostic procedures that assist teachers and students to evaluate student progress.

4. Textbooks and other tools of learning and teaching should be upgraded and updated to assure more rigorous content. We call upon university scientists, scholars, and members of professional societies, in collaboration with master teachers, to help in this task, as they did in the post-Sputnik era. They should assist willing publishers in developing the products or publish their own alternatives where there are persistent inadequacies.

5. In considering textbooks for adoption, States and school districts should: (a) evaluate texts and other materials on their ability to present rigorous and challenging material clearly; and (b) require publishers to furnish evaluation data on the material's effectiveness.

6. Because no textbook in any subject can be geared to the needs of all students, funds should be made available to support text development in "thin-market" areas, such as those for disadvantaged students, the learning disabled, and the gifted and talented.

7. To assure quality, all publishers should furnish evidence of the quality and appropriateness of textbooks, based on results from field trials and credible evaluation. In view of the enormous numbers and varieties of texts available, more widespread consumer information services for purchasers are badly needed.

8. New instructional materials should reflect the most current applications of technology in appropriate curriculum areas, the best scholarship in each discipline, and research in learning and teaching.

Recommendation C: Time

We recommend *that significantly more time be devoted to learning the New Basics. This will require more effective use of the existing school day, a longer school day, or a lengthened school year.*

Implementing Recommendations

1. Students in high schools should be assigned far more homework than is now the case.

2. Instruction in effective study and work skills, which are essential if school and independent time is to be used efficiently, should be introduced in the early grades and continued throughout the student's schooling.

3. School districts and State legislatures should strongly consider 7-hour school days, as well as a 200- to 220-day school year.

4. The time available for learning should be expanded through better classroom management and organization of the school day. If necessary, additional time should be found to meet the special needs of slow learners, the gifted, and others who need more instructional diversity than can be accommodated during a conventional school day or school year.

5. The burden on teachers for maintaining discipline should be reduced through the development of firm and fair codes of student conduct that are enforced consistently, and by considering alternative classrooms, programs, and schools to meet the needs of continually disruptive students.

6. Attendance policies with clear incentives and sanctions should be used to reduce the amount of time lost through student absenteeism and tardiness.

7. Administrative burdens on the teacher and related intrusions into the school day should be reduced to add time for teaching and learning.

8. Placement and grouping of students, as well as promotion and graduation policies, should be guided by the academic progress of students and their instructional needs, rather than by rigid adherence to age.

Recommendation D: Teaching

This recommendation *consists of seven parts. Each is intended to improve the preparation of teachers or to make teaching a more rewarding and respected profession. Each of the seven stands on its own and should not be considered solely as an implementing recommendation.*

Implementing Recommendations

1. Persons preparing to teach should be required to meet high educational standards, to demonstrate an aptitude for teaching, and to demonstrate competence in an academic discipline. Colleges and universities offering teacher preparation programs should be judged by how well their graduates meet these criteria.

2. Salaries for the teaching profession should be increased and should be professionally competitive, market-sensitive, and performance-based. Salary, promotion, tenure, and retention decisions should be tied to an effective evaluation system that includes peer review so that superior teachers can be rewarded, average ones encouraged, and poor ones either improved or terminated.

3. School boards should adopt an 11-month contract for teachers. This would ensure time for curriculum and professional development, programs for students with special needs, and a more adequate level of teacher compensation.
4. School boards, administrators, and teachers should cooperate to develop career ladders for teachers that distinguish among the beginning instructor, the experienced teacher, and the master teacher.
5. Substantial nonschool personnel resources should be employed to help solve the immediate problem of the shortage of mathematics and science teachers. Qualified individuals, including recent graduates with mathematics and science degrees, graduate students, and industrial and retired scientists could, with appropriate preparation, immediately begin teaching in these fields. A number of our leading science centers have the capacity to begin educating and retraining teachers immediately. Other areas of critical teacher need, such as English, must also be addressed.
6. Incentives, such as grants and loans, should be made available to attract outstanding students to the teaching profession, particularly in those areas of critical shortage.
7. Master teachers should be involved in designing teacher preparation programs and in supervising teachers during their probationary years.

Recommendation E: Leadership and Fiscal Support

We recommend *that citizens across the Nation hold educators and elected officials responsible for providing the leadership necessary to achieve these reforms, and that citizens provide the fiscal support and stability required to bring about the reforms we propose.*

Implementing Recommendations

1. Principals and superintendents must play a crucial leadership role in developing school and community support for the reforms we propose, and school boards must provide them with the professional development and other support required to carry out their leadership role effectively. The Commission stresses the distinction between leadership skills involving persuasion, setting goals and developing community consensus behind them, and managerial and supervisory skills. Although the latter are necessary, we believe that school boards must

consciously develop leadership skills at the school and district levels if the reforms we propose are to be achieved.

2. State and local officials, including school board members, governors, and legislators, have *the primary responsibility* for financing and governing the schools, and should incorporate the reforms we propose in their educational policies and fiscal planning.

3. The Federal Government, in cooperation with States and localities, should help meet the needs of key groups of students such as the gifted and talented, the socioeconomically disadvantaged, minority and language minority students, and the handicapped. In combination these groups include both national resources and the Nation's youth who are most at risk.

4. In addition, we believe the Federal Government's role includes several functions of national consequence that States and localities alone are unlikely to be able to meet: protecting constitutional and civil rights for students and school personnel; collecting data, statistics, and information about education generally; supporting curriculum improvement and research on teaching, learning, and the management of schools; supporting teacher training in areas of critical shortage or key national needs; and providing student financial assistance and research and graduate training. We believe the assistance of the Federal Government should be provided with a minimum of administrative burden and intrusiveness.

5. The Federal Government has *the primary responsibility* to identify the national interest in education. It should also help fund and support efforts to protect and promote that interest. It must provide the national leadership to ensure that the Nation's public and private resources are marshaled to address the issues discussed in this report.

6. This Commission calls upon educators, parents, and public officials at all levels to assist in bringing about the educational reform proposed in this report. We also call upon citizens to provide the financial support necessary to accomplish these purposes. Excellence costs. But in the long run mediocrity costs far more.

AMERICA CAN DO IT

Despite the obstacles and difficulties that inhibit the pursuit of superior educational attainment, we are confident, with history as our guide, that we can meet our goal. The American educational system has responded to previous challenges with remarkable success. In the 19th century our land-grant colleges and universities provided the research and training that developed our Nation's natural resources and the rich agricultural bounty of the American farm. From the late 1800s through mid-20th century, American schools provided the educated workforce needed to seal the success of the Industrial Revolution and to provide the margin of victory in two world wars. In the early part of this century and continuing to this very day, our schools have absorbed vast waves of immigrants and educated them and their children to productive citizenship. Similarly, the Nation's Black colleges have provided opportunity and undergraduate education to the vast majority of college-educated Black Americans.

More recently, our institutions of higher education have provided the scientists and skilled technicians who helped us transcend the boundaries of our planet. In the last 30 years, the schools have been a major vehicle for expanded social opportunity, and now graduate 75 percent of our young people from high school. Indeed, the proportion of Americans of college age enrolled in higher education is nearly twice that of Japan and far exceeds other nations such as France, West Germany, and the Soviet Union. Moreover, when international comparisons were last made a decade ago, the top 9 percent of American students compared favorably in achievement with their peers in other countries.

In addition, many large urban areas in recent years report that average student achievement in elementary schools is improving. More and more schools are also offering advanced placement programs and programs for gifted and talented students, and more and more students are enrolling in them.

We are the inheritors of a past that gives us every reason to believe that we will succeed.

A WORD TO PARENTS AND STUDENTS

The task of assuring the success of our recommendations does not fall to the schools and colleges alone. Obviously, faculty members and administrators, along with policymakers and the mass media, will play a crucial role in the reform of the educational system. But even more important is the role of parents and students, and to them we speak directly.

To Parents

You know that you cannot confidently launch your children into today's world unless they are of strong character and well-educated in the use of language, science, and mathematics. They must possess a deep respect for intelligence, achievement, and learning, and the skills needed to use them; for setting goals; and for disciplined work. That respect must be accompanied by an intolerance for the shoddy and second-rate masquerading as "good enough."

You have the right to demand for your children the best our schools and colleges can provide. Your vigilance and your refusal to be satisfied with less than the best are the imperative first step. But your right to a proper education for your children carries a double responsibility. As surely as you are your child's first and most influential teacher, your child's ideas about education and its significance begin with you. You must be a *living* example of what you expect your children to honor and to emulate. Moreover, you bear a responsibility to participate actively in your child's education. You should encourage more diligent study and discourage satisfaction with mediocrity and the attitude that says "let it slide"; monitor your child's study; encourage good study habits; encourage your child to take more demanding rather than less demanding courses; nurture your child's curiosity, creativity, and confidence; and be an active participant in the work of the schools. Above all, exhibit a commitment to continued learning in your own life. Finally, help your children understand that excellence in education cannot be achieved without intellectual and moral integrity coupled with hard work and commitment. Children will look to their parents and teachers as models of such virtues.

To Students

You forfeit your chance for life at its fullest when you withhold your best effort in learning. When you give only the minimum to learning, you receive only the minimum in return. Even with your parents' best example and your teachers' best efforts, in the end it is *your* work that determines how much and how well you learn. When you work to your full capacity, you can hope to attain the knowledge and skills that will enable you to create your future and control your destiny. If you do not, you will have your future thrust upon you by others. Take hold of your life, apply your gifts and talents, work with dedication and self-discipline. Have high expectations for yourself and convert every challenge into an opportunity.

A FINAL WORD

This is not the first or only commission on education, and some of our findings are surely not new, but old business that now at last must be done. For no one can doubt that the United States is under a challenge from many quarters.

Children born today can expect to graduate from high school in the year 2000. We dedicate our report not only to these children, but also to those now in school and others to come. We firmly believe that a movement of America's schools in the direction called for by our recommendations will prepare these children for far more effective lives in a far stronger America.

Our final word, perhaps better characterized as a plea, is that all segments of our population give attention to the implementation of our recommendations. Our present plight did not appear overnight, and the responsibility for our current situation is widespread. Reform of our educational system will take time and unwavering commitment. It will require equally widespread, energetic, and dedicated action. For example, we call upon the National Academy of Sciences, National Academy of Engineering, Institute of Medicine, Science Service, National Science Foundation, Social Science Research Council, American Council of Learned Societies, National Endowment for the Humanities, National Endowment for the Arts, and other scholarly, scientific, and learned societies for their help in this effort. Help should come from students themselves; from parents, teachers, and school boards; from colleges and universities; from local, State, and Federal officials; from teachers' and administrators' organizations; from industrial and labor councils; and from other groups with interest in and responsibility for educational reform.

It is their America, and the America of all of us, that is at risk; it is to each of us that this imperative is addressed. It is by our willingness to take up the challenge, and our resolve to see it through, that America's place in the world will be either secured or forfeited. Americans have succeeded before and so we shall again.

Members of the National Commission on Excellence in Education

David P. Gardner (Chair)
President, University of Utah and
President-Elect, University of California
Salt Lake City, Utah

Yvonne W. Larsen (Vice-Chair)
Immediate Past-President
San Diego City School Board
San Diego, California

William O. Baker
Chairman of the Board (Retired)
Bell Telephone Laboratories
Murray Hill, New Jersey

Anne Campbell
Former Commissioner of Education
State of Nebraska
Lincoln, Nebraska

Emeral A. Crosby
Principal, Northern High School
Detroit, Michigan

Charles A. Foster, Jr.
Irnmediate Past-President
Foundation for Teaching Economics
San Francisco, California

Norman C. Francis
President, Xavier University of Louisiana
New Orleans, Louisiana

A. Bartlett Giamatti
President, Yale University
New Haven, Connecticut

Shirley Gordon
President, Highline Community College
Midway, Washington

Robert V. Haderlein
Immediate Past-President
National School Boards Association
Girard, Kansas

Gerald Holton
Mallinckrodt Professor of Physics and
Professor of the History of Science
Harvard University
Cambridge, Massachusetts

Annette Y. Kirk
Kirk Associates
Mecosta, Michigan

Margaret S. Marston
Member, Virginia State Board of
Education
Arlington, Virginia

Albert H. Quie
Former Governor, State of Minnesota
St. Paul, Minnesota

Francisco D. Sanchez, Jr.
Superintendent of Schools
Albuquerque Public Schools
Albuquerque, New Mexico

Glenn T. Seaborg
University Professor of Chemistry and
Nobel Laureate
University of California
Berkeley, California

Jay Sommer
National Teacher of the Year, 1981–82
Foreign Language Department
New Rochelle High School
New Rochelle, New York

Richard Wallace
Principal, Lutheran High School East
Cleveland Heights, Ohio

Notes

INTRODUCTION

1. Albert Shanker, "A Landmark Revisited," 9 May 1993. Online at www.aft. org/stand/previous/1993/050993.html

CHAPTER ONE   *Riding Waves, Trading Horses: The Twenty-Year Effort to Reform Education*

1. See Lorraine McDonnell and Susan H. Fuhrman, "The Political Context of Education Reform" in Van D. Mueller and Mary P. McKeown, eds., *The Fiscal, Legal, and Political Aspects of State Reform of Elementary and Secondary Education* (Cambridge, MA: Ballinger, 1985), pp. 43–64.
2. See National Governors' Association, *A Time for Results: The Governors' 1986 Report on Education* (Washington, DC: Author, 1986).
3. See William H. Clune, Paula A. White, and Janice H. Patterson, *The Implementation and Effects of High School Graduation Requirements: First Steps toward Curricular Reform* (New Brunswick, NJ: Center for Policy Research in Education, 1989).
4. See Richard F. Elmore, Penelope L. Peterson, and Sarah J. McCarthey, *Restructuring in the Classroom: Teaching, Learning, and School Organization* (San Francisco: Jossey-Bass, 1996); Susan A. Mohrman and Priscilla Wohlstetter, eds., *School-Based Management: Organizing for High Performance* (San Francisco: Jossey-Bass, 1994).
5. See National Council of Teachers of Mathematics, *Curriculum and Evaluation Standards for School Mathematics* (Reston, VA: Author, 1989).
6. See Marshall S. Smith and Jennifer A. O'Day, "Systemic School Reform" in Susan H. Fuhrman and Betty Malen, eds., *The Politics of Curriculum and Testing, 1990 Yearbook of the Politics of Education Association* (Washington, DC: Falmer Press, 1991), pp. 233–267.
7. See Martin Carnoy and Susanna Loeb, "Does External Accountability Affect Student Outcomes? A Cross-State Analysis" in Susan H. Fuhrman and Richard F. Elmore, eds., *Redesigning Accountability Systems* (New York: Teachers College Press, in press); David Grissmer and Ann Flanagan, *Exploring Rapid*

Achievement Gains in North Carolina and Texas (Washington, DC: National Education Goals Panel, 1998).

8. See Katrina Bulkley, "Educational Performance and Charter School Authorizers: The Accountability Bind," *Education Policy Analysis Archives* 9, no. 37 (2001); Katrina Bulkley and Jennifer Fisler, *A Decade of Charter Schools: From Theory to Practice* (Philadelphia: Consortium for Policy Research in Education, 2002).

9. See Patrick McEwan, *The Potential Impact of Large-Scale Voucher Programs* (New York: National Center for the Study of Privatization in Education, Teachers College, Columbia University, 2000).

10. See Katrina Bulkley, *Balancing Act: Educational Management Organizations and Charter School Autonomy.* Paper prepared for CPRE Conference on Educational Issues in Charter Schools, Washington, DC, 2001.

11. See "New Reports on Michigan Charter Schools" by Standard and Poor's School Evaluation Services. Press release available online at http://www.ses.standardandpoors.com/

12. See Susan H. Fuhrman and Richard F. Elmore, *Takeover and Deregulation: Working Models of New State and Local Regulatory Relationships* (New Brunswick, NJ: Consortium for Policy Research in Education, 1992).

13. Michael W. Kirst, *Mayoral Influence, New Regimes, and Public School Governance* (Philadelphia: Consortium for Policy Research in Education, 2002), p. 15.

14. See Margaret E. Goertz, Mark C. Duffy, and Kerstin Carlson Le Floch, *Assessment and Accountability Systems in the 50 States: 1999–2000* (Philadelphia: Consortium for Policy Research in Education, 2001).

15. Ibid.

16. See Susan H. Fuhrman and Richard F. Elmore, "Understanding Local Control in the Wake of State Education Reform," *Educational Evaluation and Policy Analysis* 12, no. 1 (1990), 82–96.

17. See Linda Darling-Hammond and Barnett Berry, *The Evolution of Teacher Policy* (Santa Monica, CA: RAND Corporation, 1988).

18. See Frank Johnson, *Revenues and Expenditures for Public Elementary and Secondary Education: School Year 1997–98* (Washington, DC: National Center for Education Statistics, 2000).

19. Brian Rowan, *The Ecology of School Improvement: Notes on the School Improvement Industry in the United States.* Paper prepared for the conference on the Social Geographies of Educational Change: Contexts, Networks, and Generalizability, Barcelona, Spain, 2001.

20. See Craig D. Jerald and Richard M. Ingersoll, *All Talk, No Action: Putting an End to Out-of-Field Teaching* (Washington, DC: Education Trust, 2002).

CHAPTER TWO   *Change and Improvement in Educational Reform*

1. See, for example, Larry Cuban, *How Teachers Taught: Constancy and Change in American Classrooms, 1890–1990*, 2d ed. (New York: Teachers College Press, 1993); Seymour B. Sarason, *The Predictable Failure of Educational Reform* (San Francisco: Jossey-Bass, 1991); David B. Tyack and Larry Cuban, *Tinkering toward Utopia: A Century of Public School Reform* (Cambridge, MA: Harvard University Press, 1995); David B. Tyack, *The One Best System: A History of American Urban Education* (Cambridge, MA: Harvard University Press, 1974).

2. See Diane Ravitch, *The Great School Wars: A History of the New York City Public Schools* (Baltimore: Johns Hopkins University Press, 2000); Diane Ravitch, *Left Back: A Century of Failed School Reforms* (New York: Simon and Schuster, 2000).

3. See Arthur Powell, Eleanor Farrar, and David Cohen, *The Shopping Mall High School* (Boston: Houghton Mifflin, 1985); Ernest Boyer, *High School: A Report on Secondary Education in America* (New York: Harper and Row, 1983).

4. "The Thirteenth Man: Ted Bell and the U.S. Department of Education" (Teaching Case, Harvard Graduate School of Education, 1995).

5. See Susan Fuhrman, ed., *From the Capitol to the Classroom: Standards-Based Reform in the States* (Chicago: University of Chicago Press, 2001).

6. See Richard F. Elmore, *Building a New Structure for School Leadership* (Washington, DC: Albert Shanker Institute, 2000).

7. See Margaret Goertz and Mark Duffy, *Assessment and Accountability Across the 50 States* (Philadelphia: Consortium for Policy Research in Education, 2001).

8. See Frederick Hess, *Spinning Wheels: The Politics of Urban School Reform* (Washington, DC: Brookings Institution Press, 1999); Elmore, *Building a New Structure for School Leadership*.

9. Hess, Ibid.

10. See Michael Fullan, *The New Meaning of Educational Change*, 3d ed. (New York: Teachers College Press, 2001).

11. See Charles Abelmann, Richard F. Elmore et al., *When Accountability Knocks Will Anyone Answer?* (Cambridge, MA: Consortium for Policy Research in Education, 1999).

12. See Richard F. Elmore, *Bridging the Gap between Standards and Achievement: The Imperative for Professional Development in Education* (Washington, DC: Albert Shanker Institute, 2002); David K. Cohen and Heather C. Hill, *Learning Policy: When State Education Policy Works* (New Haven, CT: Yale University Press, 2001).

CHAPTER THREE   *The Academic Imperative: New Challenges and Expectations Facing School Leaders*

1. See Patricia Albjerg Graham, "What America Has Expected of Its Schools Over the Last Century," *American Journal of Education* 101, no. 2 (February 1993), 83–98.
2. Patricia Albjerg Graham, "Educational Reform—Why Now?" Paper presented at the meeting of the American Philosophical Society, 2000.
3. Timothy Knowles, "The Principal and the Academic Imperative" (Ed.D. diss., Harvard Graduate School of Education, 2002), pp. 29–30.
4. Ellwood P. Cubberley, *Public School Administration* (New York: Houghton Mifflin, 1929), p. 295.
5. Joseph Murphy and Lynn Beck, "Restructuring the Principalship: Challenges and Possibilities" in Joseph Murphy and Karen Seashore Louis, eds., *Reshaping the Principalship: Insights from Transformational Reform Efforts* (Thousand Oaks, CA: Corwin Press, 1994), p. 10.
6. Joseph Murphy, *The Landscape of Leadership Preparation: Reframing the Education of School Administrators* (Newbury Park, CA: Corwin Press, 1992), p. 116.
7. See Richard F. Elmore, "Teaching, Learning and Organization: School Restructuring and the Recurring Dilemmas of Reform." Paper presented at the annual meeting of American Educational Research Association, Chicago, 1991.
8. Knowles, "The Principal," p. 109.
9. Ibid., p. 111.
10. Ibid., p. 112.
11. Ibid., p. 114.
12. Ibid., p. 97.
13. Ibid., p. 117.
14. Ibid., p. 117.
15. Mildred Collins Blackman and Leslie T. Fenwick, "The Principalship," *Education Week*, 29 March 2000, pp. 68, 46.
16. Knowles, "The Principal," p. 145.

CHAPTER FOUR   *A Principal Looks Back: Standards Matter*

1. See Michael Rutter et al., *Fifteen Thousand Hours: Secondary Schools and Their Effects on Children* (Cambridge, MA: Harvard University Press, 1979).
2. Ronald Edmonds, "Effective Schools for the Urban Poor," *Educational Leadership* 37, no. 1 (October 1979), 15–24.
3. Kim Marshall, "How I Confronted HSPS (Hyperactive Superficial Principal Syndrome) and Began to Deal with the Heart of the Matter," *Phi Delta Kappan* 77 no. 5 (January 1996), 336–345.

4. This power cycle is based on the most recent work by Jeff Howard's Efficacy Institute: the Self-Directed Improvement System.

CHAPTER FIVE   *Teaching: From* A Nation at Risk *to a Profession at Risk?*

1. See William L. Sanders and June C. Rivers, *Cumulative and Residual Effects of Teachers on Future Student Academic Achievement* (Knoxville: University of Tennessee Value-Added Research and Assessment Center, 1996).

2. National Commission on Excellence in Education, *A Nation at Risk: The Imperative for Educational Reform* (Washington, DC: U.S. Department of Education, 1983), p. 23. [In this volume, see pp. 182–183]

3. Ibid., p. 30. [188]

4. Ibid., p. 23. [182]

5. Holmes Group, *Tomorrow's Teachers* (East Lansing, MI: Author, 1986), p. ix.

6. See Maynard C. Reynolds, ed., *The Knowledge Base for the Beginning Teacher* (New York: Pergamon Press, 1987).

7. See Linda Darling-Hammond, *Beyond the Commission Reports: The Coming Crisis in Teaching* (Santa Monica, CA: RAND Corporation, 1984).

8. See John I. Goodlad, *Teachers for Our Nation's Schools* (San Francisco: Jossey-Bass, 1990).

9. National Commission on Teaching and America's Future (NCTAF), *What Matters Most: Teaching for America's Future* (New York: Author, 1996), p. vi.

10. See Darling-Hammond, *Beyond the Commission Reports;* also Richard J. Murnane, Judith D. Singer, John D. Willett, James J. Kemple, and Randall J. Olsen, *Who Will Teach? Policies That Matter* (Cambridge, MA: Harvard University Press, 1991).

11. NCTAF, *What Matters Most*, p. 15.

12. See Teaching and California's Future, *The Status of the Teaching Profession 2001* (Santa Cruz, CA: Center for the Future of Teaching and Learning, 2002).

13. U.S. Department of Education, *Meeting the Highly Qualified Teacher Challenge: The Secretary's Annual Report on Teacher Quality* (Washington, DC: U.S. Government Printing Office, 2002), p. 40.

14. For an overview of this research, see Suzanne M. Wilson, Robert E. Floden, and Joan Ferrini-Mundy, *Teacher Preparation Research: Current Knowledge, Gaps, and Recommendations* (Seattle: Center for the Study of Teaching and Policy, University of Washington, 2001).

15. Richard M. Ingersoll, "Teacher Turnover and Teacher Shortages: An Organizational Analysis," *American Education Research Journal* 38, no. 3 (2001), 501.

16. Goodlad, *Teachers,* pp. 94–95.

17. See "Scripted Learning: A Slap in the Face or Blessing from Above?" *California Educator,* April 2002.

18. Gary Sykes, "Public Policy and the Problem of Teacher Quality" in Lee S. Shulman and Gary Sykes, eds., *Handbook of Teaching and Policy* (New York: Longman, 1983), p. 120.

19. See Hamilton Lankford, Susanna Loeb, and James Wyckoff, "Teacher Sorting and the Plight of Urban Schools: A Descriptive Analysis," *Educational Evaluation and Policy Analysis* 24, no. 1 (2002), 37–62.; Stephen W. Raudenbush, Randall P. Fotiu, and Yuk Fai Cheong, "Inequality of Access to Educational Resources: A National Report Card in 8th Grade Math," *Educational Evaluation and Policy Analysis* 20, no. 4 (1998), 253–267.

20. See Teaching and California's Future, *The Status of the Teaching Profession 2001.*

21. Regents Task Force on Teaching, *Teaching to Higher Standards: New York's Commitment* (Albany: New York State Department of Education, 1998), p. 10.

22. Linda Darling-Hammond, "Standard Setting in Teaching: Changes in Licensing, Certification, and Assessment" in Virginia Richardson, ed., *Handbook of Research on Teaching,* 4th ed. (Washington, DC: American Educational Research Association, 2001), p. 771.

CHAPTER SIX *Still at Risk: The Causes and Costs of Failure to Educate Poor and Minority Children for the Twenty-First Century*

1. These numbers improve only slightly for black eighth graders, with 87 percent below proficiency in 1998 (the last year for which results are available), and twelfth graders, with 82 percent below.

2. But this is not something most people can own up to in public. A whole lexicon has grown up as polite cover: these children are "underprivileged," "unmotivated," they "carry too much baggage," or are otherwise burdened by disqualifying circumstances or characteristics. The giveaway is that their more blessed counterparts, the affluent and middle-class kids who come to school knowing their colors and letters (and sometimes much more), are referred to as "the bright ones" or those with "high ability."

3. David A. Bositis, *1999 National Opinion Poll, Education* (Washington, DC: Joint Center for Political and Economic Studies, 1999), pp. 8–9,

4. David A. Bositis, *2000 National Opinion Poll, Politics* (Washington, DC: Joint Center for Political and Economic Studies, 2000), p. 9.

5. "The Business of Education," *Education Update,* February 2002.

6. Jeff Howard and Ray Hammond, "Rumors of Inferiority," *New Republic,* 9 September 1985, pp. 17–21.

7. The latest is *The Bell Curve* by Richard J. Herrnstein and Charles Murray (New York: Free Press, 1994).

8. The fact that proficiency includes the demonstration of application skills undercuts the complaint of many educators that the end-of-year proficiency examinations administered by most of the states require teachers to spend most of the year "teaching to the test." That complaint makes sense only if we are assessing rote memorization alone. If we are assessing a student's ability to acquire *and* use knowledge in the real world, then "teaching to the test" is exactly what all good educators should be doing.

9. By "normal" I have something very specific in mind. A normal child is one who proved capable of learning to communicate in a human language by the age of three. That feat of prodigious learning is unequalled by anything most of us do for the rest of our lives. Any child who can speak in a human language and be understood, and be spoken to and understand, has already demonstrated the intellectual capacity to learn anything in the gifted and talented or advanced placement curriculum later.

10. While I do not accept IQ as an adequate measure of intelligence, long-term changes in measures like IQ can indicate significant changes in some aspects of mental functioning.

11. See Richard Rothstein, "Lessons: Look at the Way Intelligence Flowers," *New York Times*, 20 December 2000.

12. See K. Anders Ericsson and Neil Charness, "Expert Performance: Its Structure and Acquisition," *American Psychologist* 49, no. 8 (August 1994), 725–727.

13. See Douglas B. Reeves, *Holistic Accountability* (Thousand Oaks, CA: Corwin Press, 2002), for an extended discussion of the centrality of evidence based on data in the development of effective educational strategy and the intelligent allocation of educational resources.

14. One element of curriculum *should* be dictated by central office administrators to ensure consistency across all classrooms and schools: *all* children (not just those designated as "gifted and talented") should work with curricula that are aligned to proficiency standards, for each subject, at every grade level. Aligned curricula transmit knowledge, and provide children the opportunity to *apply* knowledge to problems and real-world situations.

15. See Jon Saphier and Robert Gower, *The Skillful Teacher: Building Your Teaching Skills* (Carlisle, MA: Research for Better Teaching, 1997).

CHAPTER SEVEN   *The Limits of Ideology: Curriculum and the Culture Wars*

1. The Askwith Education Forum "Beyond the Reading Wars" was held at the Harvard Graduate School of Education on 8 April 1999.

2. The quotation is attributed to E. D. Hirsch, Jr., in "A Tribute to Jeanne Chall," *American Educator* 25, no. 1 (Spring 2001), 16.

3. See "Introduction to the Third Edition" in Jeanne S. Chall, *Learning to Read: The Great Debate,* 3d ed. (New York: Harcourt Brace, 1996).

4. Ibid.

5. See E. D. Hirsch's critique of the Romantic underpinnings of progressivism in *The Schools We Need and Why We Don't Have Them* (New York: Doubleday, 1996).

6. See an interview with Lemann in "The President's Big Test," *Frontline,* 28 March 2002. Online at ww.pbs.org/wgbh/pages/frontline/shows/schools/nochild/lemann.html

7. Honig is quoted in Nicholas Lemann, "The Reading Wars," *Atlantic Monthly* 280, no. 5 (November 1997), 128–134.

8. National Research Council, *Everybody Counts* (Washington, DC: Author, 1989).

9. Romesh Ratnesar et al., "This Is Math? Suddenly, Math Becomes Fun and Games," *Time,* 25 August 1997, pp. 66–67.

10. See Andreae Downs, "Will New Standards Quiet the Math Wars?" *Harvard Education Letter* 16, no. 6 (November/December 2000), 4–6.

11. Quoted in Barbara Matson, "Whole Language or Phonics? Teachers and Researchers Find the Middle Ground Most Fertile," *Harvard Education Letter* 12, no. 2 (March/April 1996), 3.

12. Diane Ravitch provides an overview of the debate in "It Is Time to Stop the War" in Tom Loveless, ed., *The Great Curriculum Debate* (Washington, DC: Brookings Institution Press, 2001).

13. See G. Reid Lyon's statement to the U.S. Senate's Committee on Labor and Human Resources on reading and literacy initiatives, 28 April 1998. Lyon is chief of the Child Development and Behavior for the National Institute of Child Health and Human Development.

14. See Ellen H. Brinkley, "What's Religion Got to Do with Attacks on Whole Language?" in Kenneth S. Goodman, ed., *In Defense of Good Teaching* (Portland, ME: Stenhouse, 1998).

15. California Department of Education, "Teaching Reading: A Balanced, Comprehensive Approach to Teaching Reading in Prekindergarten through Grade Three," Program Advisory (Sacramento: Author, 1996).

16. Chall, *Learning to Read,* pp. 288–300.

17. Matson, "Whole Language or Phonics?"

18. See Catherine E. Snow, "Preventing Reading Difficulties in Young Children: Precursors and Fallout" in Tom Loveless, ed., *The Great Curriculum Debate,* p. 229–246.

19. Preface to the third edition of Catherine E. Snow, M. Susan Burns, and Peg Griffin, *Preventing Reading Difficulties in Young Children* (Washington, DC: National Academy Press, 2000). Online at http://www.nap.edu/reading room/books/prdyc/

20. See David Tyack and William Tobin, "The 'Grammar' of Schooling: Why Has It Been So Hard to Change?" *American Educational Research Journal* 31, no. 3 (Fall 1994), 478.

21. Matson, "Whole Language or Phonics?"

22. David K. Cohen and Heather C. Hill, *Learning Policy: When State Education Reform Works* (New Haven, CT: Yale University Press, 2001), pp. 70–71.

23. Downs, "Will New Standards Quiet the Math Wars?"

24. Cohen and Hill, *Learning Policy*, p. 71.

25. Mark Clayton, "Flaws in the Evaluation Process," Christian Science Monitor, 23 May 2000.

26. National Reading Panel, *Teaching Children to Read*; Kathleen Kennedy Manzo, "New Panels to Form to Study Reading Research," *Education Week*, 30 January 2002, p. 5; Kathleen Kennedy Manzo, "Reading Panel Urges Phonics for All in K–6," *Education Week*, 19 April 2000, pp. 1, 14; also of interest is Thomas Newkirk, "Reading and the Limits of Science," *Education Week*, 24 April 2002, p. 39.

27. Richard Rothstein, "Reading Factions Should Make Amends," *New York Times*, 5 September 2001, p. B7.

28. Cohen and Hill, *Learning Policy,* pp. 71–72.

29. See Liping Ma, *Knowing and Teaching Elementary Mathematics* (Mahwah, NJ: Lawrence Erlbaum, 1999), pp. 144–153.

30. Downs, "Will New Standards Quiet the Math Wars?"

31. "Arming New Teachers with Survival Skills," *Harvard Education Letter* 18, no. 5 (September/October 2002), 8.

32. Cohen and Hill, *Learning Policy,* p. 3.

33. John I. Goodlad, "Producing Teachers Who Understand, Care, and Believe," *Education Week*, 5 February 1997, p. 36.

34. Catherine E. Snow, M. Susan Burns, and Peg Griffin, *Preventing Reading Difficulties in Young Children* (Washington, DC: National Academy Press, 1998), p. 273. Online at http://www.nap.edu/readingroom/books/prdyc/

35. Ibid, p. vi.

CHAPTER EIGHT   *Missed Opportunities: Why the Federal Response to A Nation at Risk Was Inadequate*

1. Launor F. Carter, "The Sustaining Effects Study of Compensatory and Elementary Education," *Educational Researcher* 13 (August/September 1984), 4–13; Samuel Halperin, "ESEA: Decennial Views of the Revolution, the Positive Side," *Phi Delta Kappan* 57 (1975), 147–151; Milbrey Wallin McLaughlin, "Implementation of ESEA Title I: A Problem of Compliance," *Teachers College Record* 77 (1976), 397–415; Milbrey Wallin McLaughlin, *Education and Reform: The Elementary and Secondary Education Act of*

1965, Title I (Cambridge, MA: Ballinger, 1975); Maris A. Vinovskis, "Do Federal Compensatory Education Programs Really Work? A Brief Historical Analysis of Title I and Head Start," *American Journal of Education* 107 (May 1999), 187–209.

2. Ellen Condliffe Lagemann and Lamar P. Miller, eds., Brown v. Board of Education: *The Challenge for Today's Schools* (New York: Teachers College Press, 1996); Jeffrey Mirel, *The Rise and Fall of an Urban School System: Detroit, 1907–81* (Ann Arbor: University of Michigan Press, 1993).

3. Beryl A. Radin and Willis D. Hawley, *The Politics of Federal Reorganization: Creating the U.S. Department of Education* (New York: Pergamon Press, 1988).

4. Jay R. Campbell, Clyde M. Reese, Christine O'Sullivan, and John A. Dossey, *NAEP 1994 Trends in Academic Progress: Achievement of U.S. Students in Science, 1969 to 1994; Mathematics, 1973 to 1994; Reading, 1971 to 1994; Writing, 1984 to 1994* (Washington, DC: Educational Testing Service, 1996).

5. Stanley Elam, *The Gallup/Phi Delta Kappa Polls of Attitudes toward the Public Schools, 1969–88: A 20-Year Compilation and Educational History* (Bloomington, IN: Phi Delta Kappa, 1989).

6. Thomas Toch, *In the Name of Excellence: The Struggle to Reform the Nation's Schools, Why It's Failing, and What Should Be Done* (New York: Oxford University Press, 1991), p. 17.

7. Numan V. Bartley, *The New South, 1945–1980: The Story of the South's Modernization* (Baton Rouge: Louisiana State University Press, 1995); Bruce J. Schuman, *From Cotton Belt to Sunbelt: Federal Policy, Economic Development, and the Transformation of the South, 1938–1980* (New York: Oxford University Press, 1991).

8. Charles Flynn Allen, "Governor William Jefferson Clinton: A Biography with a Special Focus on his Educational Contributions" (Ph.D. diss., University of Mississippi, 1991); Jennie Vanetta Carter, "How Three Governors Involved the Public in Passing Their Education Reform Programs" (Ed.D. diss., Vanderbilt University, 1992).

9. Committee for Economic Development, *Investing in Our Children: Business and the Public Schools* (New York: Author, 1985).

10. Paul R. Abramson, John H. Aldrich, and David W. Rohde, *Change and Continuity in the 1980 Elections* (Washington, DC: Congressional Quarterly Press, 1982); Elizabeth Drew, *Portrait of an Election: The 1980 Presidential Campaign* (New York: Simon and Schuster, 1981); Jack W. Germond and Jules Witcover, *Blue Smoke and Mirrors: How Reagan Won and Why Carter Lost the Election of 1980* (New York: Viking Press, 1981); Gerald Pomper, *The Election of 1980: Reports and Interpretations* (Chatham, NJ: Chatham House, 1981).

11. Martin Anderson, *Revolution* (New York: Harcourt Brace Jovanovich, 1988); Lou Cannon, *President Reagan: The Role of a Lifetime* (New York: Si-

mon and Schuster, 1991); David A. Stockman, *The Triumph of Politics: The Inside Story of the Reagan Revolution* (New York: Harper and Row, 1986).

12. General Accounting Office, *Education Information: Changes in Funds and Priorities Have Affected Production and Quality* (Washington, DC: U.S. Government Printing Office, 1987); Deborah A. Verstegen, "Educational Fiscal Policy in the Reagan Administration," *Educational Evaluation and Policy Analysis* 12 (Winter 1990), 355–373; Deborah A. Verstegen and David L. Clark, "The Diminution in Federal Expenditures for Expenditures for Education during the Reagan Administration," *Phi Delta Kappan* 70 (October 1988), 124–138.

13. Terrel H. Bell, *The Thirteenth Man: A Reagan Cabinet Memoir* (New York: Free Press, 1988).

14. National Commission on Excellence in Education, *A Nation at Risk: The Imperative of Educational Reform* (Washington, DC: U.S. Government Printing Office), pp. 39–41.

15. Ibid., p. 5. [In this volume, see p. 167]

16. Ibid., p.15. [175–176]

17. Ibid., p. 15. [176]

18. Ibid., p. 15. [176]

19. Ibid., p. 23. [183]

20. Ibid., p. 27. [187]

21. Ibid., p. 29. [188–189]

22. Ibid., pp. 32–33. [192–193]

23. For example, see Lawrence C. Stedman and Marshall S. Smith, "Recent Reform Proposals," *Contemporary Education Review* 2 (Fall 1983), 85–104. For a critical analysis of the rhetorical style of *A Nation at Risk*, see Jean Laura Dehart, "A Rhetorical Analysis of the Perpetuation of an Educational Crisis: 1980–1989" (Ph.D. diss., University of Georgia, 1992).

24. On the response to *A Nation at Risk*, see U.S. Department of Education, *The Nation Responds: Recent Efforts to Improve Education* (Washington, DC: U.S. Government Printing Office, 1984).

25. David N. Plank, ed., *Commissions, Reports, Reforms, and Educational Policy,* (Westport, CT: Praeger, 1995).

26. Ellen Condliffe Lagemann, *An Elusive Science: The Troubling History of Educational Research* (Chicago: University of Chicago Press, 2000); Donald R. Warren, *To Enforce Education: A History of the Founding Years of the United States Office of Education* (Detroit: Wayne State University Press, 1974).

27. Maris A. Vinovskis, *Revitalizing Federal Education Research and Development: Improving the R&D Centers, Regional Educational Laboratories, and the "New" OERI* (Ann Arbor: University of Michigan Press, 2001).

28. Richard Elmore, "Follow Through: Decision-Making in a Large-Scale Social Experiment" (Ed.D. diss., Harvard Graduate School of Education, 1976);

Maris A. Vinovskis, *History and Educational Policymaking* (New Haven, CT: Yale University Press, 1999), pp. 89–114.

29. Alice M. Rivlin and P. Michael Timpane, "Planned Variation in Education: An Assessment" in Alice M. Rivlin and P. Michael Timpane, eds., *Planned Variation in Education: Should We Give Up or Try Harder?* (Washington, DC: Brookings Institution Press, 1975), p. 18.

30. Ellen Condliffe Lagemann, "Contested Terrain: A History of Education Research in the United States, 1890–1990," *Educational Researcher* 26 (December 1997), 5–17; Lee Sproull, Stephen Weiner, and David Wolf, *Organizing an Anarchy: Belief, Bureaucracy, and Politics in the National Institute of Education* (Chicago: University of Chicago Press, 1978).

31. Vinovskis, *Revitalizing Federal Education Research and Development.*

32. Philip Phaedon Zodhiates, "Bureaucrats and Politicians: The National Institute of Health and Educational Research under Reagan" (Ed.D. diss., Harvard Graduate School of Education, 1988).

33. Verstegen and Clark, "The Diminution in Federal Expenditures."

34. Vinovskis, *Revitalizing Federal Education Research and Development.*

35. Bill Clinton, "Foreword" in Samuel B. Bacharach, ed., *Education Reform: Making Sense of It All* (Boston: Allyn & Bacon, 1990), p. xi.

36. Beatrice Gross and Ronald Gross, eds., *The Great School Debate: Which Way for American Education?* (New York: Simon and Schuster, 1985).

37. Alan L. Ginsburg, Jay Noell, and Valena White Plisko, "Lessons from the Wall Chart," *Educational Evaluation and Policy Analysis* 10 (Spring 1988), 1. On opposition to the wall chart, see Thomas Toch, "E.D. Issues Study Ranking on Education," *Education Week*, 11 January 1984. Online at http://www.edweek.org

38. On the changes in NAEP during these years, see Maris A. Vinovskis, *Overseeing the Nation's Report Card: The Creation and Evolution of the National Assessment Governing Board* (Washington, DC: U.S. Government Printing Office, 1998).

39. For some useful analyses of the trends in student achievement after the mid-1980s, see Jay R. Campbell, Clyde M. Reese, Christine O'Sullivan, and John A. Dossey, *NAEP 1994 Trends in Academic Progress* (Washington, DC: National Center for Education Statistics, 1996); Christopher Jencks and Meredith Phillips, eds., *The Black-White Test Score Gap* (Washington, DC: Brookings Institution Press, 1998).

40. Chester E. Finn, Jr., *We Must Take Charge: Our Schools and Our Future* (New York: Free Press, 1991), p. 40.

41. Toch, *In the Name of Excellence*, p. 4.

42. Maris A. Vinovskis, *The Road to Charlottesville: The 1989 Education Summit* (Washington, DC: National Education Goals Panel, 1999).

43. John F. Jennings, *Why National Standards and Tests? Politics and the Quest for Better Schools* (Thousand Oaks, CA: Sage, 1998); Diane Ravitch, *Na-*

tional Standards in American Education: A Citizen's Guide (Washington, DC: Brookings Institution Press, 1995); Robert Rothman, *Measuring Up: Standards, Assessment, and School Reform* (San Francisco: Jossey-Bass, 1995).

44. Sam Stringfield, Steven Ross, and Lana Smith, eds., *Bold Plans for School Restructuring: The New American Schools Designs* (Mahwah, NJ: Lawrence Erlbaum, 1996).

45. Vinovskis, *Revitalizing Federal Education Research and Development.*

46. Jennings, *Why National Standards and Tests?*; Ravitch, *National Standards in American Education*; Rothman, *Measuring Up.*

47. On the origins and meanings of systemic reform, see Vinovskis, *History and Educational Policymaking*, pp. 171–202.

48. Jennings, *Why National Standards and Tests?*; Ravitch, *National Standards in American Education*; Rothman, *Measuring Up.*

49. Lynn Olson, "An Unusual Alliance Presents United Front on Title I Revisions," *Education Week*, 10 February 1999. Online at http://www. edweek.org

50. "Republicans Snub Clinton ESEA Bill," *Title I Monitor* 4 (July 1999), 1–2, 7; Joetta L. Sack, "Ed-Flex's Sponsors Gave Bill a Push Before Media Storm," *Education Week*, 28 April 1999. Online at http://www. edweek.org

51. On the 2000 election, see James W. Ceaser and Andrew E. Busch, *The Perfect Tie: The True Story of the 2000 Presidential Election* (New York: Rowman and Littlefield, 2001); Larry J. Sabato, ed., *Overtime: The Election 2000 Thriller* (New York: Longman, 2002); Gerald Pomper, ed., *The Election of 2000: Report and Interpretations* (New York: Chatham House, 2001).

52. Elisabeth Bushmiller, "Focusing on Home Front, Bush Signs Education Bill," *New York Times*, 9 January 2002, p. A16; Dana Milbank, "With Fanfare, Bush Signs Education Bill," *Washington Post*, 9 January 2002, p. A3; Lynn Olson, "States Gear Up for New Federal Law," *Education Week*, 16 January 2002, pp. 1, 24–25; Bill Sammon, "Bush Hails Education Reform," *Washington Times*, 9 January 2002, pp. A1, A10.

53. Lynn Olson and Debra Viadero, "Law Mandates Scientific Base for Research," *Education Week*, 20 January 2002. Online at http://www. edweek.org

54. For analyses of the use of randomized trials in education, see Frederick Mosteller and Robert Boruch, eds., *Evidence Matters: Randomized Trials in Education Research* (Washington, DC: Brookings Institution Press, 2002).

55. For an analysis and discussion of the issue, see Richard J. Shavelson and Lisa Towne, eds., *Scientific Research in Education* (Washington, DC: National Academy Press, 2002).

56. Debra Viadero, "Research Bill Clears House without Fuss," *Education Week*, 8 May 2002. Online at http://www.edweek.org

CHAPTER NINE   *The Emerging State Leadership Role in Education Reform: Notes of a Participant-Observer*

1. Terrel H. Bell, *The Thirteenth Man* (New York: Free Press, 1988), pp. 127–131.
2. Task Force on Education for Economic Growth, *Action in the States* (Denver: Education Commission of the States, 1984).
3. Denis P. Doyle and Terry W. Hartle, *Excellence in Education: The States Take Charge* (Washington, DC: American Enterprise Institute, 1985), pp. 17–18.
4. National Governors' Association, *Time for Results* (Washington, DC: Author, 1986), pp. 3–4.
5. Ibid, p. 8.
6. Task Force on Teaching as a Profession, *A Nation Prepared: Teachers for the 21st Century* (New York: Carnegie Forum on Education and the Economy, 1986).
7. National Governors' Association, *Time for Results, 1987* (Washington, DC: Author, 1987).
8. Maris A. Vinovskis, *The Road to Charlottesville: The 1989 Education Summit* (Washington, DC: National Education Goals Panel, 1999), p. 17.
9. Ibid, pp. 19–21.
10. Ibid, pp. 28–36.
11. Robert B. Schwartz and Marian A. Robinson, "Goals 2000 and the Standards Movement," *Brookings Papers on Education Policy 2000* (Washington, DC: Brookings Institution Press, 2000), pp. 173–214.
12. Diane Massell, Michael Kirst, and Margaret Hoppe, *Persistence and Change: Standards-Based Reform in Nine States* (Philadelphia: Consortium for Policy Research in Education, 1997).
13. Unfortunately, no one briefed Paul O'Neill, then CEO of Alcoa, on the script, which led to the most amusing and authentic exchange at the summit. After Thompson and Gerstner opened the meeting by asserting the responsibility of each state to set its own standards, O'Neill observed that Alcoa has plants not only in many states, but all over the world, and as far as he knew in all of these jurisdictions nine times nine equals 81, so why should Maine's standards be different from Mississippi's? Gerstner gave a classic New York shrug and said, "Paul, what can I tell you? It's not rational, it's political."
14. See Achieve, *A Review of the 1996 National Education Summit* (Washington, DC: Author, 1996), pp. 5–6.
15. All of Achieve's benchmarking reports are available online at http://www.achieve.org
16. In addition to the individual reports on these states, see *Gaining Ground*, also online at www.achieve.org
17. "Public Agenda: Reality Check 2001," *Education Week*, 21 February 2001.

CHAPTER TEN   *The American Way of School Reform*

1. See Richard Rothstein, "How U.S. Punishes States with Higher Standards," *New York Times*, 18 September 2002.
2. Jeffrey Mirel, "Unrequited Promise," *Education Next* 2, no. 2 (Summer 2002), 64–73.
3. See Joseph P. McDonald, Thomas Hatch, Edward Carbo, Nancy Ames, Norris M. Haines, and Edward T. Joyner, *School Reform Behind the Scenes* (New York: Teachers College Press, 1999).
4. Report by the Consortium on Chicago School Research, quoted in David T. Gordon, "Moving Instruction to Center Stage," *Harvard Education Letter* 18, no. 5 (September/October 2002), 5.

Contributors

Richard F. Elmore is the Gregory R. Anrig Professor of Educational Leadership at the Harvard Graduate School of Education. His research focuses on the effects of federal, state, and local education policy on schools and classrooms. He is currently exploring how schools of different types and in different policy contexts develop a sense of accountability and a capacity to deliver high-quality instruction. Elmore is a senior research fellow with the Consortium for Policy Research in Education (CPRE), a five-university collaborative engaged in research on state and local education policy and school finance. He is coauthor of *Restructuring in the Classroom: Teaching, Learning, and School Organization* (with Penelope L. Peterson and Sarah J. McCarthey) and coeditor of *The Governance of Curriculum* (with Susan H. Fuhrman).

Susan H. Fuhrman is the Dean and George and Diane Weiss Professor of Education at the Penn Graduate School of Education in Philadelphia. She is also Chair of the Management Committee of the Consortium for Policy Research in Education, a five-university collaborative that conducts research on state and local education policies and on school finance. Fuhrman received bachelor's and master's degrees in history from Northwestern University, and a Ph.D. in political science and education from Columbia University. She has written widely on education policy and finance; among her edited books are *From the Capitol to the Classroom: Standards-Based Reform in the States* and *Designing Coherent Education Policy: Improving the System*. She is a former Vice President of the American Educational Research Association, and serves on the editorial boards of *Educational Evaluation and Policy Analysis, Education Policy,* and the *American Education Research Journal*. Her current research includes work on high school responses to accountability pressures and on the use of instructional assistance in six states. She resides in Westfield, New Jersey, with her husband, Dr. Robert Fuhrman; they have three sons.

Nathan Glazer is Professor of Education and Sociology, Emeritus, at Harvard University. His many books include *We're All Multiculturalists Now, Beyond* *the Melting Pot* (with Daniel P. Moynihan), *The Limits of Social Policy,* and *The Lonely Crowd* (with David Riesman and Reuel Denney). Glazer has received John Simon Guggenheim Foundation Fellowships, been a fellow of the Center for Advanced Study in the Behavioral Sciences, and is a member of the American Academy of Arts and Sciences as well as the American Academy of Education. He is a cofounder and coeditor of the journal *The Public Interest.*

David T. Gordon is the Editor of the award-winning *Harvard Education Letter,* a bimonthly publication about K–12 education research and practice written in a jargon-free way for school administrators, teachers, parents, and policy-makers. He has edited the book *The Digital Classroom: How Technology Is Changing the Way We Teach and Learn* and special reports about Violence Prevention and Conflict Resolution, Minority Achievement, and Teaching as a Profession. Before coming to Harvard in 1999, he was an associate editor at *Newsweek,* where he wrote about education, foreign affairs, culture, and technology. He holds degrees from Columbia University and Emerson College, where he has taught in the School of the Arts.

Patricia Albjerg Graham is the Charles Warren Research Professor of the History of American Education at the Harvard Graduate School of Education, where she joined the faculty in 1974 and served as Dean from 1982 to 1991. She began her teaching career in Deep Creek, Virginia, and later taught in Norfolk, Virginia, and New York City. She has also served as a high school guidance counselor. From 1965 to 1974, she directed Barnard College's Education Program. She has served as Dean of the Radcliffe Institute and as Vice President of Radcliffe College. President Jimmy Carter appointed her Director of the National Institute of Education, then the federal government's educational research agency, where she served from 1977 to 1979. From 1991 to 2000, she served as President of the Spencer Foundation, the nation's only philanthropic organization committed solely to funding education research. She is the author of numerous articles and books, including *Progressive Education: From Arcady to Academe* and *SOS: Sustain Our Schools.*

Pam Grossman is a Professor at Stanford University's School of Education, where she specializes in English education and teacher education and serves as the cochair of the area of curriculum and teacher education. Her research interests focus on teacher learning across the career, from teacher education programs through professional development, and the teaching of secondary English. Her publications have appeared in *Teachers College Record, American Educational Research Journal, Educational Researcher,* and *Review of Educational Research,* and others. She serves as the Vice President of Division K,

Teaching and Teacher Education, of the American Educational Research Association.

Jeff Howard is Founder and President of The Efficacy Institute, Inc. He has more than twenty-five years of experience as a staff developer and consultant to school and community leaders on systemic education reform, and as a consultant to corporate executives and senior managers of Fortune 1000 companies in the arena of diversity and human development. Over the past two decades, The Efficacy Institute has developed a comprehensive set of field-tested training programs, consulting services, and materials for adults and youth. The Efficacy Institute's mission is to promote the academic and social development of children by helping educators, parents, and human-service providers operate from a simple belief: that all children can learn at very high levels if the process of education is effectively organized. The Efficacy Institute has trained over 30,000 educators in more than fifty school districts throughout the United States. Howard holds an A.B. from Harvard College and a Ph.D. in Social Psychology from Harvard University. He has been published in the *The New Republic, Daedalus, Education Week*, The National Urban League's *The State of Black America,* and the *Boston Globe.*

Timothy Knowles currently serves as Deputy Superintendent for the Boston Public Schools. He also served as the codirector of the Boston Annenberg Challenge, a five-year school reform effort focused on improving instruction throughout Boston Public Schools. Prior to coming to Boston, he lived and worked in New York City, where he started and directed a K–8 public school in Bedford-Stuyvesant, Brooklyn. He also founded the New York office of Teach for America. He has taught American and African history in Cambridge and Boston, Massachusetts, and in Botswana. He earned a B.A. from Oberlin College and a doctorate from the Harvard Graduate School of Education. He lives in Brighton with his wife and three daughters.

Kim Marshall graduated from Harvard College in 1969 and taught in a Boston middle school until 1980. He returned to Harvard for an Ed.M. and then worked in the central office of the Boston Public Schools as assistant to the Superintendent, curriculum director, and planning director. In 1987, Marshall began fifteen years as principal of Boston's Mather Elementary School. In the summer of 2002, he resigned from the Boston schools and began working with New Leaders for New Schools, which recruits, trains, and supports urban principals. He has written extensively about his teaching and administrative experience, and has also published a series of books of classroom materials. He is married to Rhoda Schneider and has two children, one in college and one in high school.

Robert B. Schwartz was President of Achieve, a nonprofit organization created by the nation's governors and corporate leaders to help states implement standards-based reform, from 1996 to 2002. He has also been a lecturer on education at the Harvard Graduate School of Education since 1996. Over the past forty years, Schwartz has been a high school teacher and principal, education advisor to Boston Mayor Kevin White and Massachusetts Governor Michael Dukakis, an assistant director of the National Institute of Education, and director of the Boston Compact. From 1990 to 1996, he led the education grant-making program at the Pew Charitable Trusts, a Philadelphia-based private foundation that has been a major funder of national education reform initiatives.

Maris A. Vinovskis is the Bentley Professor of History, a senior research scientist at the Institute for Social Research, and a faculty member of the Gerald R. Ford School of Public Policy at the University of Michigan. He served as the research adviser to the Office of Educational Research and Improvement (OERI) in the first Bush and the Clinton administrations. His latest book is *Revitalizing Federal Education Research and Development: Improving the R&D Centers, Regional Educational Laboratories, and the "New" OERI*, and he has just completed a book manuscript entitled "The National Education Goals and Federal Compensatory Education Policies from Ronald Reagan to George W. Bush."

Acknowledgments

I am grateful to Patricia Albjerg Graham and Richard F. Elmore for their generous encouragement and thoughtful advice throughout the process of putting together this book. It benefited greatly from their suggestions. And thanks to the authors for delivering such insightful articles on a very tight schedule. Their graciousness and enthusiasm made my job an easy one.

I owe special thanks to my colleagues at the Harvard Education Publishing Group for their professional support, no-nonsense guidance, and good humor. These include director Douglas Clayton, production manager Dody Riggs, marketing director Karen Walsh, as well as Alice Swinden Carter, Laura Clos, Marilyn Lofaro-O'Neill, Wendy McConnell, Michael Sadowski, and Meg Wilson. You make a terrific team.

Index